EDGAR CAYCE
And The

ETERNAL FEMININE

To Jean—
Best Wishes,
Writer!
December 20, 2007

𝕰DGAR 𝕮AYCE
And The

~~~~~~~~~~~~~~~~~~~

𝕰TERNAL 𝕱EMININE

Lynn Rogers M.A.

LYNN ROGERS, MA

Illustrations by LYNN ROGERS, MA

We Publish Books

Chicago, Illinois — Las Vegas, Nevada — Newark, Delaware
Palm Desert, California — San Diego, California

Copyright © 1993 by Lynn Rogers. All rights reserved. No part of this book may be reproduced in any form, except for brief review, without the express permission of the publisher.

Edgar Cayce Readings copyrighted Edgar Cayce Foundation © 1971, 1993, 1994, 1995, 1996. All rights reserved. Used by permission.

For further information, you may write or e-mail:

>We Publish Books
>P.O. Box 1814
>Palm Desert, Ca 92255
>
>www.wepublishbooks.com
>E-mail: LynnRogers@wepublishbooks.com

Library of Congress Cataloging in Publication Data:

Rogers, Lynn
Edgar Cayce And The Eternal Feminine
Includes bibliographical references

>Edgar Cayce And The Eternal Feminine/ by Lynn Rogers
>1. Mind, Body & Spirit 2. Spirituality 3. General
>   OCC 036000

ISBN 1-929841-02-7

Printed in the United States

First Printing, 2004

We Publish Books

"The roots of present-day holism go back 100 years to the birth of Edgar Cayce in Hopkinsville, KY. By the time he died in 1944, Cayce was well recognized as a mystic who entered sleep trances and dictated a philosophy of life and healing called 'reading'. His base was established in Virginia Beach, VA, now the headquarters of the Cayce Foundation."

Editorial
Journal of the American Medical Assoc.
March 16, 1979 Vol. 241 No. 11

DEDICATION

To Jessica, now in Spirit, who loved
the Edgar Cayce Work
with all her heart

Jessica Madigan 1911-1986

"Only those become conscious of same that have attuned themselves to that which is in accord, or seeking to know—His will; for each soul, every soul, should seek to attune its mind, its soul—yea, its body vibrations—to that He, the Son of man, the Mother-God in Jesus the Christ, lived in the earth. Tune into that light and it becomes BEAUTIFUL; in that you think, that you are, that you live!"

—Edgar Cayce, 254-68

Jessica Madigan, Edgar Cayce and Lynn Rogers
Sketch by Lynn Rogers

ACKNOWLEDEMENTS

The help and interest of all those who contributed to this book is sincerely appreciated. Special appreciation is expressed in particular to:

Joe,Haddox who, like Hephaestus- god of the forge – tirelessly lent all his support—especially his skills as the computer craftsman, to this project.

Vanessa, born with the lifelong disability of autism, whose bright soul teaches everyone who knows her that there is more than one way to be fully human.

Megan, who at age four, heard the author praying aloud to God and finally said, "You can be quiet now Mommy, She's heard you," thus opening new possibilities.

Hermetic figure Lawrence Rouse, PhD, for his mercurial moments as a catalyst; past life Marx sister and solitary scholar, Nancy Payne, for vital facts from her depth research; Dionysian Robert Houseman for his mystic insights before he left this world.

The members of the author's master's thesis committee at Atlantic University, Margaret Irby, PhD, Rev. Robert Danner, and especially Rev. Pamela Bro-Benetz—who shared a dream.

Louise Vernon, who taught, "it's already been written somewhere in time," then helped mortals discover that place.'

The Atlantean priestesses who reemerged along with the Eternal Feminine including:

Sisters from the past met one by one in the journey to Virginia Beach: Jeannie Holcombe and Ellen Hylton who opened their homes, Grethe Tedrich, Suzanne Keehn and Stase Michaels.

And to those in California who helped with this project, including Judy Martin and especially Vicky Borba, a new friend from the Azores—once a remnant of Atlantis—who reappeared in the nick of time to keep a promise from long ago.

**Joe Haddox at the A.R.E. Library's
Andrew Jackson Davis Room
intuitively locating research material for Lynn Rogers 1991**

Finally, to the Women in the Edgar Cayce Work who were the subjects of this study, from 102 year-old Irene Seiberling Harrison to 14 year-old Deja Elizabeth Howard. Special thanks to the Cayce family for allowing the author to better glimpse the character and key roles, and listen to the voices of the first Women in the Work.

Contents

Acknowledgements	ix
List of Tables	xiii
A Note From The Author	xv
Preface	xvii
Introduction	xxi

Section 1: Literature Review — 1
- Chapter One   Creation — 5
- Chapter Two   The Way of the Mother — 39
- Chapter Three   Future Horizons — 73

Section 2: Direct Research — 101
- Chapter Four   The Circle of Light/Moon Cycle Process — 105
- Chapter Five   Women In the Work: Multigenerational Interviews — 129

Evaluation and Reflection — 153

Appendix A	Developmental Sequence: Circle Of Light/Moon Cycle Process	155
Appendix B	Process Leaders	157
Appendix C	Circle Of Light Process Correlated to the Seven Chakras	159
Appendix D	Sally Cayce Interview	165
Appendix E	Representative Responses to Questionnaire	185
Appendix F	Akashic Record Reading by Jessica Madigan	211
References		219
About the Author		229

Tables

		Chapter
Table 1.	The Five Ages of Atlantis	2
Table 2.	Correlations of Alternate Cayce Planetary Associations With Goddess and God Systems	4
Table 3.	The Four Directions and Typologies	4
Table 4.	The Four Elements in the Circle of Light/Moon Cycle Process	4
Table 5.	The Three Aspects of the Eternal Feminine and Cyclicity	4
Table 6.	Sample Scrying/September 11, 1990/Moon Circle/ 84th Street Beach/Virginia Beach/ Facilitator; Lynn Rogers	4
Table 7.	Correlations of Approximate Number of Participants per Facilitator in Varied Settings	4
Table 8.	Summary of Main Themes as Noted by Process Developer	4
Table 9.	Summary of Main Themes as Noted by Student Teacher A	4
Table 10.	Summary of Main Themes as Noted by Student Teacher B	4
Table 11.	Summary of Main Themes as Noted by Student Teacher C	4
Table 12.	Themes Ranked by Frequency	4
Table 13.	Multigenerational Interview Subjects	5
Table 14.	Subjects Sorted by Chronological Generations	5
Table 15.	Subjects Sorted by Generations in the Work	5
Table 16A.	Total Subjects by Generations in the Work	5
Table 16B.	Total Subjects by Chronological Generations	5
Table 16C.	Total Subjects by East vs. West	5
Table 17.	Interview Questions	5

A Note From The Author

In 1989, after years experimenting with intuition and Goddess Spirituality under the oak tree in my back yard, I came to Edgar Cayce's Atlantic University on a quest. Where was the Divine Feminine in this great work? People there said Cayce had missed the boat on the Goddess. I didn't think so. What resulted was my graduate thesis which has evolved into this new book, Edgar Cayce And The Eternal Feminine. Since then, I have continued to lead participants under the oak tree and before the fireplace, blending Goddess magic and ageless Cayce insights into new wisdom for the Aquarian Age of Mary.

Lynn Rogers Leading A Circle of Light in front of the old Cayce Hospital building in Virginia Beach 1990

**Edgar Cayce dreamed of a University
for the study of the human spirit**

**Lynn Rogers at Graduation from Atlantic University
Master's Program in Transpersonal Studies**

PREFACE

EDGAR CAYCE AND THE ETERNAL FEMININE

An Overview of the Relationship Between the Emerging Divine Feminine and the Edgar Cayce Readings

This book undertakes to determine the points of connection between the emerging body of knowledge regarding the Eternal Feminine and the Edgar Cayce material. The literature review suggests the connections between the two systems in the following areas:

The "Creative Forces" described in the Edgar Cayce material suggest Father/Mother God, which includes the Divine Feminine. Parallel scholars present various ideas of Creation that include feminine, or androgynous beginnings, and then male rebellion figures, which evolve into later patrifocal themes about the Creator.

Next, the Edgar Cayce creation story is examined and compared with cross-cultural creation myths from the five races as delineated by the Cayce sources. The Cayce creation account refers to androgynous beings who separated into twin souls. The motif of an eternal complement is repeated through myth and in the arts.

The Cayce readings also trace the Eternal Feminine historically from Creation through Atlantis to early Egypt and India, through Goddess-worshipping societies that preceded today's patrifocal religions and cultures.

Today, the submerged Eternal Feminine principle is reemerging around the world through: new ideologies, including ecology, gender equity and planetism; partnership ideals in work and home, and new religious forms which are springing up in answer to the earth's call for a new agenda. Such forms synthesize feminine and masculine Co-Creative Forces, help individuals discover the Divine within and become empowered with, instead of over, others.

The direct studies illustrate the connections between the Eternal Feminine traced in the literature review and the Edgar Cayce philosophy in two distinct ways.

First, the preliminary study of the Circle of Light Moon Cycle Process I developed, translates the language of each system of knowledge into that of the other through an integrative experiential process which serves to heighten intuitive phenomenon and the perception of feminine imagery associated with the Divine.

Second, the preliminary multigenerational interview study allows women associated with the Edgar Cayce Work to voice their direct experiences. These experiences suggest areas of connection as well as apparent disconnection between the Eternal Feminine and the Edgar Cayce Work.

For example, most women found answers to fundamental life questions within the Cayce philosophy and many experienced a sense of belonging and commitment to the Work, yet there were instances of alienation where women felt undervalued or ostracized by either the material or the established organizations. Both circumstances are epitomized in my mentor, the late Jessica Madigan's experience.

Today humanity may be approaching a synthesis of early matrifocal and later patrifocal traditions towards the Oneness of Creative Forces as described in the Edgar Cayce material. The Edgar Cayce philosophy as it connects to the emerging body of knowledge regarding the Eternal Feminine can provide a conceptual bridge towards such future synthesis by providing ideals of gender partnership and spiritual equality.

**Lynn Rogers in front of Portrait of Edgar Cayce
located in the A.R.E. library in Virginia Beach**

Lynn Rogers and Dr. Charles Thomas Cayce at Atlantic University in Virginia Beach 1989

Lynn Rogers sitting on Cayce's Couch at the Edgar Cayce Foundation in Virginia Beach 1989

INTRODUCTION

An emerging body of literature regarding the Eternal Feminine points to the need for a more balanced understanding of ourselves, our world and The Creative Forces or what we call the Divine. However, this body of knowledge has not yet been related to the Edgar Cayce readings. The intent of this book is to provide an historical overview and to determine the points of intersection—the relationships between the Edgar Cayce insights and the reemerging Goddess tradition. The points of intersection will be demonstrated through literary review and direct research.

Definitions

The Edgar Cayce Readings

Edgar Cayce (1877–1945), America's "sleeping prophet", gave 14,000 discourses in an altered state of consciousness similar to self-hypnosis. These discourses are called readings. He answered questions on a variety of subjects— including health, past lives, dreams, spiritual ideals, soul mates, the mythical Atlantis and more. I believe the Edgar Cayce readings are a body of material that was produced and created through the interaction of various factors, including the influx of Universal Forces, the religious, cultural and psychological zeitgeist, the temporal mind set of the petitioner, Edgar Cayce, and other associates and influences. (What people thought made a difference in what he could receive.) Thus the readings appear to comprise varying depths of perception. Despite these variables, certain themes occur consistently through the readings for specific subjects.

Creative Forces

Creative Forces is the term often used in the Edgar Cayce readings as synonymous with Father/Mother God, or the creative energy of the Universe.

Archetypes

According to Carl Jung, an archetype is "an archaic or primordial image that has existed since the remotest times". (Jung, 1959, p. 5) Further, Jung states that "Life wants to create new forms, and ... when a dogma loses its vitality, it must ... activate the archetype that has always helped man to express the mastery of the soul ... the psychic archetype makes it possible for the divine figure to take form and become accessible to understanding. Only experience can establish which archetype has become operative." (Jung, 1963, p. 347)

It appears to me there are both temporal and eternal feminine and masculine archetypes. (Temporal are back and forth ideas about what is masculine or feminine, eternal is the deep forever truth underneath.) Some of these temporal archetypes, or temporary images, change with the cultural wind. What we think of as feminine, changes depending upon what people want and who's in charge at a given time.

For example, people thought women should be plump in the eighteen nineties because that meant they had more food to eat and were wealthier and less sickly. After World War One, when men celebrated their comrades in arms, women tried to look like boys with no breasts showing. After so many lives were lost in world war two, motherhood and family was in. Breasts meant motherhood, women wore pointy bras. These images of women are temporal or temporary archetypes.)

Temporal archetypes reflect oscillating cultural megacycles. (Meaning a thing can seem to be true because we've thought that way for a long time.) Thus, a temporal archetype could have seemed to reappear since the remotest times of the patriarchal epoch. (From the time men dominated, an evocative women could be seen as temptress or whore, a motherly women who would take care of men seen as Madonna or good. But in the times of the Goddess, an evocative woman could be seen as a healing priestess and a motherly woman as an expression of The Mother who gave birth to the stars and should be worshipped.)

Introduction

Eternal archetypes express the unifying ideal that transcends time in terms of gender epochs. (Eternal means the truth of what's masculine or feminine that's always so and doesn't get skewed based on who's in charge. History at one time being written by men, these eternal feminine archetypes are hard to find.) Nonetheless, such eternal feminine and masculine archetypes are similar to Plato's forms, the Cayce material's concept of spiritual ideals versus mental ideas. (257-181, 1739-6), or possibly Psycho synthesis' concept of the Self versus sub-personalities. (Assagioli, 1965)

The Eternal Feminine

One of two co-creative forces comprising the One, with applications in spiritual, psychological and cultural domains. The Eternal Feminine can be described in two ways: first, as a transcendent deity (the Divine Feminine); second, as an immanent archetype (the Universal Feminine). (Transcendent is above us, beyond us, immanent is within us, a part of us.) To further clarify: According to the Cayce material, male and female were first one spiritually and then physically. Then the entities split into male and female as two physical entities.

Webster's Dictionary (1957) defines masculine and feminine as having qualities characteristic of males or females. In my opinion, some human attributes such as reason and feeling may belong to the original state of Oneness and are not gender-linked. Further, different qualities have been regarded as feminine or masculine in matrifocal (mother-focused) or patrifocal (father-focused) epochs. (In the matrifocal epoch, the deity was female and name and property passed through the mother's line. In the patrifocal epoch, the deity was male and name and property passed through the father's line.) Thus, for example, in Goddess-worshipping societies, primordial feeling was an attribute of the horned god (the Goddess's male complement). It seems that the gender in ascendancy assigns certain attributes to themselves and others to the more submerged gender.

Many persons believe they have both feminine and masculine characteristics, an idea originally popularized by Carl Jung as the anima and animus (1959) and now absorbed into group consciousness. In my opinion, often such characteristics are defined according to prevailing patrifocal cultural stereotypes.

Reuther (1983) addresses the dubiousness of gender linking certain human faculties such as reason or intuition. She states "there is no valid biological basis for labeling certain psychic capacities, such as reason, 'masculine' and others, such as intuition, 'feminine'.... Thus the labeling of these capacities as masculine and feminine simply perpetuates gender role stereotypes." (Reuther, 1983, p. 110) Further, C. Whitmont, Jungian analyst and Chairman of the Board for the C. G. Jung Training Center, believes that "femininity and masculinity are *a priori* structural patterns of psychic, no less than biological, functioning. But in respect to identifying their specific contents, we still need to retain open minds and be prepared to revise our views." (Whitmont, 1980, p. 121) (Feminine and masculine are deep forces, but there's nothing in our bodies that says men reason and women feel. These are unfair labels; let's search for fresh truth.)

I believe The Eternal Feminine is one of two co-creative forces comprising the One. The Eternal Feminine is the timeless ideal expression (of one of the two forces or principles) underlying both matrifocal and patrifocal patterns. Divine Feminine relates to the deity as the Mother or Goddess. Universal Feminine is the Divine Feminine immanent or residing or existing within persons and relates to those qualities that might be most closely associated with female persons cross-culturally and throughout time. Such qualities include: attunement with and holistic perspective regarding the life cycle; appreciation of relatedness and connectivity (a partnership model versus a hierarchical mentality); and the ability to reconcile and unify seeming opposites or polarities. However, because researchers still stand in a predominantly patrifocal period, looking back to glimpse distant matrifocal periods, it is difficult to determine absolutely which qualities are feminine (or masculine). I believe humanity stands on the brink of a new era in which the Eternal Feminine will be more consciously experienced and better understood.

Twin Souls

For the purposes of this study, twin souls are defined in accord with numerous references in the Cayce readings as follows: Twin souls are male and female polarity entities who were once part of a larger spiritual androgynous entity. This entity first projected itself into each of the five human races (red, brown, black, yellow and white) and became five androgynous physical beings. Then each of these androgynous physical beings later separated into one male and one female physical being called twin souls. Each entity was a complete soul unto itself, while retaining an underlying Oneness of spirit. Either entity within the couple may or may not be incarnated on earth at any one time. If incarnated together, the souls may be in any relationship: father and daughter, mother and son, husband and wife, brother and sister, friends. According to Madigan (1965), from the time of separation, each half of the twin soul couple represents more the masculine or the feminine pole of the total soul and so more often incarnates in a body of corresponding gender. However, either soul can incarnate in the body of the opposite pole.

The Goddess Tradition

The Goddess tradition is the history—or "her-story"—along with the theology—or "thea-ology"—of the worship of the deity or Creator as Mother—called the Goddess. According to Walker (1983), "every female deity in the present encyclopedia may be correctly regarded as only another aspect of a female Supreme Being." (Walker, 1983, p. 346) (Or, called by many names, she is One)

Limitations

Because of the varying depths of perception contained in the Edgar Cayce readings, the references to the Divine Feminine are often implicit as well as explicit—both of which I will address. (Sometimes he hints at Her, other times She shines through).

Atlantic University fulfills one of Edgar Cayce's dreams

Lynn Rogers with family, daughter Megan Flautt and Joe Haddox

Lynn Rogers beneath portraits of Gladys Davis, Edgar Cayce and Hugh Lynn Cayce

Lynn Rogers researching Cayce and the feminine in the A.R.E. library at Virginia Beach, VA

Lynn Rogers at the Cayce gravesite in Hopkinsville, KY where she researched the women in Edgar Cayce's life

SECTION I

LITERARY REVIEW

SECTION ONE

LITERATURE REVIEW

In the first section of this book, a wide body of existing literature on the Eternal Feminine is reviewed. Sources include readings from the fields of history, religion, and transpersonal psychology with correlations to the Edgar Cayce material and work. Specific topics reviewed are: Creation, including Creative Forces, cross-cultural myths and twin souls. Next is the Goddess tradition, including its roots in Cayce's Atlantis, Egypt and India, its theology, and its submergence by patrifocal culture. And finally, Future Horizons, including the reemergence of the Goddess in the modern world through Mary's appearances and new ideologies and religious forms which incorporate ideals of gender partnership.

CHAPTER ONE
CREATION

CHAPTER ONE

CREATION

This chapter summarizes the creation story in the Edgar Cayce readings in light of the Divine Feminine. Cross-cultural creation myths are compared. The Divine Feminine can be traced through legendary Lemuria where souls first used free will, to the separation of the angel Amilius into twin souls Adam—and Eve who would become Mary, a powerful pattern for women today.

What the Edgar Cayce sources call the Creative Forces has been imaged as both or either Mother or Father throughout time. The Edgar Cayce readings on Creation will be correlated with the works of diverse authors such as Walker, Starhawk, Pagels and Fox, in order to demonstrate the Oneness of the two Co-Creative Forces.

Creative Forces and Themes

The Edgar Cayce sources often refer to the Creative Forces: "Spirit that uses matter, that uses every influence in the earth's environ for the glory of the Creative Forces, partakes of and is a part of the universal consciousness." (3508-1); "For heaven is that place, that awareness where the Soul, with all its attributes, its mind, its body—becomes aware of being in the presence of the Creative Forces—or one with same. That is heaven." (262-88); "For each entity—as a portion of the stream of creative energy, as it flows through the activities to come to the presence of the maker—is a part of the universal consciousness, the universal energies that we worship or know as god." (648-1) The terms Creative Forces, Creator and God seem to mean the same thing.

In my opinion, the term Creative Forces also suggests Father/Mother God, a description sometimes used in the readings. "Peace that passeth understanding can come only with the heart being (in) at-onement with the Father-Mother God." (4087) As is demonstrated, The Creator has been viewed by humans as either Mother or Father throughout history. I further believe that the rhythmic dance of the masculine and feminine Creative Forces existed before the beginning of time. Some of the

Edgar Cayce readings corroborate this theme. For example, speaking of male and female, Edgar Cayce stated that in the beginning they were one in mind, body and spirit. (364-7) When asked to explain the Immaculate Conception, the Cayce source gave the following:

> "As flesh is the activity of the mental being (or the spiritual self and mental being) pushing itself into matter, and as spirit—as He gave—is neither male nor female, they are then both—or one." (5749-7)

The Oneness described in the Edgar Cayce readings is also described by other sources. For example, the early Christian Gnostics, or Knowers, who eschewed dogma for the inner experience of Christ, left material that parallels the Edgar Cayce readings when it refers to the Creator as both Mother and Father. Like the Cayce material, Gnosticism comprises a variety of themes that link earliest Christianity to Eastern religion. The ground breaking author of *There Is A River*, Tom Sugrue, asked the sleeping Cayce: "The eleventh problem concerns a parallel with Christianity. Is Gnosticism the closest type of Christianity to that which is given through this source?"

Each person who asked for a reading was assigned a number for anonymity. In Tom Sugrue's fourteenth reading, Cayce answered: "This is a parallel . . . " (5749-14) Gnostic writings are more inclusive of the Eternal Feminine than later Biblical versions. According to Gnostic author and Princeton professor Elaine Pagels, PhD, the Gnostics understood the Divine in three ways:

> Some insisted that the divine is to be considered masculofeminine—the great 'male-female power'. Others claimed that the terms were meant only as metaphors, since in reality the divine is neither male nor female. A third group suggested that one can describe the primal Source in either masculine or feminine terms, depending on which aspect one intends to stress. Proponents of these diverse views agreed that the divine is to be understood in terms of a harmonious, dynamic relationship of opposites—a concept that may be akin to the Eastern view of yin and yang . . . (Pagels, 1979 p. 51)

Further, this Oneness is reflected in cross-cultural creation myths, was articulated in Cayce's Atlantis, and has been recapitulated in many forms in subsequent history.

Yet, the commonly held view of male/female qualities as polarities in the present patrifocal culture defines the male polarity as light, reasoning, and active and the female polarity as dark, feeling and intuitive, and passive. Starhawk states in the *Spiral Dance: A Rebirth of the Ancient Religion of the Great Goddess*, that it is important to separate the concept of polarity from our culturally conditioned images of male and female. The Chinese concept of yin and yang, she states, is somewhat similar to the male/female concepts of the ancient Goddess religion, but the description of the forces is very different. Neither force, for example, is "active" or "passive". Moreover, the female is seen as the life-giving force, the power of manifestation, of energy flowing into the world to become form. The male is seen as the death force in a positive, rather than negative sense; the force of limitation that is the necessary balance to unbridled creation. (Starhawk, 1979) Therefore, rather than polar opposites, male and female are part of a cycle, each dependent upon the other.

The ancients did not see the Eternal Feminine as only including the qualities of feeling or intuition. For example, according to Pagels (1979), Valentinus, Gnostic poet and teacher of Ptolemy, begins with the premise that God is essentially indescribable. Then he suggests that the divine can be imagined first as the "Mother of All" or as a masculine and feminine dyad, or pair. Similarly, Hippolytus describes the Creator as a great power, as illustrated in the following:

> Mind of the Universe, which manages all things, and is male, and a Great Intelligence, which is female and produces all things. These powers joined together are Mind in Intelligence, and these are separable from one another, and yet are one, found in a state of duality. Thus this divine power is divided above and below; generating itself, making itself grow, seeking itself, sister of itself, spouse of itself, daughter of itself, son of itself—mother, father, unity, being a source of the entire circle of existence. (Pagels, 1979, p. 51)

Clearly, the quality of intelligence is associated with female creativity by the ancients for whom the Creative Forces were a dyad.

The Creative Forces described by Edgar Cayce are like the dyad of Father/Mother God. Sjoo and Mor (1987), state, "... yin and yang constantly complement each other to maintain cosmic harmony." I believe the universes came into being through the rhythmic dance—the interplay—of this eternal, archetypal dyad. Temporally, these forces appear to be separate and yet are eternally one.

Several themes recur in creation stories. These include: a Mother giving birth to Creation; souls conceived in original goodness as co-creators (correlated with the idea that souls fell from grace through self-will that conflicted with the wisdom of the Creator—versus the idea that souls were conceived in original sin); an androgynous deity or Divine Couple creating a human male/female pair; and the rebellion of the created against the Creator. In one form or another these themes further serve to illustrate the dual Mother/Father nature of the Creative Forces.

Creation Myths of Birth and the Feminine

The theme of God as Birther of Creation is evident in ancient writings, was discussed by early scholars such as the Sethian Gnostics, medieval Catholic mystic, Hildegarde of Bingen, and has been revived by modern scholars such as Walker (1983), Fox (1983), Stone (1976), Starhawk (1979) and others.

In these ancient writings, the Creator was often seen as the Mother from whom all life arose, as the following illustrates:

> Hear O ye regions, the praise of Queen Nana; magnify the Creatress; exalt the dignified; exalt the Glorious One; draw nigh to the Mighty Lady. —Sumer, Nineteenth Century, B.C.

> To the Queen of Heaven, the Goddess of the Universe, the One who walked in terrible Chaos and brought life by the law of Love, And out of Chaos brought harmony, and from Chaos Thou has led us by the hand. — Babylon, Eighteenth to Seventh Centuries B.C.

> In the beginning there was Isis, Oldest of the Old, She was the Goddess from whom all Becoming Arose. She was the Great Lady, Mistress of the Two Lands of Egypt, Mistress of Shelter, Mistress of Heaven, Mistress of the House of Life, Mistress of the Word of God. She was the Unique. In all Her great and wonderful works She was a wiser magician and more excellent than any other God. —Thebes, Egypt, Fourteenth Century B.C. (Stone, 1976, p. x)

According to Walker (1983), myths of creation generally present a symbolic view of birth. Images of a uterine environment are often used. Often there is the suggestion of one entity inside another.

> When there was neither the creation, nor the sun, the moon, the planets, and the earth, and when darkness was enveloped in Darkness, then the Mother, the Formless One, Maha-Kali, the Great Power, was one with Maha-Kala, the Absolute. (Walker, 1983, p. 183)

Sethian Gnostics explain that heaven and earth have a shape similar to a womb. (Pagels, 1979) The 12th Century nun, Hildegarde of Bingen, wrote that:

> The earth is at the same time mother; she is mother of all that is natural, mother of all that is human. She is mother of all, for contained in her are the seeds of all.
> (Fox, 1983, p. 57)

The Bible, Walker states, continues a form of the birth myth that is derivative of earlier versions. From Genesis 1:2, we read, "the earth was without form, and void; and darkness was upon the face of the Deep". The Deep was the Mother's womb—called "tehom"—derived from Tiamat, the Babylonian name of the Goddess. "In Egypt, she was Temu, mother of the abyssal elements: Water, Darkness, Night, and Eternity." (Walker, 1983, p. 183)

In these themes the feminine is represented by images related to the womb. In other cases, the Creator is clearly seen as a female deity and Mother. Thus, in ancient accounts, Creation and birth were inseparable from the figure of the Goddess.

The Edgar Cayce readings could be interpreted to imply themes of birth and of one entity within another insofar as they refer to "the desire of companionship as innate in the Creator, that brought companionship into creation itself" (364-5), and that they describe created physical entities that are "both male and female in one" (288-6).

Creation Spirituality and Ideas of the Fall

Dominican Father Matthew Fox has redefined an ancient tradition called Creation Spirituality which includes the Divine Feminine and which is like the Goddess tradition, in that neither female nor male are linked to sin, and that the body is viewed as sacred. Fox describes later Fall/Redemptive creation theories as those in which souls are conceived in original sin, the body is viewed as base, and women are blamed for sin. Fox states that the creation-centered spiritual tradition is not the Fall but the creative energy or word of God. In Creation Spirituality, creative energy is continuous and never stops. (Fox, 1983)

Threads of Creation Spirituality and Fall/Redemptive Spirituality can be seen in the Bible. Walker (1983) points out that the Book of Genesis unfolds two distinct creation myths. The E version speaks of plural creators, Elohim, male and female deities who blessed their creations. The J version describes Jehovah, the God of gods and refers to the fall where Eve disobeys Jehovah and she and Adam are driven out of the Garden of Eden. The E version does not refer to the Fall. Through the E and J

Biblical threads, both Creation Spirituality and Fall/Redemptive themes are evident.

In my opinion many of the Edgar Cayce readings fall within the Creation Spirituality tradition. For example:

> Spirit that uses matter, that uses every influence in the earths environ for the glory of the Creative Forces, partakes of and is a part of the universal consciousness. (3508-1)

Paradoxically, the Cayce readings describe a falling away from original co-creativity or what I might term Original Wisdom. (Gnostic sources, as cited by Barnstone (1984), are closer to the Cayce concept of a fall, although in the Gnostic sources a male figure is blamed.) The Cayce concept of the fall is not entirely equivalent to the Fall/Redemptive concept because both the Cayce sources and the Creation Spirituality scholars, as researched by Fox, believe that creation is blessing.

The Cayce material generally states that souls were intended to be co-creators with the Divine. Given the free will to make choices, souls chose for selfish motives at the expense of others and became enmeshed in the physical results of such choices, thus necessitating a reincarnational cycle of births and deaths. The principle of karma or cause and effect allows each entity to meet itself, or the karmic results of its choices. Souls can always choose to act in accord with the Christ Consciousness (or spirit of love and forgiveness) within and bring grace in the meeting of such circumstances. Even a karmic stumbling block—such as a child's condition of mental retardation—can become a steppingstone to blessings. "Then turning within, through those influences of the Christ Consciousness, know that thou doest with thy might will have its blessings in thy life and those that ye serve." (811-2) Thus the Cayce concept of the soul's journey toward at-onement with the Father/Mother God is still anchored in original blessing, and keys to grace are found within.

In summary, the Creation Spirituality creation themes differ from the Fall/Redemptive creation themes in that humanity's legacy is original blessing rather than original sin. Fox states that God the Creator, like any artist, is not indifferent or neutral to his/her work of art. Like any parent, God loves her creation and that love, which is unconditional sending forth into existence, is blessing. (Fox, 1983)

Consistently the Edgar Cayce readings state that the destiny of souls is at-one-ment with the blessings of the Creative Forces.

> For each soul seeks expression. And as it moves through the mental associations and attributes in the surrounding environs, it gives out that which becomes

> either for selfish reactions of the own ego—to express—or for the I AM to be at-one with the Great I AM THAT I AM. (987-4)

Thus the Cayce material partakes of the tradition of Creation Spirituality in that the soul's journey in the earth is to "find self and its relationships with the Creative Forces" (5356-1), which brings "the exhilarating feeling of nearness to that Creative Energy" (1877-1), or original blessing.

The Divine Couple and the Separating Andrognune

The oldest myths make the Goddess not only the birther of heaven and earth, but of people as well. In Sumerian legend, for example, the Goddess had created people in male/female pairs. (Stone, 1976) The Gnostic Secret Book states that "(She is) . . . the image of the invisible, virginal, perfect spirit . . . She became Mother of everything, for she existed before them all, the mother-father (matropater) . . . " (Pagels, 1979, p. 52) In some Gnostic myths the Goddess is paired with a male God figure as for example, Sophia and Saboath. (Barnstone, 1984)

It appears to me that there is a Divine Couple, or Mother/Father Creator, who birth or create a separating andrognune—or human couple, like Adam and Eve. This idea finds corroboration in the Edgar Cayce material. For example, "The first cause was, that the created would be the companion for the Creator . . . " (5733-1) In a Sunday school lecture Edgar Cayce stated: "These beings were male and female in one; they were images of that God-spirit which moved and brought Light into being." (Sanderfur, 1988, p. 44) Regarding the separation of the androgynous entity Amilius into Adam and Eve, the readings state that Adam and Eve were to be helpmeets to each other, not just companions of the body, as each was a portion of the other because of the original Oneness.

> . . . and when there was that turning to the within, through the sources of creation, as to make for the helpmeet . . . then, from out of self—was brought that as was to be the helpmeet, not just the companion of the body. (364-7)

Thus the Edgar Cayce material gives new insight into the myth of Adam and Eve as twin souls. The Cayce material also parallels the Gnostic accounts of the Oneness of the separating andrognune in creation myths from around the world. It appears that this pattern of the separating andrognune is repeated in various cultures. This will be discussed later in the text. Moreover, there may be two sets of Divine Couple myths. An evolution is apparent from the Creative Source as the Goddess—or the female deity—to the dual creative forces of male and female in a Divine Couple.

The earliest myths describe the Goddess as the Birther of the Universe with a male figure symbolizing rebellion against Her, as She is the will of the Divine. Later myths reverse this theme, with a male God and a feminine rebel, as in Eve. (This will be explored further below in the discussion of "Rebellion".) For example, the Gnostic "The Creation of the World", from *The Other Bible*, (Barnstone, 1984) reverses the traditional Adam and Eve myth.

This tractate describes Sophia Zoe, who is beside, or paired with Sabaoth as a Divine Couple. Sophia cast a drop of light. It floated upon the water. First the drop became a female body, then an androgynous being. From this androgynous being, Adam and Eve were born. After the fortieth day, Sophia sent her daughter Zoe, called Eve (of Life) to raise up Adam, in whom there was no soul. When Eve saw her co-likeness cast down, she pitied him, and she said, "Adam, live! Rise up on the earth!" Immediately, her word became a deed. For when Adam rose up, he opened his eyes. When he saw her, he said, "You will be called the 'mother of the living' because you are the one who gave me life." (Barnstone, 1984, p. 70)

Thus, these accounts all suggest the dual nature of the Creator and the created as both feminine and masculine. The suggestion is made by the pairing of male and female Creators, as well as by the separation of an androgynous being into distinct male and female entities.

Rebellion

Another key creation theme is that of rebellion of the created against the Creator. In many early accounts, the Divine Feminine was emphasized and referred to as the Creator or the original source of life, associated with God as Birther. For example, even the Romans made the connection with the Mother as the Source quite clear: "Juno Lucina was . . . the Mother who brought 'light' to the eyes of the newborn. The Biblical God who said 'Let there be light' (Fiat lux) copied the word from the Goddess." (Walker, 1983, p. 184) I speculate that the emphasis upon the Divine as Mother may have resulted in the submerged male force rearing up in its shadow aspect. Carl Jung defines the shadow as the unacceptable and unacknowledged parts of self. (Jung, 1959) Here we see the male figure as the arrogant rebel against his Mother's wisdom.

As part of the rebellion against the Mother, later Biblical versions of the creation story finally erased the more inclusive Elohim and any suggestion of the Divine Feminine. However, the notion of the Divine Feminine as the ground of being has remained an undercurrent even in patrifocal religion. According to Gutpa, for example, the feminine ground of the divinity has a certain primacy over the male, since it is the source out of which the male Trinitarian Procession emerges. (Gutpa, 1987)

The Gnostic accounts describe a time of early rebellion against the Eternal Feminine. According to the Gnostics, Jehovah claimed to be the only God because he had forgotten the Mother who brought him into being. (Walker, 1987) They say he believed that he had made everything by himself. In reality, he had created the world because Wisdom, his mother, had infused him with energy and implanted into him her ideas. According to some Gnostic accounts, Jehovah's Mother grieved over his rebellion then withdrew herself into the upper regions of the heavens in distress when he became arrogant. The Gnostic Secret Book of John illustrates Jehovah's rebellion against Mother Wisdom:

> ... I am a jealous God, and there is no other God beside me.' But by announcing this he indicated to the angels ... that another God does exist; for if there were no other one, of whom would he be jealous? ... becoming arrogant in spirit, boasted he himself over all those things that were below him, and exclaimed, 'I am father, and God, and above me there is no one.' But his mother, hearing him speak thus, cried out against him, 'Do not lie, Ialdabaoth ... '

Often in these Gnostic texts, the creator is castigated for his arrogance, nearly always by a superior feminine power. According to the *Hypostasis of the Archons*, discovered at Nag Hammadi, both the mother and her daughter objected when ...

> Jehovah became arrogant, saying, 'It is I who am God, and there is no other apart from me' ... And a voice came forth from above the realm of absolute power, saying, 'You are wrong, Samael' (which means, 'god of the blind'). And he said, 'If any other thing exists before me, let it appear to me!' And immediately, Sophia (Wisdom) stretched forth her finger, and introduced light into matter, and she followed it down into the region of Chaos ... And he again said to his offspring, 'It is I who am the God of All.' And Life, the daughter of Wisdom, cried out; she said to him, 'You are wrong, Saklas!' (Pagels, 1979, p. 58)

In 1960, mythologist Joseph Campbell commented upon the prevalent Biblical Adam and Eve story as a "curious mythological idea", and upon the still more curious fact that "for two thousand years it was accepted throughout the Western World as the absolute dependable account ... " (Stone, 1976, p. 7–8) Campbell believes that this event exemplifies the "influence of conspicuously contrived, counterfeit mythologies and the inflections of mythology upon the structure of human belief and the consequent course of civilization." (Stone, 1976, p. 8) Ironically, Sophia's daughter, Eve, whose Gnostic name was Zoe—or Life—, comes to symbolize the Fall rather than the male figure rebelling against the Mother's wisdom. Here the rebellion against the Mother is complete, in that the Divine Wisdom of the Eternal Feminine has become associated with sin in the "curious mythological idea" of Adam and Eve.

However, even in the Judeo-Christian tradition there are alternative accounts of the Adam and Eve myth. In the Hebrew Talmud and the Kabala, Lilith was the first wife of Adam, for example. Created from the ground with Adam, she was his equal. According to Christ and Plaskow (1979), Adam did not like this and wanted her to be beneath him. She was forced to flee from her home, since she insisted upon love in mutual respect or not at all. Lilith, or Nin-lil on the Sumerian tablets, is described as the Hand of Innana, thus linked to the Goddess. Lilith birthed the moon and the darkness of the Nether World. It appears to me that Lilith became the Lady of the Night after she was forced out of Paradise. Could Lilith be a symbol for the saga of the Eternal Feminine in the earth when she was pushed from empowerment into the lunar unconscious? Stone (1984) suggests that this might be the first account of Goddess suppression.

The Lilith and Eve myths suggest to me a splitting of the Eternal Feminine into the polarities of dangerous rebel and passive handmaiden. Perhaps the reason the relationship of the Eternal Feminine to creation has not been understood over the last three to five thousand years is because of the lengthy cultural inclusion of what Campbell describes as politically contrived pseudo-myths, or what might be termed temporal archetypes.

Even in modern psychology, the theme of male rebellion resulting in fear of the feminine is suggested. Born from woman's flesh, entering her womb in love, DeBeauvoir suggests that male fear and hatred of women may occur because he comes upon the "dreaded essence of 'the mother' in the woman he possesses; he is determined to dissociate these two aspects of femininity." (Sjoo and Mor, 1987) I wonder if such collective fear and hatred are not the result of the suppression of the once-beloved Divine Mother. The Cayce material suggests that fear often results from guilt.

Rebellion of a different sort is also highlighted in the Cayce material. The readings speak of androgynous souls attracted to the earth plane who misused their creative energies, thereby rebelling against the Creative Forces' intent or wisdom. Here, neither male nor female figures are isolated as the rebels.

> For the Spirit of God moved and that which is in matter came into being, for the opportunities of His

associates, His companions, *His sons, His daughters, These are ever spoken of as One.* (Author's italics)

> Then there came that as sought for self-indulgence, self-glorification; and there was the beginning of warring among themselves for activity—still in Spirit. (262-114)

These rebellious souls created "thought forms" by intermingling spiritual forces with animal and plant forms. Mermaids, Cyclopes, centaurs and other distorted forms resulted.

> These, then, are the manners in which the *entities*, those *beings*, those *souls*, in the beginning partook of, or developed. Some brought about monstrosities, as those of its (the entity's) association by its projection with its association with beasts of various characters. Hence those of the ... satyr, and the like; those of the sea, or mermaid; those of the unicorn, and those of the various forms ... (364-10)

The Cayce readings seem to equate selfishness with rebellion for all souls—whether male or female.

The theme of rebellion is common to many creation stories, as illustrated by the preceding accounts. After the rebellion against the Divine Feminine, female creativity came to be feared and The Eternal Feminine was submerged. This was not always the case. In earlier creation accounts, the Creative Forces were frequently imaged as both feminine and masculine. The idea of God as Birther was preeminent, and therefore the Creator was often seen as the Mother, source of Life and Wisdom. Even the subsequent rebellion against the Wisdom of Sophia could not completely eliminate the underlying Oneness of forces described in the Edgar Cayce material.

Tracing the Eternal Feminine Through Cross-Cultural Creation Myths

The Eternal Feminine emerges in many cross-cultural creation myths. Myths related to the Eternal Feminine will be highlighted from each of the mythological five races, as described by Edgar Cayce. First, the creation story given in the Cayce material will be delineated.

The Edgar Cayce creation story provides a bridge, under girding ancient and modern scholarship in tracing Eternal Feminine through cross-cultural creation myths.

We find (the entity) in the beginning, when the first of the elements were given, and the forces set in motion that brought about the sphere as we find called earth-plane, and when the morning stars sang together, and the whispering winds brought the news of the coming of man's indwelling, of the spirit of the Creator, and he, man, [sic] became the living soul. (294-8)

In the beginning, as was outlined, there was presented that that became as Sons of God, in that male and female were as in one, with those abilities for those changes as were able or capable of being brought about. (364-7)

My interpretation of the Cayce saga on Creation is, "entities", or souls were destined to be co-creators with God—or the Creative Forces. Amilius was the prototype of such souls who embodied the masculine and feminine principles in one. (364-5) These souls may have been given guardianship over the natural forms on earth. In a spirit of curiosity and rebellion, they created thought projections without concern for the effect on these creatures—described as mermaids, Cyclopes, centaurs and other distorted forms. In my opinion, these souls acted like what would be described today as dysfunctional parents, denying responsibility for their children.

Lynn Rogers' A.R.E Survey Lecture – Psychic Forces and the Soul

The legend of Lemuria, which pre-history scholar Jery Vincent Stier says is submerged beneath the Pacific Ocean, typifies this fourth to third dimensional stage of soul evolution. By the same token, Atlantis, the mythic land submerged below the Atlantic, would become the place for souls to begin again.

Because of the misuse of their creativity in the service of self-will, the host of celestial beings (262-52) with Amilius chose to incarnate in true human form to work through their karmic responsibilities in fleshly bodies that could reproduce themselves across the earth. (Madigan, 1970) The Cayce readings gave the number five as the number of humanity in the earth. (Shelley, 1965, 1976) Each of the five races corresponds to one of the five senses and to a lesson related to one of these senses. First there was a separation into the five races and later the division into male and female for the purposes of reproduction.

The separation of each angelic soul into the five human races can be imaged as a five-pointed star. Later, each androgynous point of the star separated itself into male and female in the second division. Thus, twin souls emerged who had been one in the beginning and would be complementary in purpose throughout time. Numerous Edgar Cayce readings (such as 364-5) suggest that the entity, Amilius, would become Adam and Eve and state that Adam and Eve later incarnated as Jesus and Mary. In my view, Jesus and Mary are the Wayshowers, with Mary the link to the Divine Feminine.

It appears that by the second Atlantean age, the "adamic" projection (into the races) had occurred. Adamic projection meant that like a five pointed star, each androgynous soul in the group of "fallen angels" split itself into the five races, and later each of the five points separated itself into it's own "Adam and Eve" twin soul couple. In this creation myth, human body forms came into being at this point through souls overshadowing evolving animal forms—through an integration of evolution and divine influx.

According to the Cayce readings, Amilius separated into five Adams and Eves in each of the five racial Gardens of Eden: the red race in Atlantis or the Americas; the black race in the Sudan or Africa; the yellow race in the Gobi; the white race in the Carpathians; and the brown race in the Andean (or what we call the South American land.) Thus Amilius, the androgynous soul from which Mary and Jesus would emerge, became the red Adam and Eve in Atlantis with brother-sister souls in the other four races. Regarding the appearance of the races, the Cayce readings state:

Q: Was Atlantis one of the five points at which man appeared in the beginning, being the home of the red race?
A: One of the five points. (364-9)

Q: Did the appearance of what became the five races occur simultaneously?
A: Occurred at once. (364-13)

Thus the Cayce creation account delineates five root races.

Highlights from creation stories emphasizing the Eternal Feminine (as taken from the five root races) will be discussed. The Eternal Feminine is referred to by various names in the following cross-cultural myths, all of which suggest the Eternal Feminine in Her Divine (transcendent) or Universal (immanent) aspects.

The Red Root Race

Stone (1984), Downing (1987), and others offer red race accounts of "Our Grandmother". Although varied, they all suggest the Eternal Feminine in Her Divine and immanent aspects.

To the Shawnee Indians of the eastern woodland of America, the Goddess is described as the Creator of the World, of other divinities, and of human beings. According to the Shawnee account, the Great Goddess descended from above and created a great turtle for the earth to rest upon. She was assisted through her grandson, Rounded-side, a hero-trickster figure, who slew dangerous monsters but also flooded the world on one occasion.

One of Her creations is the Corn Goddess, who once fled from earth to her Mother in Heaven but was persuaded to return to earth to feed the Shawnee people. The Great Corn Mother herself became a pervasive figure from Chicomecaatl, Mexico to the Southwestern United States. This myth closely parallels the story of Persephone and Demeter from the Greek.

The Hopi Indians of Arizona—with whom I lived for a month as a high school student—are the oldest, continuous inhabitants of North America. Different Hopi clans have different myths. According to one myth, the world was created at the command of the Sun God. In another myth, Spider Woman gave life to the world. So in Hopi Indian legend, human beings have, in addition to their immediate parents, Father Sun and Spider Woman.

Another Hopi story is similar to the Cayce account of Atlantis. According to the centuries-old teachings of the Hopi elders at Old Oribi, Arizona, the earth has already turned over three times in major upheavals. Depending on humanity's choices in regard to the Hopi people and Mother

Earth, another great upheaval could be imminent or can be averted. The Hopis respect Mother Earth and the feminine principle and they believe all humanity must come to share this respect, thereby ensuring survival of the planet.

The Navajo people are the Hopi's near neighbors in Arizona. Changing Woman is the Creator of the Navajo people. She is the Mother of All. She is Mother Earth, She is the seasons, and She is Iyatiku who brings forth All Life, Mother Nature in all that She unfolds. She teaches the flow of life and its cycles. Humanity cannot defy Her patterns, for to try to change the ways of Changing Woman is to destroy all life. "But those who understand the ways of Changing Woman, forever walk the Trail of Beauty." (Stone, 1984, p. 292)

Author Lynn V. Andrews quotes a modern-day Native American medicine woman—Agnes Whistling Elk: "There are no medicine men, without medicine women. A medicine man is given power by a woman, and it has always been that way. A medicine man stands in the place of the dog. He is merely an instrument of woman. It doesn't look that way any more, but it is true." And, "It is a law that all things must be born in woman, even things invented by men." Agnes Whistling Elk (Andrews, 1981 pp. 61, x)

The various red root race creation stories emphasize the Eternal Feminine. Recurrent themes indicate a deep reverence for the earth, the Divine Couple and feminine empowerment. As Edgar Cayce suggested, the Atlanteans were a red race. (364-13) It seems to me that these red root race creation themes are timeless.

The Black Root Race

The Creator is seen as female in various African creation stories. She is called by different names as she takes many forms. These black race myths, with roots in the African culture, have widespread influence in other cultures.

Addressing students at Fox's Institute in Culture and Creation Spirituality on September 11, 1990, Black-American author, Luisah Teish, raised one of the biggest questions in African folklore: "Who is the Mother of Elegba, the Chief Magician?" she asked. Elegba is a trickster figure according to Teish. Hermes is frequently linked in mythology with the trickster. The Edgar Cayce sources gave that Jesus had lived before as the Nubian or African Hermes. (281-10) I speculate that Elegba and the black Hermes are the same figure.

Teish said the Mother of Elegba is so old they don't know her name. She is referred to as Na Na Baruka, but that is not Her name. The Dahomy say that She is a self-impregnating female who had twins. The twins mated and gave birth. Thus, She is Mawu, Mother of All Created, of the mountains and the rivers. It is said that the serpent carried Her in his giant reptilian jaw when She created the world. Thus, the curve of the mountains and the rivers reflect her path. She also created fire, why She created All, All, All. (Payne, 1991)

According to Stone (1984), further African creation myths include the following: In Nigeria the Goddess is the Provider of Life and the Mother who receives again in death. She proclaims law for moral human behavior. She is Holy Mother Earth. Her Sacred Womb is the Pocket of All. The Ibo people live by her laws.

To the Zulu of Natal, She is Mbaba Mwana Waresa, the Sacred Goddess of the light that streaks across the heavens, the Sacred Goddess who beats upon the drums of heaven. She pours the waters from her heavenly home roofed with rainbow arches. She taught the people how to sow and reap. She brought them beer to celebrate times of joy. She chose a mortal youth most beautiful and wise when none in the heavens took her fancy. She is Yemay-Olokun, Mother of the Sea, the Great Water, Womb of Creation; She is the veiled Isis. (Stone, 1984)

African Creation Goddesses affected the world. Early matriarchal Africans traveled throughout the ancient world. The Cayce material described such matrifocal Nubians. (816-3) (Refer below to the section on Egypt.) In Europe—especially Eastern Europe—in Spain, France and Italy, there are Black Madonnas. According to Sjoo and Mor (1987), once the Goddess ruled Africa, and from thence, much of the world.

A.R.E. Librarian, Jeremiah Hoggard, whose grandfather was a holistic healer, shared insights with Lynn Rogers, reminding her of Cayce's Nubian Hermes.

The Yellow Root Race

Asian creation myths often present the Divine Feminine as part of a pair. The masculine and feminine principles complement and complete one another. These emphasize the balancing of polarities.

In Japan, the primal Divine Couple is Izanagi and Izanami. They created the eight-island country. Then they gave birth to many deities, the principal one being Amaterasu, the Sun Goddess. Although part of a trinity, She is most often paired with Susanoo, an earthly Dionysian god, according to Kyoko Nakamura. In one legend, Susanoo was unhappy with his assignment to the ocean and ascended to the heavens to disturb his sister, Amaterasu. Amaterasu has become an arch symbol in Japan. (It appears that the myth of the Eternal Feminine, encloistered in the heavens, and the arrogant God, on earth, is a temporal archetype linked to the patrifocal period that is repeated cross-culturally.) Nakamura states that the pattern seems to be towards dichotomy rather than tripartism. Thus deities are paired, and shrines to divine couples abound in Japan. (Olson, 1987)

Kuan-Yin is the Savior and Savioress in Chinese Pure Land Buddhism, according to Paul (Olson, 1987) Kuan Yin is derived from K'uai—earth, and Yin—woman. She is the Holy Mother of Compassion, who achieved ultimate enlightenment, yet chose to return to us when we called in times of trouble—to the Merciful Mother, Most Holy Kuan Yin. (Stone, 1984)

In Confucianism, Heaven and Earth were considered a divine creative pair and a continuum. The Taoist yin/yang wheel depicted the relativity of all values; the yin/yang symbol epitomizes the complementing and counterbalancing of polarized principles. (Smith, 1958) "Know the Strength of Man, But Keep a Woman's Care! Be the Stream of the Universe!" (Geng and English, 1989, p.7)

The creation myths of the yellow root race exhibit recognition of opposites and emphasize the balancing of these. They illustrate the view that opposites should work together as complements. Although one Japanese story contains tripartism as well as the theme of male rebellion, in the majority, the Divine Couple—the union of polarities—appears most often.

The White Root Race

In the white root race, examples are found of inclusion of the female within androgynous deities. In other cultures, such as among the Druids of the British Isles, the Goddess was once the religious focus, with female figures in myth personifying Her attributes.

According to hereditary British Druid, Sybil Leek, "In the Midrasch, Rabbi Samuel-bar-Nachman says 'Adam, when God created him, was a man-woman (andrognune).' The learned Maimonides supported this, saying that 'Adam and Eve were created together, co-joined by their backs but this double being God-divided and taking one half (Eve) gave her to the other half (Adam) for a mate.'" Leek further states that in the Brihadaranyaka Upanishad, the evolution of Brahm is described: In the beginning, Brahm was a large being, encompassing man and wife together. "He then made this self into two and thence husband and wife. He said, 'We are as alike as a split pea.'" (Leek, 1971, p. 176)

In Scandinavia, the Goddess spun the golden threads of the universal design of past, present and future. She was often shown as having the sexual organs of both sexes, standing with bow in one hand and sword in the other. Her husband is Odin and the legends surrounding her son, Balder, can be compared to other myths of dying sons or lovers of the Goddess in the Near East. (Leek, 1971, p. 176)

The Syrian Baal was also often depicted as androgynous as well—in combination with Astarte. A popular invocation was "Hear us Baal... whether thou be god or goddess." (Leek, 1971, p. 177)

In Greece, Aphrodite, Adonis, Dionysus—even Zeus at times—were described in hermaphroditic terms. Aphrodite was also known as Aphroditos (in the Louvre in Paris she is depicted standing with masculine organs). Often, Adonis was petitioned as "Thou with thy gracious hair, both maiden and youth, Adonis." Aristides wrote that the god Dionysus is male and female, with form true to his nature, since everywhere in himself he is like a double being. (Leek, 1971, p. 177)

In Robert Graves' translation of Roman writer Apuleius' *The Golden Ass*, the Goddess herself appears and speaks:

> I am Nature, the universal Mother, mistress of all elements, primordial child of time, sovereign of all things spiritual, queen of the dead, queen also of the immortals, the single manifestation of all gods and goddesses that are. My nod governs the shining heights of Heaven, the wholesome sea breezes, the lamentable silences of the world below. Though I am worshipped in many aspects, known by countless names, and propitiated with all manner of different rites, yet the whole round earth venerates me. (Stone, 1976, p. 22)

Goddesses associated with the British Isles include Morgan le Fay and the Lady of the Lake, who were honored in England and Wales (as well as France and Italy.) Queen Morgan was the Holy Goddess of Fortune or Fate. The Goddess Bridget was once Supreme Goddess of the Brigantes, though later canonized as a Christian saint. Bridget's powers were celebrated at the Celtic ritual of Imbokon on February First. The fire at Bridget's shrine in County Kildare in Ireland was originally tended by priestesses and later cared for by Catholic nuns until the decree of a bishop declared this practice to be pagan and ordered that the fire be extinguished—in 1280 A.D. (Stone, 1984)

In early white root race creation myths, either the Goddess or androgyny is emphasized. This emphasis on the female appears pervasive. These myths were later supplanted by patrifocal Judeo/Christian culture that superimposed their own versions. In many instances a merging of myths occurred—as in the story of Catholic Saint Bridget who bears a close resemblance to a Celtic fire goddess by the same name.

The Brown Root Race

These earliest myths from the brown root race also illustrate androgynous deities, and many emphasize the Divine Feminine. Pantheons of female deities are common. Also, the Edgar Cayce material suggests that this root race—like the red root race—has continued the wisdom of Atlantis. (497-1)

Colonel James Churchward recounts a version of the creation given on an ancient Mexican tablet. Discovered in 1584 it said human beings were created with the dual principle, masculine and feminine. The Creator caused this entity to pass into a sleep, and while sleeping, "the principles were severed by cosmic forces." When awakened, born again, the entity was two—man and woman. (Madigan, 1965, p. 1)

According to Downing (1987), the Huichol Indians of Jalisco and Nayarit have a pantheon of goddesses. One is the mother of the Pacific Ocean. She separated the living from the dead. The great Goddess of the Huichol is known as "Our Great-Grandmother". She is a towering goddess who also turns up as male. She brings life and fertility and is depicted as surrounded by snakes. In this way she resembles the Aztec Goddess Chiuacoatl, "Serpent Woman", who was always surrounded by snakes. Downing includes Hultkrantz's speculation that "this pantheon with its female dominance . . . could be likened to the pantheons that preceded the complicated theological systems of the Maya, Toltec, and Aztec high cultures. Maybe the Huichol religious structure be, at least in part, a leftover from those ancient times, but there is no consensus on that point." (Downing, 1987, p. 214)

The Goddess Coatlicue of Aztlan (Atlantis?) was the Mother of all Aztec deities. She gave of all life and took again in death. The necklace of skulls she wore was a reminder that in time, all would return to Her, all would return to the Source of Being.

Interestingly, the Edgar Cayce readings describe the Mayan and Aztec cultures as the repository of Atlantean wisdom. Atlanteans sought to establish the Law of One in these lands when Atlantis was breaking up. (497-1) It appears to me that ancient myths and theologies from cultures where the Atlanteans settled contain Atlantean wisdom. Certainly, the brown root race creation myths emphasize the Eternal Feminine. The Eternal Feminine was often included or suggested by the Edgar Cayce material on Atlantis, as discussed later in the text.

These varied, yet similar creation myths involving the Eternal Feminine from the five root races as delineated by the Edgar Cayce material suggest that, indeed:

> Our history as a species is stored in our genes; and no matter how hard patriarchy tries to suppress our past matriarchal history, it keeps bobbing to the surface in

worldwide archaeological ruins, icons, and myths, as in our dreams. (Sjoo and Mor, 1987, p. 384)

In conclusion, the Edgar Cayce source described five root races. From each of these root races appear cross-cultural myths that strongly incorporate the Eternal Feminine. Further, there are potential connections between some of these creation accounts and the Cayce material, such as the parallel between the Black Elegba and Cayce's Nubian Hermes, many accounts of separating andrognunes in the white and yellow races, and possible links between the emigrating Atlanteans and the surviving red and brown root race creation myths.

I'll never forget what Jessica Madigan (1911-1986) said about twin souls. For each lonely person there was one forever love. In a given lifetime, twin souls could be family to each other, sweethearts if lucky; even after death, one could be the guardian angel to the other. Twin souls intrigued the romantic in me.

Now I see from meeting mine, twin souls are not just the romantic concept of my youth, but a crucible for soul growth. And yet I still believe Jessica's prediction will come true. In this millennium we will find our true complement, and together, reach for the Light.

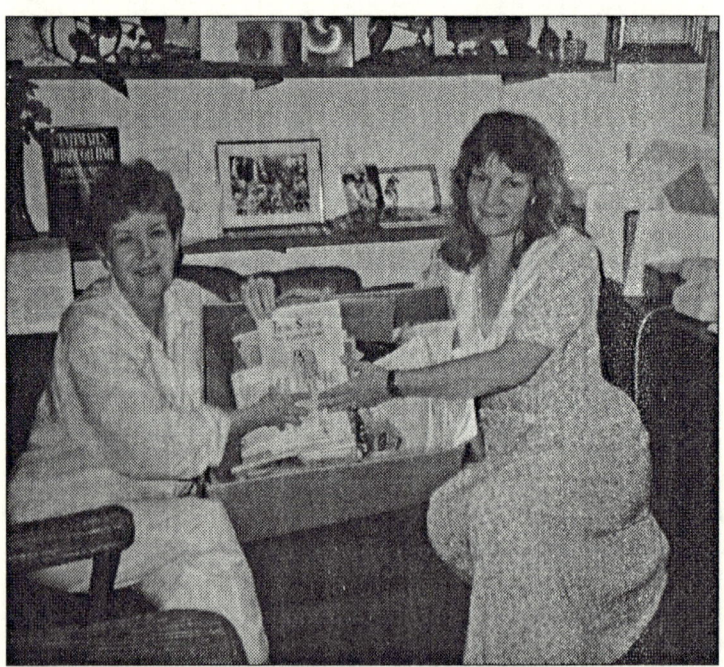

Jeanette Thomas receiving Jessica Madigan's material contributed to the Edgar Cayce Foundation. Presentation given on the couch where Edgar Cayce gave Readings.

Twin Souls—Eternal Balance and Partnership

Another concept that shows the important role of the Eternal Feminine is the idea of twin souls. From around the world stories arise of androgynous beings who separate into twin souls. There are also examples throughout history of the intense love of people who appear to be twin souls.

The Edgar Cayce readings describe Amilius as an androgynous being who separated in Atlantis to become Adam and Eve. Adam became Jesus, the Wayshower, and Mary links us to Divine Feminine.

The Cayce twin soul concept embodies eternal balance and partnership of the feminine and masculine principles as twin souls had been one in purpose from the beginning of time.

> In this then, also comes that as is held by many who have reached especially to that understanding of how *necessary*, then, becomes the *proper* mating of those souls that may be the *answers* one to another of that that may bring, through that association, that companionship, into being that that may be the more helpful, more sustaining, more the *well-rounded* or experience of those that are a *portion* one of another. Do not misinterpret, but knowing that all are of one—yet there are those divisions that make for a *closer* union, when there are the proper relationships brought about. (364-7)

Further, when asked by one young man whether a particular young woman would be best suited to him for a successful life, the Cayce source answered: "May be made so in each. No one is suited exactly in the beginning unless it has been foreordained throughout ages of mating of each." (416-1)

Writing Friends. Close souls often look alike.

Young close souls Sam Mossman and Megan Flautt 1991

St. Francis and St. Clare

For example, the readings gave Edgar Cayce and Gladys Davis as twin souls who had known many relationships through time. Reading 288-6 referred to their incarnations together in Persia as the visionary desert chieftain Uhjltd and his Persian wife Illya. The readings stated that there were present-day echoes of the emotions from the Persian experience when "There is the realizing of, or awakening to, the oneness of their souls in the [desert] plain." (288-6) In the Persian lifetime, as throughout ages of being soul mates, "the answering of spirit and soul gave the answering with the body beautiful . . . and the crying of the soul's desire—both in the carnal and the answering of the oneness in each." (288-6) Subsequent readings appear to offer counsel for these twin souls who could not be in the relationship of husband and wife in the present lifetime:

> These two have ever been together, you see, except in the American forces when there was the soon return in that of the wanderer, and in the Grecian period . . . e thou faithful unto the end and receive that crown that is ever for the faithful in heart soul and body. Be kind, affectionate, loving, ever giving, ever preferring the other. (294-9)

Finally, reading #288-6 suggested that:

> They need only remain in the future faithful one to the other, ever giving, ever retaining those joys of the relations that bring and give of self in service to others; and these bring joy, peace, and again uniting of body, soul and spirit in the next. Remain faithful, therefore, to the end; gaining those joys through daily acts of selflessness for and with others, remembering that in these manifestations they (and all souls) become knit one with the other.

Thus information offered by the Cayce source for both Edgar Cayce himself, and his twin soul, Gladys Davis, suggests a universal pattern for all twin souls who are answers to each other and who long for reunion.

Robert and Elizabeth Browning who resemble Hugh Lynn Cayce and Jessica Madigan

(Next page) Hugh Lynn's letter to Jessica thanking her and her husband for tireless efforts on behalf of A.R.E. Like Edgar Cayce and Gladys Davis, Jessica and Hugh Lynn were, in the opinion of many, close souls who complimented each other in a common purpose.

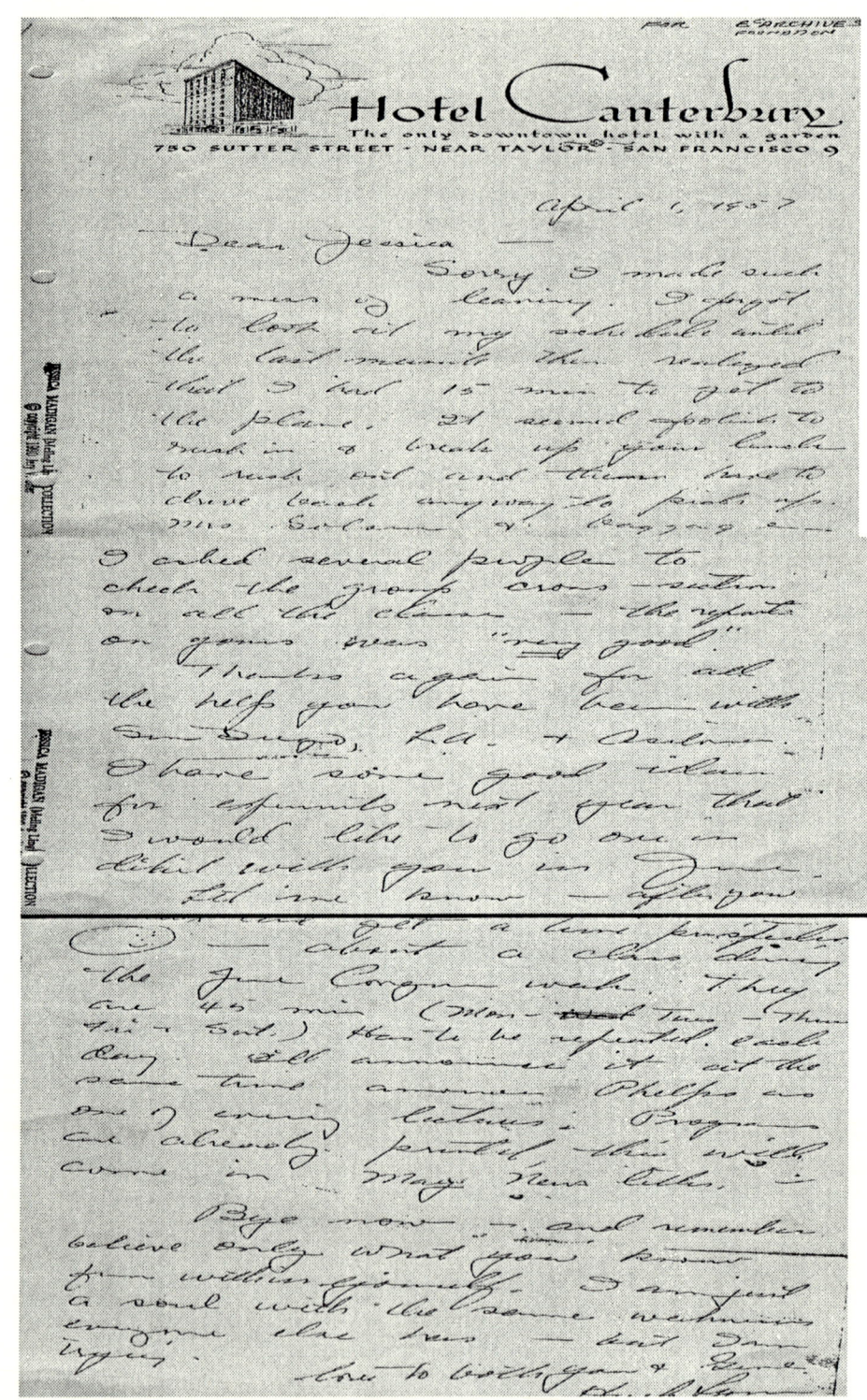

Author and clairvoyant Gladys V. Jones states that "the love which soul mates have for each other is a pure, imperishable love which was imprinted upon their consciousness in the form of an eternal pattern for love and marriage and was buried in their soul memory never to be forgotten." Further, though we may have "psychic affinities" through karmic memories with others, "soul mates are already joined and pledged together as one and their love is impervious to all other loves." (Jones, 1979, p. p. 146)

From the Gnostic treatise on the Origin of the World we read that when this first entity ate of the tree of life, his mind was opened "so that he became enamored of his co-likeness, and condemned other alien likenesses, and loathed them." (Barnstone, 1984, p. 68) According to early Association of Research and Enlightenment (A.R.E.) lecturer and author Jessica Madigan (1965), twin souls often incarnate in complementary roles, for example: Mother and son, father and daughter, sister and brother, teacher and student, husband and wife. Sometimes one even might stay out of the body as a guardian to the other.

A.R.E. author and lecturer Lynn Sparrow suggests that twin souls may not incarnate at the same time. Moreover, Sparrow asserts, "Even when they are, it may or may not be best for their development to be together at any given time." In Sparrow's opinion, sometimes the mental "commonality of purpose" shared by twin souls living on earth brings them together for needed strength, and in "other contexts" would not be necessary. (Sparrow, 1988, p. 44)

Mary and Jesus, according to the Cayce sources, are twin souls. (5749-8) Madigan writes that the awareness of an eternal love does not come until the soul seeks it . . . even though it is hidden in the heart from the beginning of time. And this is true, she states, for all men who have lived upon the earth—for all men follow the pattern of Christ, who was One with the Beloved Mother.

> The story, then, of Amilius/Amelia who became Mary and Jesus is the story of our journey throughout the earth. They have taken the road ahead of us; they have pointed out the rough places which we may tread. They have brought the eternal principles into manifestation. (Madigan, 1970, p. 104)

Madigan discussed with me the idea that Mary, like her twin soul, Jesus, could have lived a number of earthly lives in her soul's journey toward perfection. And that if understood, Mary's earthly joys and struggles and soul choices in past lives could become a helpful pattern for all women.

Possible examples of other historic and legendary twin souls could include: Adam and Eve, Abraham and Sarah, Tamar and Amnon, Jonathon and David, (with Jonathan, the feminine polarity choosing a masculine vehicle to enter the battlefield with David), Cupid and Psyche, Diana and Apollo, Guinevere and Lancelot, Benedict and Scholastica, St. Francis and St. Clare, Heloise and Abelarde, Nathaniel and Sophia Hawthorne, Elizabeth and Robert Browning, Jean Paul Sartre and Simone De Beauvoir, George Burns and Gracie Allen, John and Yoko Lennon. (Madigan and Lynn Rogers)

Richard Bach describes his novel, *The Bridge Across Forever*, as a "tale of the one adventure that matters most . . . in any age." In the novel, the Bach character sees his soul mate for the first time.

> Joy exploded through me and I tore apart, atom from atom, in the love of it, a matchstick fallen into sun. Joy too intense to bear, not another instant? I choked. Please, no! . . .
>
> Love! So intense! If it were green, it would be a green so transcendently green that even the Principle of Green couldn't have imagined . . .
>
> LOVE, not the fake broken syllables, but Love that IS! like no love I've ever imagined . . . (Bach, 1984, pp. 118–119)

In addition to the joy, there were hurdles and obstacles in Bach's journey toward his soul mate.

Similarly, Linda Goodman describes the reunion of twin souls in our age:

> During the weary search for one's own Twin Soul, there will be many side trips, many relationships that at first appear to be genuine, then fade into disinterest and boredom. Even when the Soul Mate is at last discovered, there are often many complications and testing of worthiness which cause temporary pain. Only in continually and consistently practicing tolerance and forgiveness can the hurt be alleviated. To return pain for pain only creates the future certainty of a like reaction, of more pain, through the workings of karmic cause and effect . . . (Goodman, 1978 p. 5)

As with Bach, Goodman tells of the double-edged sword of the love of twin souls with its attendant tests and trials.

Tom Sugrue, who wrote *There Is A River*, the biography of Edgar Cayce, also wrote the following in his autobiographical book, *Stranger In The Earth*:

> A man's search is for a woman to whom he can give his mind... and such a woman is rarely found... She is the Virgin of the World. She is the symbol of Holy Wisdom (Sophia) to whom Everyman offers the sign of his virtue, the intelligence with which he carries forward the labor of his resurrection; with her alone he is safe; in her arms he can rest, his weapons put aside. She will not betray his soul or stop his heart while he sleeps. He must be certain it is she, however, before he capitulates, just as a woman must have marriage before she gives up the entrance to her womb, for if he is wrong, he is lost. That is why a man may lie all his life with women and never give his mind. He gives his body as he gives kindness, or friendship, or bread, but the chalice of his thought is kept for the bride of his soul...

(Madigan, 1965, p. 28)

The love story of the 19th century English poets Elizabeth and Robert Browning has been told countless times. In the early years of their marriage, Elizabeth, an invalid, shyly gave Robert a group of sonnets she had written out of her love and devotion to him. Tennyson called these the most beautiful sonnets since the time of Shakespeare. They are simply written from her heart.

> 'How do I love thee? Let me count the ways. I love thee to the depth and breadth and height My soul can reach — and if God choose, I shall but love thee better after death.' (Madigan, 1965, p. 34)

"Twenty-eight years after her demise, when an English writer criticized her slightly, Robert Browning wrote a poem in retaliation which blisters the pages... ending it by saying that he would 'spit upon the man', except that his own lips had once been 'sanctified by hers'. In his only proposal to another woman many years after Elizabeth's death, he wrote his prospective fiancé that even if they should marry, he would have her know that his 'heart would ever be buried in Italy with Elizabeth'." (Madigan, 1965, p. 38) This story demonstrates the intensity of love and devotion that twin souls who have the opportunity to be mates may express for one another.

Franciscan Father Murray Bodo (1979) reflects in modern day Assisi, Italy, about 12th century Francis and Clare whose names are so often linked in legend. St. Bonaventure stated that "She was the first flower in Francis' garden, and she shone like a radiant star, fragrant as a flower blossoming white and pure in springtime." (p.x) Bodo suggests that Clare and Francis' love for God makes Assisi a magnetic paradise seven and a half centuries later. Together, the saints consecrated their lives to creating a Camelot, which welcomed lepers and beggars. Bodo describes this paradise as:

> ... a new Eden where men and women walked in the cool of evening hand in hand with God... You two, so removed from one another are so much closer than the lovers I watch walking hand in hand in the Piazza del Comune. How weak my mind becomes; how insufficient even poetry to explain this. (Bodo, 1979, p. 102)

Charismatic young Francis had become sick of the "glamorous" crusades, his merchant father's materialism and the decadence within the Catholic Church. He had a vision at the abandoned chapel of San Damiano that he should rebuild God's church. He'd taken the vision literally, renounced his former life and begun to repair the chapel, brick by brick, but his real work was greater than he'd dreamed.

Clare was an aristocratic girl who was quickened by Francis' dream. She fled her comfortable home by night, cut off her long golden hair, and established the Order of the Poor Clares. She argued with the Pope that women should have the right to live a life of poverty in the pattern of Christ. Clare rebelled against papist authority in the name of Father God.

Throughout Francis' life, Clare's love never failed him. "Their names are linked together," Professor J. Herkless, D.D., states "like Jerome and Paula, Benedict and his sister Scholastica, in ecclesiastical history: like Dante and Beatrice, Petrarch and Laura, in literature; and many have deemed the affection of Francis and Clare more than spiritual, an offering on that altar of God which not seldom has received the sacrifice of the most tender love." (Herkless, 1901, p. 77)

She was his guide in a life dedicated to Lady Poverty. Francis' consummate Canticle to the Creatures was written during the rare time Francis spent with Clare while she nursed his afflicted eyes. Bodo (1979) speculates that Brother Sun and Sister Moon are images of Francis and Clare on one level. Clare herself was an impassioned writer. Could the Canticles have been a co-creative effort? Certainly they suggest the motif of twin souls, of the eternal feminine and masculine principles through time. The English poet Matthew Arnold offered the following translation:

> Praised be my Lord God with all His creatures,
> and specially *our brother the sun*, who brings us the day

and who brings us the light; fair is he, and shines with a very great splendor: O Lord, he signifies to us Thee?

Praised be my Lord, for *our sister the moon*, and for the stars, which He has set clear and lovely in heaven.

Praised be my Lord for *our brother the wind*, and for air and cloud, calms and all weather, by which Thou upholdest life in all creatures.

Praised be my Lord for *our sister water*, who is very serviceable to us, and humble and precious and clean.

Praised be my Lord for *our brother fire*, through whom Thou givest us light in the darkness; and he is bright and pleasant and very mighty and strong.

Praised be my Lord for *our mother the earth*, she which doth sustain us and keep us and bringeth forth divers fruits and flowers of many colours, and grass . . . (Herkless, 1901, p. 69) (author's italics)

It seems to me that this canticle is in the tradition of Creation Spirituality. Masculine and feminine imagery intertwine in the Oneness of forces described by the Edgar Cayce sources.

Transpersonal phenomena are associated with Francis and Clare's relationship. Bodo (1979) recounts the following legend. Often lonely, Clare loved to walk with Francis, but unpleasant insinuations were made. "'We have to walk apart,' he said one winter day as they wound through the snow-covered Valley of Spoleto. 'Francis, when will we see each other again?' Francis answered gently, 'When summer comes and roses are in bloom.' Clare stood open-mouthed and trembling. From the snow-covered tops of bushes and small trees, roses began to appear in full bloom." (Bodo, 1979, p. 53)

Carl Jung suggested that synchronistic events occur when kindred souls come together. How else may we recognize the twin soul? Indications given by Madigan (1965) include the following:

PHYSICAL ATTRACTION would be almost overwhelming. It is the SAME BODY, according to Plato.

You view life in much the same manner.

The spiritual work is the same.

> You have the same soul purpose throughout the earth.
>
> There is a feeling of ONENESS all of the life, physically, mentally, emotionally. A prominent writer who lost her husband of many years wrote that it was as if a portion of her BODY and MIND had been cut off from her.
>
> You 'click'. This is the best friend, lover, parent, child. You respond to each other—you are ANSWERS one to the other. (Madigan, 1965, p. 42)

Finally, Madigan states that "One of the most beautiful readings in the Edgar Cayce file gives this answer. When it was asked by a very young girl who hoped to meet her 'true love', he answered by saying 'The heart knoweth . . . the soul never forgeteth'". (Madigan, 1965, p. 4)

In this chapter on Creation, discussion of the Creative Forces, cross-cultural creation myths and accounts of twin souls show connections between the Edgar Cayce material and the Eternal Feminine. These connections can be summarized as follows:

Creative Forces described in the Edgar Cayce material are elucidated through recurrent themes found in other creation stories across many times and cultures. These include: myths of God as Birther; souls' beginnings in original blessing versus original sin; the separation of the Divine and Universal feminine and masculine principles at the transcendent and immanent levels; and the rebellion of the created against the Creator, with either a male or female rebel rising up against the Mother's wisdom or the Father's authority, respectively.

The Edgar Cayce creation story sets the stage for tracing the Eternal Feminine through cross-cultural creation myths and in the motif of twin souls. Each of the five root races, as described by the Edgar Cayce material, contain creation myths which include the Divine Feminine in many forms, as well as references to spiritual and physical androgyny in the form of Divine Couples and andrognunes. Further, the twin soul motif concretizes the idea of the separating androgynous being through the accounts of the life patterns of individual couples through the present day. Creation themes, overall, help to provide a foundation of understanding about the relationship between the Eternal Feminine and the Edgar Cayce concepts.

I'd awakened to Cayce's truths in my late teens. By the mid-eighties I started a ministerial training program. I woke one day to the realization that male diety language excluded me.

I became aware of it everywhere. Even Edgar Cayce once said, "If God wants to make trouble for a man, he sends a woman." I called my teacher Jessica who comforted me, said Cayce had a hard go at times, living in the same house with his wife and twin soul both. In that reading, his human self bled through. But I'd tossed the book toward the fireplace.

Like many women in this crisis of exclusion, I threw out all the male only systems. Into this temporary vacuum came new truth. I read how God had been a woman once—in pagan times, I was part of the Divine.

But the bridge back to metaphysical Christianity was a surprise to me, a non-Catholic. I discovered Mary and came to my church with lots to share. One Sunday for my student talk, I decorated the altar with fig leaves and asked my young daughter, my minister's wife and an elder woman to stand up as maiden, mother and wise woman. In those days, some parishioners asked the minister, "Does she have to do that again?" Years later, they were all part of it.

Lynn Rogers in front of the old Cayce Hospital Building at Virginia Beach

CHAPTER TWO
THE WAY OF THE MOTHER

CHAPTER TWO

THE WAY OF THE MOTHER

Several years ago my young daughter asked, "Is God a man or a woman or both?" Her question prompted research into ancient religious traditions. I was surprised to discover that in ancient times people worshipped the Goddess.

Reawakening awareness of the Divine Feminine to balance current masculine imagery regarding the Creator, means that we are all made in the image and likeness of the Divine. Only by understanding Her transcendent aspect can we answer the children of tomorrow who ask, "Is God a man or a woman or both?"

In this chapter, the history of Goddess worship is examined and traced through Atlantis, India, and Egypt to its eventual submersion by invading patrifocal peoples. Interrelationships between the Goddess tradition and the Edgar Cayce material are illustrated.

The Goddess was worshipped for over 25,000 years as the core Deity. This ascendancy of the feminine principle had tremendous implications for the social system as well as humanity's way of relating to its natural environment. For example, in this matrifocal worldview with the Goddess at the center, as opposed to the pinnacle, of the religious gestalt, females enjoyed high social status yet there were fully developed roles for males as well. Nature was seen as integrated with human life instead of as a mechanical object to be manipulated. The final overturning of matrifocal by patrifocal religion shifted the religious and social emphasis to a hierarchical system of sky gods where, according to Gadon (1989), the "world where life became less free, less creative and less joyful." (Gadon, 1989, p. 110)

Atlantis

Could this Goddess worship have begun in that faraway land Edgar Cayce described as Atlantis? The Edgar Cayce readings imply that women enjoyed an elevated spiritual status in Atlantis:

> In the one before this we find in that country now submerged, and the entity among those of the high priestess' to the then worshipped or worshipful position held by such. (37-1)
>
> The entity was a priestess in the temple of the Law of One. (1206-3)

In my opinion, it seems natural to assume that when the deity is conceptualized as female, or includes the Eternal Feminine, then female persons enjoy greater status. This assumption is validated by examples from both later Goddess-worshipping societies and more recent patrifocal cultures as well.

The Eternal Feminine can be traced through Atlantis in the account rendered by the Cayce sources. Individual life readings by Edgar Cayce, as well as the work of Atlantean historians, such as Stier, Hall and contemporary Cayces (Edgar Evans and Gail) describe aspects of the Eternal Feminine.

Numerous Edgar Cayce readings state that Atlantis was a prehistoric civilization that existed for 200,000 years in the area we now call the Atlantic Ocean. Before its final destruction its seers took its spiritual secrets into new lands. It appears to me that the Cayce account of Atlantis is significant on three levels: archaeological, prophetic and archetypal.

Research scientists are in the process of substantiating Atlantis archaeologically. An example of their findings related in Venture Inward Magazine, is that in 1989 a shark-shaped sand mound of indeterminate age was sighted on the east side of Bimini Island in the Atlantic. Interestingly, the Cayce material states that Bimini is the highest portion left above the waves of a once great continent; when earth changes begin, these portions will be among the first to rise. (996-1) and (587-4) Other prophesies contained in the readings suggested that, by the end of the last century, when the selfish world motives would be broken up, we would discover the records of Atlantis. Recent discoveries of submerged structures off the coast of Cuba support this claim. (Van Hoose, personal communication, 2003)

Until Atlantis is uncovered, its themes are relevant psychologically and figuratively in regard to this question: What part did the Eternal Feminine play in Atlantis and how has this principle carried over into the world today?

> ... if we are to accept such as being a fact or fiction, may truly depend upon ... what contribution would such information be to the minds of individuals, as

to knowing or understanding the better or closer relations to the Creative Forces? (364-1)

According to Jery Stier, Director of the Society for Mystic Prehistory Studies, there were five major Atlantean ages, with either the masculine or the feminine principle accentuated until the last age when a synthesis of the two prevailed. Throughout the five ages there had been a gradual descent from fourth dimensional to third dimensional consciousness. (See Table 1 below). The Age of Magic and the Mental Age were the realms of eternal archetypes where thought was crystallized. "As to their forms in the physical sense, they were rather like thought forms . . . " (364-3)

What Stier calls the First (masculine) Age was destroyed after 50,722 B.C. when the Great Council met to attempt to eradicate the overrunning beasts that had been created as thought projections of earlier Lemurian cycles. Stier believes that the use of huge crystals, or lasers, triggered the breaking up of the land. After this breakup the Second (feminine) Age unfolded on five great islands and ended in 28,000 B.C. It appears that either the yang or the yin force carried too far is an extreme and necessitates the balancing influence of the other —thus the oscillating masculine and feminine ages.

According to Merlin Stone (1978) and Riane Eisler (1987), authors of *When God Was A Woman* and *The Chalice and the Blade*, respectively, archaeological evidence suggests that Goddess worship begins in the Upper Paleolithic period. It occurs to me that this is the same time the Cayce sources gave for the destruction of the second Atlantean Age—the "feminine" age, according to Stier. One woman was told by the Cayce source that she had been a priestess in the Atlantean land (just before the second destruction) "when there were those periods of activity in which there was the changing of individuals from the double sex, or the ability of the progeneration of activities from self." She aided the people and came to be worshipped. (2390-1)

Curiously, all known Goddess scholarship places the origins of Her worship from the Upper Paleolithic Period—approximately 28,000 B.C. (See "The Goddess" below.) The Edgar Cayce material further suggests, at the time of the destructions of each Atlantean age, different forms of exoduses occurred.

> The entity was in Atlantis when there was the second period of disturbance—which would be 22,500 before the periods of the Egyptian activity covered by the exodus; or it was some (28,000) before Christ, see? (470-22)

I speculate that "known" Goddess worship is the remnant of more complex Atlantean worship of the Creative Forces.

By the Third Age the single Atlantean continent had been broken up by previous destructions, from five great islands in the Second Age, into three major islands. These islands were given by the Cayce sources as Aryan, Og, and Poseidia. Mu, a Lemurian remnant, also still existed. In reading #509-1 a woman was told that she had,

> ... not far from the land in which the entity in this sojourn first saw the light—(that must in the near future fade again into those joinings with the land of Mu)—established a temple of worship for those that escaped from the turmoil of the shifting of the earth at that particular period.

AGE	APPROXIMATE TIMES	GEOGRAPHY	COMMENTS
Age of Magic	200,000 BC -100,000 BC		4th dimensional
Mental Age			
1st Age (Masculine)	100,000 BC -50,000 BC	1 large continent	3rd dimensional
2nd Age (Feminine)	50,000 BC -28,000 BC	5 islands	
3rd Age (Synthesis)	28,000 BC -10,000 BC	3 islands	

Table 1. The Five Ages of Atlantis

> The entity, in the name Oeueou, established near Santa Barbara the temple to the sun and the moon; for the satellite of the moon had not faded then, *and there was enjoined as to the entity in the worship as the goddess to the moon and the sun* (author's italics). (509-1)

According to Stier, the last age of Atlantis was the spiritual high point. In one of her life readings given by Edgar Cayce, an individual identified as (288) was told that she had lived before with her twin soul as an androgynous flesh being named "Asule/Aczine" in the late Atlantean epoch as a ruler in Poseidia. In 12,800 B.C., she and her twin soul incarnated together in the body of a female. "In *flesh-form* in earth's plane we find the first in that of the Poseidian forces, when both were confined in the body of the female; for this being the stronger in the then applied or expressed forces found manifestations for each in that form . . . " (288-6) Despite cycles of masculine or feminine ascendancy the two principles are One. The Edgar Cayce source concluded reading 288-6 by telling Miss 288 that she and her twin soul were one in Poseidia in 12,800 B.C. "The desire remained in the One, for which the Oneness was created." (288-6)

Similarly, regarding Mary the Beloved Mother—twin soul of Jesus, in Atlantis, Madigan (1970) writes that:

> Mary, in the Atlantean culture when women were of equal and like status to men, sometimes assumed the dominant role. Once, as the daughter of a king, she ruled. Again, as a high priestess in the Temple of Light, she brought the principle of the masculine-feminine polarity into the sacred literature of Atlantis. Centuries later, Ram brought this very teaching into the land that became India. (Madigan, 1970, p. 101)

Madigan's premise regarding Mary's status in Atlantis is illustrated by the following subjective account. In a "Re-Search" reincarnation series conducted by the author and hypnotherapist Alexi MacKinnon, more than one audio-taped hypnotic regression subject "saw" Mary as a great spiritual leader in latter day Atlantis. One individual described Mary in the Poseidian Hall of Flowers. She appeared as a tall Being of Light who was "like the Christ." (Rogers and MacKinnon, 1987)

Many women were told by the Cayce source that they had been priestesses in Atlantis in service of the Law of One, or the Creative Forces—Father/Mother God. To a young woman, aged 24, it was given:

> Through that particular period of experiences in Atlantis, the children of the Law of One—including this entity, Rhea, as the high priestess—were giving periods to the concentration of thought for the use of the universal forces. . . . (2464-2)

To a woman aged 56 who sought guidance from the Cayce sources it was given:

> Then the entity was in the name Asamasama, and of those lines of priestesses and priests in those holy lands, that found aid and help from compliance to the Law of One. (2402-2)

These individual life readings provide clues to the expression of the Universal Feminine in Atlantis by showing the choices and activities of individual women in regard to the Creative Forces in terms of their dedication to the Law of One.

The Cayce material on other cultures that existed at the same time as Atlantis shows a similar pattern where women are concerned. Before Atlantis was destroyed, there was communication with other cultures existing in the world, including the City of Gold in the Gobi. According to the Cayce material, the Gobi had been an entry point for one of the simultaneous appearances of Adamic humanity on earth. (364-13, 1210-1, 5748-1) "For the entity was as a minister or teacher, or princess; and journeyed to many of these lands (from the City of Gold to Egypt, India, from Atlantis, Mu, Lu-Lemuria—Nordic) relating all truths as one truth." (1648)

Interestingly, the Gobi period, according to the Cayce account, was one of equality of the genders with female rulership. "The association or activity in the experience was with a companion chosen from the Gobi land; yet—in that period of experience—the female *ruled rather than the male*." (Author's italics) (2067-4); "There was equality between the sexes during that experience . . . The rights of each were that of the other." (877-1) Here the Cayce material is in exact accord with recent scholarship regarding the Goddess, in that such scholarship suggests that when society was Goddess centered, it was (paradoxically) founded on ideals of gender partnership. (See "The Goddess" below.)

Many Cayce readings on the Gobi period highlight the role of the Eternal Feminine as illustrated by the following readings given for women today who had been women leaders in the Gobi land:

The Way Of The Mother

**One of Lynn Rogers' Survey Lectures
at A.R.E in Virginia Beach 1989**

Before that the entity was in the Indo-China land, when the queen or princess rose to authority and power. The entity was an associate, a companion of that entity 'the golden girl', or the golden princess. (2762-1)

... the entity gained and gained through this experience, for many peoples worshipped the entity, yet the entity gave self in service without desiring worshipfulness. (31-1)

... entity's activities were in the Temple Beautiful that was established in Taoi, which may some day be brought to light—when there have been those concentrated efforts in the direction to uncover the activities that will make for a greater correlation of the facts that Truth is that which grows in the hearts of men to make them more aware of *their* relationship to their maker. (1037-1)

I believe the Edgar Cayce life readings on the Gobi period further correlate and uncover the truth of the role of the Eternal Feminine in the earth.

Life readings for those who had past lifetimes in other lands that existed at the same time as Atlantis, follow this pattern. For example, a woman was told that she had lived in the Peruvian country (before the destruction of Atlantis) and brought sun worship. She was "made high priestess, for the entity was worshipped as highest in that period." (2688) Another woman was told that she gave the Peruvian peoples self-government and that today she is "one given to control many peoples. One given to know the greater scope not given to detail forces." (2801-5) Thus the Edgar Cayce material further demonstrates the role of the Eternal Feminine in Atlantis and contemporary cultures before its final demise.

Ultimately, the selfish nature manifested by the "Sons of Belial", opposing the Children of the Law of One, brought the final destructions to Atlantis. According to Hugh Lynn Cayce (1971), the sons of Belial believed in self-gratification without respect for others. Ironically, this destructive self-emphasis at the expense of others is antithetical to one of the principles, which appears to have been most closely associated with the Eternal Feminine cross-culturally and throughout time; namely, relatedness as expressed through equal regard for and respect for others.

Edgar Cayce gave a talk in 1931 about the misuse of the mind forces by the Atlanteans for self-gratification at the expense of others in which clear warnings are given about such selfishness and the domination of others:

> Many of you who have studied something of the history of Atlantis know that these mental forces were highly developed there. Many individuals were able to think with such concentration that they brought material things into existence by the mere power of their thought. But to use such a force, as they did, for selfish interests can result in evil. The greatest sin in the world today is selfishness, and the domination of one individual will by another. (Cayce, 1946)

The following reading describes one woman's role at the time of the final conflict between the forces of selflessness and selfishness as the Atlantean period draws to a close:

> Before that we find the entity was in the Atlantean land, in those periods when there first began the withdrawing from the Law of One, those establishing of the sons—or of the son Belial in that experience.
>
> The entity made for a foregathering with these for power, having been of the priestesses of the land; and through the activities of Belial became the priestess in the temple that was built in opposition to the ones—or the sons of the *ONE* (author's italics). (263-4)

Here the Cayce material also implies the loss of the synthesis, the Oneness, and the beginnings of another cycle of gender polarization—as they stress the "—son of Belial". Today, after a long "Way of the Father", we are re-membering the Goddess for the first time in over 3,000 years as we approach a new age of synthesis. What was the Way of the Mother?

The Goddess

Historians now believe that the Goddess was worshipped for over 25,000 years. As previously stated, Goddess worship began around the time of the second destruction of Atlantis. (See Atlantis above.) It appears that every historic goddess is an aspect of the core concept of the Divine Feminine. According to Riane Eisler, Goddess-worshipping, matrifocal societies were gyno-centric, with fully developed roles for men as well as women. Name and property passed through the mother's line. Sexual violence and child sexual abuse were almost non-existent; the birth of daughters was a special blessing.

Scholars such as James (1935), Graves (1948), Stone (1976), Eisler (1987), Olson (1987), and Gadon (1989) cite archaeological, historical and mythological evidence of Goddess worship for a period over 25,000 years. As previously stated, the Eternal Feminine can be described in two ways: first, as a transcendent deity (the Divine Feminine); second, as immanent within female persons (the Universal Feminine). When She is both, she is a model for human wholeness.

Transpersonal psychologists such as Carl Jung have helped us to glimpse the immanent aspects of the Goddess. The Goddess incarnate unifies the duality of life and death. She fuses pairs of opposites—motherhood and virginity, femininity and masculinity, birth and death. Erich Neumann called her the goddess of opposites. (Eisler, 1987, p. 111) The unity of such opposites is expressed and celebrated through rituals emphasizing the Oneness of Being.

Downing believes that the earliest Goddess traditions imaged Her as androgynous. The Goddess represented the unity that encompassed gender duality as it encompassed kindness and cruelty or life and death. Thus, Downing states, once upon a time the Goddess was the most potent exemplification of divine power. (Downing, 1987) This first Goddess concept of androgynous unity parallels the Edgar Cayce account of the Oneness at the time of Amilius.

> As flesh is the activity of the mental being (or the spiritual self and mental being) pushing itself into matter, and as spirit—as He gave—is neither male nor female, they are both—or one. (5749-7)

In high school, my only glimpse of the Goddess was of a portly, headless fertility figure. If the feminine principle played a part in history at all, it was in a primitive and rudimentary form. More recent scholarship paints a startlingly different picture. Here we find a transcendent being. Mythologist Robert Graves (1948) states, "The Great Goddess was regarded as immortal, changeless, omnipotent." (Stone, 1976, p. 23)

To many women and men today this concept is electrifying and empowering. We have worshipped the masculine—Father God, but we've only glimpsed the other, Divine Feminine face of the Creator.

As my daughter, then a teenager, put it:

> Men have always been able to identify with a masculine god and be that much closer to 'heaven's gates' simply because of their gender. Women have not been able to see themselves in the image of the divine because of the lack of a feminine deity. (Flautt, 1991, Personal Communication)

Z. Budapest, Goddess Movement pioneer and President of Women's Spirituality Forum, recently received a letter: "Thank you for giving us back our divinity. —Glenna". (Budapest, 1990, p. 3)

Lynn Rogers' daughter Megan Althea Flautt who helped make Lynn aware of the Goddess.

Her Nature

According to Merlin Stone, one of the first voices in the newly emerging body of Goddess scholarship, the original status of the Goddess was as supreme deity. She was linked to the sun, heaven, the universe, the source of all life. It was She who brought forth the Heavens and the Earth, the first people. (Stone, 1976)

Barbara Walker states that although male writers through the centuries broke the Goddess figure down into innumerable "goddesses", she was to the ancients "a full-fledged cosmic parent figure who created the universe and its laws, ruler of Nature, Fate, Time, Eternity, Truth, Wisdom, Justice, Love, Birth, Death, etc." (Walker, 1983, p. 364) Further, She was Mother, the author of being and the deity who infused all creation with the vital blood of life. In reality "every female divinity in the present encyclopedia may be regarded as only another aspect of the core concept of a female Supreme Being." (Walker, 1983, p. 346)

Thus, the Sumerian goddesses Ishtar and Inanna, the Egyptian goddesses Isis and Hathor, the Greek Gaia—Goddess of the Beginning, the Canaanite-Hebrew goddesses Asherah and Anath, the Gnostic Sophia, the medieval Virgin Mary, a host of Indian goddesses including Kali and Radha Sri Lakshmi, the Chinese Kuan-Yin, the Japanese Amaterasu, the African goddess Oshun, the Eskimo sea goddess Sedna, the Sioux Buffalo Calf Woman, the Corn goddess of the Iroquois and Hopi and the Mexican Huichol earth goddesses—are all aspects of the Divine Feminine.

Stone states that it is difficult to grasp the immensity and significance of the reverence paid to the Goddess over a period of 25 thousand years, cutting across national boundaries and vast expanses of sea; yet, it is vital to do that in order to comprehend the widespread power and influence of this religion prominent 20,000 years before Moses was born. (Stone, 1976) Such comprehension will also help to incorporate the Divine Feminine into the lives of peoples and societies in the present day.

Reasons for a Female Rather than a Male Deity

According to mythologist Robert Graves, the concept of fatherhood had not yet been introduced into religious thought at the time of the development of Goddess worship. (Graves, 1948) Frazer, Margaret Mead, and other anthropologists agree that early peoples did not understand the secret of human fecundity. Thus, "the human female was revered as the giver of life. Only women could produce their own kind, and man's part in this process was not as yet recognized". (Stone, 1976, p. 11)

Jeremy Taylor states that the facts of life were told from woman to woman in the ancient Mediterranean societies so that secret knowledge of conception was kept from men in a "secret and binding oath". (Taylor, 1983, p. 17) Gross (edited by Olson) asserts that the ancient Hindus "had a keen perception of the awesomeness of female sexuality and the female sex organs, particularly the *yoni* but sometimes the breasts. They are venerated in and of themselves as awesome and creative." (Olson, 1987, p. 226) This keeping of secret knowledge effectively perpetuated female power.

Joseph Campbell stated that in earliest times it was the women who showed themselves supreme—not only as the bearers of children but also the chief producers of food. By realizing that it was possible to cultivate as well as to gather, they had made the earth valuable and they became, consequently, its possessors. (Campbell, 1959)

> Hear O ye regions, the praise of Queen Nana; Magnify the Creatress; exalt the dignified, exalt the Glorious One, draw nigh to the Mighty Lady.
> —Sumer, Nineteenth Century B.C. (Stone, 1976, p. x)

Not only was the Creator once female in Sumer, but also in Egypt, Crete, Greece, Ethiopia, Libya, India, Elam, Babylon, Anatolia, Canaan, Ireland, Mesopotamia, and even in ancient Judah and Israel, to name but a few. The deifications of the Goddess in the ancient world were variations on a theme. (Stone, 1976) Such deification increased the status of women in the ancient world.

Regarding Egypt, where Hugh Lynn Cayce sent Mark Lehner to be to be educated, Lehner (1974) writes:

> Archaeological data from the predynastic period show that women of the time held advanced social positions. The Great Mother, also symbolized by the cow, was always one of the foremost Egyptian goddesses. Early slate palettes from Gerzeh suggest that she was regarded as Queen of Heaven. Furthermore, the graves of women from the predynastic period are some of the largest and most elaborate . . . (Lehner, 1974, p. 126)

The Cayce material suggests the importance of women's leadership role in earliest Egypt. Ms. 993-3 asked the sleeping Cayce, "Was I a man at that time when among those that put up the first of the pyramids?" The Cayce source answered, "Then there was rather that as a woman, the entity was the ruler over those of man—and had many men as husbands, then." Thus this Cayce material directly supports recent Goddess scholarship, such as that of Stone (1978) regarding female empowerment in Goddess-worshiping societies.

In the Bible concurrence of worship of the popular Goddess religion is demonstrated from portions of text such as the Old Testament, Jeremiah 44:

> 15 Then all the men which knew their wives had burned incense unto other gods, and all the women that stood by, a great multitude, even all the people that dwelt in the land of Egypt, in Pathros, answered Jeremiah, saying. . . .
>
> 17 But we will certainly . . . burn incense to the queen of heaven, and to pour out drink offering to her, as we have done, we, and our fathers, our kings, and our princes, in the streets of Jerusalem: for then had we plenty of victuals, and were well, and saw no evil.
>
> 18 But since we left off to burn incense to the queen of heaven, and to pour out drink offerings unto her, we have wanted all *things*, and have been consumed by the sword and by famine.
>
> 19 And when we burned incense to the queen of heaven, and poured out drink offerings unto her, did we make her cakes to worship her, and pour out drink offerings to her, without men? (*Holy Bible, King James Version*)

We may tend to view the Goddess and her priestesses as dominant in matrifocal societies because we stand today within a hierarchical dominance structure and mind set. As Eisler suggests in *The Chalice and the Blade*, the Goddess-worshipping societies were gyno-centric. Thus the deity was represented in female form—at the center, rather than at the top, of a social system that allowed more fully developed roles for men as well as for women. (Eisler, 1987)

Ancient societies centered on the Eternal Feminine (in terms of the Divine Feminine—the female deity, and the Universal Feminine—qualities most closely associated with women) offer alternative ideas about masculinity. In matrifocal societies, the feeling aspect of males could come forth and was revered in mythic and religious imagery. For example, there are references (Stone, 1976 and Starhawk, 1979) to Father Nature, the horned god, and Brother Moon, who suggest to me the fiercely protective, earthy, wild and feeling aspect of the masculine principle.

What can men and women learn today from the immanent god of yesterday to help them today? As Robert Bly, Matthew Fox and other pioneers invite men to greater wholeness, the ancient archetypes of Brother Moon and Father Nature, Protector of the Weak, have special meaning.

> When the collective social assumptions about male-dominance remain unquestioned and unconscious, men are led to believe that they 'cannot speak' about their emotions and their internal life, even with other men. Men are persuaded that they have 'won', but only at the cost of their own self-expression and sense of multiple creative possibilities. (Taylor, 1990, p. 31)

According to Beverly Rubik, PhD., Director of the Center for Frontier Sciences, Western science too has suffered from a culturally narrow masculine attitude. Francis Bacon wrote that science would "tease and torture the secrets out of nature". (Rubik, 1990, p. 6) Science has been regarded as a masculine activity and Nature a female to be unveiled and defrocked. Physicists smash atoms, biologists kill organisms, and geneticists control and manipulate the gene pool of life. Today's dominant masculine ideology is a simple mechanical (or mechanistic) order. (Rubik, 1990) Yet the Edgar Cayce readings stated that "activities that count to every soul are the unseen forces that may *not* be measured in the crucible nor may they be taped by any meter." (476-1)

Rubik (1990) speculates about an emerging feminine scientific paradigm. Nature would not be seen as a passive mechanical object to be manipulated, but as alive, growing, and integrated with human life. Rather than the "Big Bang" we might have the image of the Cosmic Egg unfolding. Twelfth century nun and psychic healer Hildegarde of Bingen anticipated such a cosmology in her visionary art. (See Future Horizons below.) Not only has science been conceptualized through a culturally narrow masculine attitude, but religious and psychological notions about what is "archetypically feminine" reflect similar language and assumptions.

It appears to me that there are both temporal and eternal feminine and masculine archetypes. The former reflect oscillating cultural cycles, while the latter are universal. To understand the Eternal Feminine and its relationship to the Edgar Cayce material today, it is helpful to first explore civilizations and cultures that created myths so different from our own.

India and Egypt, Mothers of Religion

I assert that the Atlanteans held the Father/Mother God concept, or understood the Oneness of the two archetypal co-creative forces. Before the flood, Atlantean teachings, including those of twin souls and the eternal feminine and masculine principles, were taken to other places in the earth, such as the Peruvian and Yucatan lands, the British Isles, the Orient and Egypt and India. "India and Egypt, after Atlantis, were the two great mothers of religion, but India came first by many centuries." (Madigan, 1970, p. 71) For this reason certain mythic accounts of India and Egypt as given by the Edgar Cayce and parallel sources will be surveyed. Here we may see how awareness of the Eternal Feminine was carried from Atlantis into subsequent cultures.

India

Atlantean religious concepts are encoded in ancient Indian teachings. Male and female imagery is employed in every aspect. Each god has his goddess. The study of energy movement through the charkas is grounded in the assumption of the separation and reunion of the Creative Forces, which appear dual—yet are one.

The legend of Rama and Sita links the Edgar Cayce material and the Eternal Feminine in India. The readings suggest that the leader Ram (Rama) lived before as Amilius.

> In the period, then—some hundred, some ninety eight thousand years before the entry of Ram into India—there lived in this land of Atlantis one Amilius, who had first noted that of the separations of the beings into male and female as separate entities, or individuals. (364-3)

Madigan (1970) attempts to interpret the time discrepancy given in this reading:

> Atlantis existed for about 200,000 years. If Edgar Cayce meant 198,000 years, then Ram would have entered India about two thousand years before Hermes, the Nubian (a later incarnation of Jesus) entered Egypt with Ra Ta. If Edgar Cayce meant 98,000 years, then there would have been a very great time period between Ram and Hermes.
>
> Time is the most difficult factor in reading the Akasha. The answer is a simple one. In fourth dimensional experiences, *time* does not exist. All time is one. The East Indian civilization is far older than that of Egypt, and it may be that the 98,000 years *after* Amilius is correct. (Madigan, 1970 p. 67)

Regardless of this confusing time disparity, the story of Ram—and his wife Sita—has become deeply imbedded in Indian legend.

In 1968, Mahatma Gandhi's close friend Rajogopalachari retranslated *The Ramayana*, or Life of Ram. In this mythic account that has been handed down for generations, Ram comes from the Dynasty of the Sun and enters India by flying chariot. (This could suggest air travel from Atlantis.) Regarding Ram's female counterpart, in the words of Rajogopalachari:

> Sita is the female counterpart of the Supreme Being (Rama). She is the embodiment of compassion and grace. Compassion is the Supreme Mother and she is enthroned in the heart of the Lord ... God as Father and God as Mother are not distinct. (Madigan, 1970, p. 72)

Madigan speculated that the legend of Ram's wife Sita could have been based upon a real past incarnation of Mary. According to the Vedas, the ancient sacred literature of Hinduism, and Madigan's psychic insight, Sita was born in India.

In legend, Ram's wife Sita was found in a furrow. The Vedas describe Sita as daughter of Sri Lakshmi, Goddess who caused the pulsating universe. (Olson, 1987) Sita presides over agriculture. This association of the Goddess with agriculture has persisted through time. Sita also becomes known as Kakshmi, Loka-Mata, The World Mother, Jalandhija, Ocean-born and Padma, symbol of the Lotus.

Madigan believed the Vedas are Atlantean memory—teachings of a time when souls were not imprisoned in the flesh. The Upanishads are the "knowledge" portion of the Vedas. In the Upanishads we listen to the age-old teachings of Amilius brought by Ram from Atlantis into India.

The Upanishads describe our eternal state of consciousness as a dreamless-dream, free from evils, free from fear—as in the translation by Radhakrisshnan in the section on dreams and sleep:

> As a man when in the embrace of his beloved wife knows nothing from without or within, so the person when in the embrace of the intelligent self knows nothing within or without. That, verily, is his form in which his desire is fulfilled, in which the self is his desire, in which he is without desire, free from all sorrow. (Madigan, 1970, p. 74)

According to the Edgar Cayce material, each country had a symbolic strength and weakness. Jess Stearn, author of the pivotal *Edgar Cayce - The Sleeping Prophet* (1967) quotes the Cayce material in this regard: "Each nation, each people, have built by their very spirit a purposeful position not only in the affairs of the earth but of the universe." (Stearn, 1967, p. 85). At the time of Cayce's readings, India's weakness was the sin of self—its caste system and emphasis on karma to the exclusion of grace. On the other hand, perhaps India's strength lies in its understanding of the ageless mysteries and wisdom teachings—many of which emphasize the Eternal Feminine.

Jess Stearn and Lynn Rogers

```
                    Atlantic University
       67TH STREET AND ATLANTIC AVENUE    P.O. BOX 595    VIRGINIA BEACH, VIRGINIA 23451
                         TELEPHONE: (804) 428-3588

   FALL SCHEDULES    1989


   TS-512: TOPIC: OUR ENERGY SYSTEM-PROCESS OF HARMONIZATION/TRANSFORMATION
           Instructor:    Dr. Margaret Irby
           Class:    Tuesday 7:00 - 10:00 pm       DATE:  9/5 through 11/28
           Place:    AU-1 classroom (2nd floor Visitor's Center)
           Books:    Subtle Body    The Chakras


   TS-512: TOPIC: CREATIVE WRITING AND THE METAPHYSICAL
           Instructor:    Mr. Jess Stearn
           Class:    Wednesday 7:00 - 10:00 pm     DATE:  9/6 through 11/29
           Place:    Mini-auditorium
           Books:    Soulmates    I Judus    Maupassant    Somerset Maugham
                                                           short stories


   TS-503: ORIGINS OF CONSCIOUSNESS
           Instructor:    Dr. Scott Sparrow
           Class:    Wednesday 7:00 - 10:00 pm     DATE:  9/6/ through 11/29
           Place:    AU-1 classroom (2nd floor Visitor's Center)
           Books:    Up From Eden


   TS-501: INTRODUCTION TO TRANSPERSONAL STUDIES
           Instructor:    Dr. Henry Reed
           Class:    Monday 7:00 - 10:00 pm        DATE:  9/11 through 12/4
           Place:    AU-1 classroom (2nd floor Visitor's Center)
                     EXCEPTION   Monday Sept. 11th - Students to attend
                                 Conference Lecture The Psychic Imagination
                                 from 8:00 - 9:30 pm in the auditorium.
```

Atlantic University Courses including Jess Stearn's Creative Writing Class which stimulated Lynn Rogers' research on the Feminine

Egypt

There was a transitional period between matrifocal and patrifocal societies. The detailed mythic account of early Egypt given in the Edgar Cayce readings epitomizes this pivotal stage. Mark Lehner (1974) speculates that Ra Ta, high priest of early Egypt, came from Zu, or Sumeria. Sumeria was a land of the Goddess. Ra Ta was later exiled from

Egypt to Nubia, which the readings describe as a matriarchy "when those of the opposite (female) sex were the rulers". —816-3 (Lehner, 1974, p. 41)

The Cayce sources describe Egypt after the time Stone (1978) refers to as the Upper Paleolithic II period. The readings describe Egypt 10,500 years before Christ as the center of universal activities of nature or spiritual forces, where Creative Energies might be applied in human lives. At this time, according to the Cayce account, Atlanteans were making their way east to the Pyrenees and Egypt and west to the Peruvian and Yucatan lands in the midst of a great religious and global polar axis shift. Stier (1988) speculates that more feminine, fluid forms pervaded Egypt with more masculine angular forms in the Yucatan.

It is against this backdrop that we must see the saga of Ra Ta, high priest of Egypt. Ra Ta "was the son of a daughter of Zu that was not begotten of man."(294-147) Here the readings state that Ra Ta's mother (like Anne, the mother of Mary, I note) was immaculately conceived. Other connections occur. First, we know from Goddess scholarship that, because the Goddess was deity in Sumeria, (or what Cayce called Zu) females were held in high esteem. In Sumerian hymns the female preceded the male, women held and managed their own estates and the birth of daughters was a special blessing. (Stone, 1976).

Further, it is from Zu—or Sumeria—that Ra Ta entered Egypt with Arart and his tribe of 900. The native Egyptians were peaceful agrarians who offered little resistance. Perhaps aspects of the cultures were compatible. According to Lehner (1974), Egypt could have been chosen because there might be the least disturbances by the convulsive movements which came in the earth through the destruction of Lemuria, Atlantis—and in later periods, the flood. It is interesting to trace the Eternal Feminine through the individual lives of those souls in feminine expression during the period of Ra Ta's Egypt.

Ra Ta and his soul group brought the concept of spiritual and physical partnership of husband and wife from Atlantis. With Ra Ta they set up the Temple of Sacrifice to cleanse appendages and bodily imperfections brought over from Lemurian and Atlantean cycles of "thought projection". The Temple Beautiful became a place of healing and spiritual study and unfoldment.

Sensing extremes in Ra Ta's efforts to perfect the body, opposing priests tempted him to create a child with the dancer Isris. Even though he had a wife, Ra Ta chose to break his own ideal of one husband, one wife. Isris was the favorite of King Araaraart who then exiled Ra Ta to the Nubian lands with a band of followers. The little child Iso (companion soul through time to Ra Ta) was kept as hostage and died.

Nubia was a matriarchal society at this time in the earth when the Goddess still reigned. This matriarchal society of Nubians—"when those of the opposite sex were the rulers" (816-3)—grew closer to Ra Ta and his followers. I believe this occurred because Ra Ta—a former incarnation of Edgar Cayce—according to the readings—understood the role of the Eternal Feminine in the earth.

Here in Nubia also, Ra Ta met the black Hermes (former incarnation of Jesus). Hermes' mother, Mara, died early in his life. Madigan in her original trilogy *The Past Lives of Jesus and Mary*, (1970) speculates that Hermes' mother Mara—known as the Black Madonna—might be another incarnation of Mary, as twin souls often incarnate to be helpmeets to one another in various roles. Later, Hermes married the young Egyptian wife Seshat, whom Madigan believed could be Mara returned. Hermes-Thoth, as he is named in legend, was always paired with his alter ego, Seshat. Seshat is the goddess of writing or history. She is his double, Mistress of the house of architects, the House of Books. Moreover, in *The Book of the Dead*, Hermes and Maat, the Goddess of Truth, are paired together.

Atlanteans flooded into Egypt, including women who played significant roles in these times of change as illustrated in the following readings:

> The entity was among those of the Law of One who made their departure . . . for the preserving of the records . . .
> For the entity was a priestess in the temple in the lands of the Atlanteans. (1042-2)
> Before that we find the entity was in that now known or called the Egyptian land, during those periods when there were those journeying hither from the Atlantean land. The entity then was the princess of fire, or that one of the Law of One who acted in the capacity of the interpreter . . . (966-1)

When political conflicts resulting from this influx needed resolution, Ra Ta and the exiles were recalled. Weak in body, Ra Ta withdrew to the Temple Beautiful for regeneration. A great reconstruction period followed. Dynamic religious and cultural roles for women abounded. For, as stated in reading 294-151, the Priest gained access through Isis—the first Goddess—to the Throne itself.

> The decorations in (the) Temple Beautiful became more elaborate. These, with the supervision of Isis (now), and with the spiritual influence of Iso, brought more and more attendance of that part of man's development. (294-152)

Various Cayce readings excerpts as compiled by Lehner (1974) indicate that Ra Ta's daughters played pivotal roles. For example, Ra Ta's daughter Aris Hobeth worked in the field of medicine; another of his daughters helped to establish the center of culture in what is now called Alexandria. And I think that it was here—thousands of years later—that Mary, the mother of Jesus, came to study in the Library of Alexandria, for the Edgar Cayce sources said that:

> Josie and Mary were not idle during that period of sojourn, but worked with those records—that had been part of those activities preserved in the libraries there. This was a part of the work *that had been designated for them* (Author's italics). (1010-17)

This reading hints that Mary may have lived before in Egypt. Where? As Van Hoose (2003) points out, Alexander built the library in Alexandria in about the third century. Often a soul returns to continue former work. According to the Edgar Cayce readings, Jesus studied in the lands of his former incarnations during the "lost years". Again, because Mary is Jesus' companion soul through time, they would share a complementary pattern.

The Eternal Feminine in Egypt is further elucidated in *The Book of the Dead* through the Song of Isis, who was taught by Hermes. The Edgar Cayce readings state (281-10) that Hermes was a former incarnation of Jesus who became the Christ. Madigan (1970) quotes the Song of Isis:

> I am Isis, the mistress of every land.
> I was taught by Hermes, and by the aid of Hermes . . .
> I set down laws for all mankind,
> And we ordained the things that no one has the power to change . . .
> I, with Hermes, revealed spiritual initiations to mankind.
> I compelled women to be beloved by the husband . . .
> I, with Hermes, ordained that Truth is all of beauty.
> (Madigan, 1970, p. 15)

Ra Ta's Egypt, as presented in the Edgar Cayce material, represents one of the last periods of integration of the Eternal Feminine and Masculine Forces before the descent of the Goddess.

The cultural and religious gender integration seen in ancient India and Egypt culminates the Way of the Mother, which includes all of the historical periods in which the Eternal Feminine was either in ascendancy or in balance with the masculine principle. India and Egypt thus provide a bridge over which Atlantean ideas, including the Eternal Feminine, reach to other areas of the modern world.

Goddess "Thea-ology"

Since the Goddess tradition lasted at least 25,000 years until the closing of the last Goddess temple in Greece, it is possible that the female deity, Her theology and the cultures that surrounded Her worship took different forms at different times and in different lands. Human gender roles and myths are intertwined. Thus, prevailing myths evolve from and often reflect dominant social themes. (For example, the Sun Goddess of Wisdom and Prophesy or Brother Moon-Protector of the weak were surprising reversals of more current themes.) While a balanced androgynous ideal (a legacy of Amilius) may have been the Goddess' inception, later forms may have been distorted.

Just as with the period of male ascendancy, there could have been eternal and temporal archetypal patterns expressed. Killing off one's consort or "yearly husband" as a sacrifice to the fertility of the land, for example, is part of the mythic Goddess legacy. Budapest (1980) believes that this happened only after the influence of male-dominated religious forms. Some scholars believe that such sacrifices were symbolic rather than literal. Others, such as Campbell (1959) describe Jesus as the last in a tradition of sacrificial kings born of the Goddess.

Divine Feminine "Thea-ology" is creation-centered rather than fall-redemptive. According to Dominican priest Matthew Fox, (1983) creation spirituality is life affirming, rooted in original goodness, rather than original sin.". It starts with original blessing. When asked his thoughts about the Edgar Cayce legacy today, Matthew Fox stated to me that the Edgar Cayce work seems to be an important catalyst toward mystical thought. Fox was concerned that it might be dualistic, and hoped it would answer the call for gender equity and integrate the shadow. (Fox, personal communication, May 8, 1990)

I might interpret this comment to suggest that Fox honors the Cayce work as a stimulus to the mystic's path. Fox believes that the mystical, or esoteric heart of all great religions and philosophies is one, whereas the exoteric—or outer—belief systems appear to be in conflict. Fox's comment regarding dualism appears to me to refer to "either-or" rather than "both—and", or inclusive thinking. For example: God is Father and not Mother, rather that *both* Father and Mother—*and* more; or that the body wars against, rather than expands the soul. A beautiful example of mind/body cooperation is Hildegarde of Bingen's expression that the spirit moistens the flesh. Fox's hope for greater gender equity in the Cayce circles could mean greater emphasis on inclusive God language (Father/Mother), and greater acknowledgement of women's contributions. The suggestion for the group to integrate the shadow, or unacknowledged parts of self, could refer to looking at painful, as well as joyful feelings honestly—and being willing to walk through the Via Negativa—or dark night of the soul—for greater creativity and transformation.

According to authors such as Stone (1978), Budapest (1979), Starhawk (1979), Gadon (1989), Eisler (1987), Sjoo and Moor (1987), Tish (1990), Reuther (1990) and many others, Goddess spirituality is egalitarian, pluralistic and ecological. What does this really mean? It means justice between men and women. It means justice among the races. It means that there is more than one way to be human, including drawing from the unique contributions and experiences of the mentally and physically disabled. It means joyous respect for all the living systems upon the earth.

The Cayce philosophy is similar to Goddess spirituality in that it also emphasizes justice and kindness to others. For example, Cayce reading #3375 states that "each soul entity in the earth", of whatever shade or color, "whether with this or that disfigurement of body or mind, is in the earth by the Grace of God . . . thus if ye belittle others, what sort of tree will grow in thine own heart? Ye may be sure someone else will belittle thee. That is thy warning. . . ." (3375-2) Some readings compare the love of God for us to that of a mother who cannot disregard any of her children. Therefore, both Goddess Thea-ology and the Cayce philosophy portray ideal human relationships as compassionate and inclusive—in keeping with the Way of the Mother.

Lynn Rogers at an Edgar Cayce Study Group at the old Hospital Building. Study Groups foster ideal human relationships of cooperation and Oneness

Many of the Cayce readings encouraged fairness and a cooperative ideal between men and women. A 49-year-old housewife was told that she was innately a leader, a teacher, and an instructor to the young. "Here it would not be well to allow the idiosyncrasies of one person—even though it is the husband—to prevent the entity from fulfilling those abilities . . . for which it entered this sojourn." (3379-2) A woman was told that she could help her husband best by "Counseling with him as an equal; not as one below him, not even second best." (2602-3) A man was told that neither he nor his wife-to-be should "sit *still* and let the other do all the giving, nor all the forgiving". (752-1) Rather, they should work to complement each other and thus know peace and contentment. One woman was told that she had lived in early America. "In that experience the entity was not only a home builder, but a state and nation builder." (2425-1) Reading #457-1 stated that:

> The greater career for any soul may be that of home, and those who depend *upon* the building of same— for as is seen, in each and every individual heart comes that longing for home, even as the *eternal* home . . .

Readings such as this one—which state that the home is the greatest career for *any* soul—anticipated the greater sharing of home building that was not the norm in Cayce's time, but which is fast becoming an ideal for many couples today.

Finally, Goddess spirituality means respect for all the living systems interdependent upon the earth. It means sharing—with animals and plants and with each other. In a similar vein, Cayce reading #3374-1 the beauty of nature is a reflection of the God's care for us and should be respected:

> One may never tell a rose to be beautiful nor a violet to give off its fragrance, nor yet a sunset or the storm or the wind adds their voice to the songs of nature. Yet music and nature, and beauty of all kinds, appeal much to this entity. Have you wondered why? Have you used or abused such? These you must answer in self . . .

Matthew Fox, (1990) in his first West Coast public lecture after the Vatican had silenced him, said "the earth is calling to us with a new agenda". And according to a January 1991 San Francisco PBS television broadcast on E.I. Disease, a new "environmental illness" has been identified. Sufferers become incapacitated because of chemically produced products. Yet, organic products grown and produced in harmony with lunar (Goddess) cycles have been found to provide some relief. Interestingly, many such E.I. patients report that they now feel great empathy for endangered animal species. To them, there is no separation. ("E.I. Disease" PBS Broadcast, January, 1990)

The Way Of The Mother

Dr. Pamela Bro, Pastor of Christ Point Church in Virginia Beach, (later at Yale University,) with her husband John Benetz and daughters Kaitlyn and Chelsea. This family appears traditional, but enjoys flexible roles as Pam has written her children's book, *God Is A Mama, Too*

And like other thoughtful men of the New Millennium, John also enjoys homebuilding. Ironic, because Edgar Cayce gave Pam's mother June readings on how building a home was the greatest opportunity any soul could have

Both the Edgar Cayce readings and the Divine Feminine rituals suggest reverence for nature. The material encourages us to know the Divine through nature, "through the smile of a baby, the fragrance of the rose." (3374) We may attune to the "vibrations of the flowers, the song of the birds, the wind, the hail, the sleet, and the snow". (3374-1) The readings invite us to revivify the body by breathing the beauty of nature into our own souls.

Similarly, Divine Feminine ritual celebrations, now being revived by Budapest, Starhawk, others, and myself honor the sacred cycles of life represented in the Wheel of the Year. When God and Goddess dance together, the seasons, the cycles of the moon come into being.

Each stage of human life is also sacred. Therefore, maiden, mother and crone—or wise woman—are each honored. In our culture, the maiden and the mother are recognized, but the woman of mature years is often cast aside. In Goddess-worshipping societies, it was she alone (the crone) who could part the veil of the mysteries of life and death. In Goddess circles in ancient times as well as today, it was thought that the woman entered the last stage of her Queenship with the cessation of menstruation. Now she ceased to shed her "wise blood". Saved for herself, her energies were freed to direct toward more spiritual goals and greater achievement.

Goddess Thea-ology emphasizes respect for all interdependent living systems upon the earth. It espouses gender equity and is impartial regarding race or life circumstance—recognizing that there is more than one way to be human. Goddess Thea-ology is creation-centered and celebrates all of life's diversity.

A Blow To The Spirit

Goddess-worshipping civilizations fell in the face of waves of invasions by the male-dominated and hierarchical cultures of Indo-Europeans, as well as natural disasters such as floods and earthquakes. In *The Once And Future Goddess*, Gadon (1989) states that "by 1,500 B.C., the Indo-Europeans were firmly established in the Near East and the Mediterranean", and that wherever these invaders entered, "the Goddess would have to share her domain with male gods". (Gadon, 1989, p. 110)

Her Suppression

When the religious polar axis shifted from a matrifocal to a patrifocal system, the Goddess religion became the victim of centuries of persecution and suppression. Warring patriarchal Aryans and Indo-Iraneans brought male deities into prominence and the desire for property to be owned by the man. Male dominance was established through means that were "in some places . . . precipitous and brutal, in others gradual as her powers were co-opted one by one". (Gadon, 1989, p. 110)

According to Donna Read, director of "Goddess Remembered", a new film produced by the Canadian National Film Board and recently screened by University of California at Berkeley to over a thousand cheering women and men, the dawn of western civilization was the beginning for men and the end for women. Moreover, 25,000 years of "her-story" of the Goddess' bountiful creativity were obliterated. Man, said man, had always been the master of the earth. After 3,500 years of the recent dominator model, humankind has come collectively to honor warrior cults, to follow a sky god in a patriarchal social system with fear at its core. (Read, 1990)

In societies subsequent to those that worshipped the Goddess, Her spiritual teachings were first subsumed and incorporated into patrifocal religious systems. For example, Hinduism holds that all gods and goddesses are but part of one Source. Gradually, awareness of the Eternal Feminine was blurred and the status of women declined. Psychologies that arose out of these religions tended toward imbalance. Finally, the timeless sacred role of the Eternal Feminine as the life-giver was denied and the male role over-inflated.

In later societies Her spiritual teachings were camouflaged and encased in myths. Nowhere is this better exemplified than in the Hindu tradition. In Hindu bhakti yoga, God can be seen as parent—mother or father. The love of God is developed through myths, symbols and a rich panoply of masculine and feminine images. Thus, Hinduism offers us many masks or images of the one Source in its various aspects. The Divine Couple is a familiar image. The Hindu deities Shakti and Shiva, for example, divide and reunite in the Sacred Marriage. Shakti is the Tantric title of the Great Goddess. Her name means "Cosmic Energy". Shiva is the oldest god of the Vedic male trinity superimposed on the earlier Goddess trinity. Originally, Shiva was

> ... in a state of actualization because he is in bodily contact with his own universal energy, the Shakti, the Goddess, the feminine active principle, the efficient and material cause of the universe, the Maya that evolves the differentiated elements and beings. Shiva bears on his head the crescent of the moon. (Zimmer, 1946, p. 129-130)

Individual gods and goddesses are manifestations of the two archetypal creative aspects of the One Source. As Shiva told the man who worshipped Shiva but hated all other deities:

> Thy bigotry is unconquerable. I, by assuming this dual aspect, tried to convince thee that all gods and goddesses are but various aspects of one Absolute Brahman. (Smith, 1986, p. 88)

Unfortunately, this balance was later lost in practical application when females became property in patrifocal social systems. Small girls were physically mutilated as child brides. Widows were immolated in ritual suttee. (Daly, 1984) These horrors decried the beauty of the dance of Shakti and Shiva—first brought to India by the Atlantean Ram and his Sita.

When male deities were superimposed upon religion globally, the status of women declined. For example, in India, independent goddesses like Sri Lakshmi became dependent upon their male consorts and ultimately models of passive compliance. Societies retaining the idea of true Goddess worship seldom demonstrate child abuse or sexual violence against women, "two relatively common crimes in modern patri-focal societies", according to licensed clinical social worker Victoria Borba (personal communication, 1991).

In the Orient, the Yin/Yang wheel symbolizes the interrelationship and the Oneness of the masculine and feminine archetypes—or what might be better termed composites of pure energy essences. A young man of my acquaintance who was schooled in Tibet reported, however, that the association of yang with light and yin with dark are recent revisions. According to oral tradition, originally, dark was associated with the male who hunts by night, and light—with the female who grows grain by day. Anonymous (personal communication, July 19, 1987)

This surprising reversal corroborates Merlin Stone's (1976) research. When the Goddess was revered as supreme deity, she was often linked to the sun, wisdom and prophesies. Conversely, from these ancient religious systems such images evolved as Father Nature and Brother Moon, Protector of the Weak. It is important to recognize that prevailing myths evolve from and often reflect dominant social themes.

As stated, when a matrifocal system was replaced by a patrifocal system, the Goddess religion was persecuted and suppressed. When the Indo-Iranean invaders came into contact with ancient forms of civilized settled society, in comparison with which they were mere barbarians (James, 1935), new creation legends were written over the old. As myths changed, the Goddess who had stood alone had first a subordinate son, then a brother-husband. Finally her husband murdered her and the male deity became supreme.

The symbols connected to Goddess worship were propagandized as evil. The serpent of wisdom and prophecy became the symbol of darkness; the fruit from the tree of life, the tempting apple. Adam gave birth to Eve from his missing rib (or womb) and the ancient belief in the Goddess as the Ground of Being, the Universe from which The All emerged, was overturned.

Patrifocal Ideologies

Psychologies that arose out of these patrifocal religions tended toward imbalance. The only "normal" human model was male. Female strengths once regarded as sacred were now appropriated as male. Many subsequent theorists have reinforced this reversal. Freud, for example, thought that the little girl must be smitten with jealousy when she sees the male generative organ because it could create life, i.e. babies. (Lewin,

1984) In my opinion, this is not far from the medieval homunculus theory in which a dwarfish man was thought to exist in the male seed. Females, it was believed, had no seed and were mere vessels for the homunculus.

Medieval priest and scholar, Thomas Aquinas even believed that women were "misbegotten males" conceived when an ill wind blew. Interestingly, child monk Aquinas had virtually no contact with females after the age of seven. Thus he passed on fears of women that were prevalent among many of his day. Mathew Fox (personal communication, April, 1990)

It appears to me that these one-sided and fearful ideologies may have arisen because the ancient association of woman with the Goddess was threatening. When woman's role had reflected esteem for the Divine Feminine, name and properties passed through the mother's line. Eisler, Stone and other scholars state that the motive for the elimination of the female deity, which disempowered female persons by association, was to establish patrilineal descent or inheritance. To accomplish this, the timeless sacred role of woman as the life-giver was purposely denied and the male role over inflated.

Rosemary Ruether states, the negative and despised self is extended to socially dominated people. (Reuther, 1990) It makes sense to me, if we don't like something in ourselves we project it out, shove it onto someone less powerful. Black people, at a shameful time in this country for example, were regarded by their masters as having a penchant for "rhythm" and watermelon—or worse—seen as barely human. Regarding Black Americans, Stearn quotes Cayce:

Lynn Rogers addressing Doug Richard's Atlantic University Class, in 1991, on the Goddess tradition in ancient times

> Those who have brought servitude to him, without thought or purpose, have created that which must be met within their own principles and selves. These should be help in an attitude of their own individual fitness, as in every other form of association. (Stearn, 1967)

Numerous Edgar Cayce readings generally warned against self-aggrandizement and the selfish egotism at the expense of others.

Similarly, other patrifocal religious, psychological and consciousness theorists have tended to persist in associating femininity with their own disowned shadow. Such theorists have described the Great Mother as a whore or a morass of blood, or Adam as positive and dynamic in the "active" male gender, Eve as "passive" and assigned to assist Adam through time. One could speculate that such hostility could be construed as resulting from womb-envy—if one were to reverse Freud's concept of supposed female envy of male reproductive anatomy.

It is important to note that in the ideologies of the Way of the Mother, all parts of the human body were revered as sacred, regardless of gender. In the transitional Hindu religion, for example, there were many yoni—or female genitalia—shrines, as well as depictions of the opposite male lingam. There was no separation in such ideologies of the body from the spirit, or of the feminine and masculine principles, either in the deity or in human affairs. Thus, I assume that there was less impetus toward hostility and, therefore, greater justice between the genders during the period of the "Way of the Mother".

Such gender equity does not appear to be as prevalent in subsequent patrifocal ideologies. As Stone questions, "What else might we expect from a society that for centuries has taught young children, both female and male, that a MALE deity created the universe and all that is in it, produced MAN in his own divine image—and then, as an afterthought, created woman, to obediently help in his endeavors? The image of Eve . . . has in many ways become the image of all women." (Stone, 1976, p. xi)

Yet, the Edgar Cayce readings describe Eve as the twin soul of Adam—who would become Jesus, just as she would later become the Beloved Mother—Mary.

> In the beginning Mary was the twin-soul of the Master in the entrance into the earth. Neither Mary nor Jesus had a human father. They were one soul as far as the earth is concerned; because else she would not be incarnated in flesh, you see. (5749-8)

Additionally, reading #1738 refers to the "ideal as set by Him, in that—Though he were of the Father, yet in the Son came that relationship with man and woman that exalted, honored, glorified, womanhood!" Perhaps this glorification was in the ultimate union of purpose of these twin souls in Palestine. The insight from the Edgar Cayce readings that Mary and Jesus are twin souls holds tremendous potential for the much needed clarification of the role of the Eternal Feminine in the earth.

Former Catholic theologian and author Mary Daly expands further upon the long-standing exclusion and suppression of the Divine Feminine in patriarchal religions. Daly states that the traditional Christian Trinity that "births" the Universe is devoid of Divine Mother or Daughter. Daly also maintains that "the myth of feminine evil, expressed in the story of the Fall, is reinforced by the myth of salvation/redemption by a single human being of the male sex." (Daly, 1975, p. 7)

On the other hand, an example of inclusion of the Divine Feminine in Christianity is found in the tradition of Mary within the Catholic Church. Technically, Mary is described as human saint who was the vessel for Jesus as God to be born. However, in practice in many parts of the world Mary is prayed to directly and virtually worshipped as the Divine Feminine. It appears to me that the tradition of Mary allows the continuation of humanity's need for the Eternal Feminine to be represented.

For the most part, the coming of the patrifocal religious systems meant the loss of mythical Atlantean concepts of the God/Goddess principle and the idea of twin souls as helpmates through time. Goddess-worshipping societies had revered a wise and gentle Creator. In earliest India and Egypt the Eternal Feminine and Masculine principles stood poised in equality and balance. Where once the Divine Feminine shone forth as brightly as the torch held aloft in the Atlantean Temple of Flame, now Her flame seemed to dim in the winds of change. According to Butler and Goldstein, the Goddess has veiled her face since Atlantis. (1990) And so humanity entered The Way of the Father.

In this chapter the Eternal Feminine was highlighted through discussion of related references in the Edgar Cayce readings on Atlantis, early India, and Egypt. Later the Divine Feminine was examined in ancient religious systems where the Goddess was worshipped for over 25,000 years. She was either the supreme deity, or coupled with a male deity, and as such represented a full-fledged cosmic parent figure that created the universe and its laws.

The Goddess occupied the center, as opposed to the pinnacle, of the religious and social system, and She unified dualities and opposites through rituals that emphasized the underlying Oneness of being. This view of the deity at the center, rather than at the top of the spiritual and social order, resulted in a humane and holistic way of life. Thus, the Way of the Mother meant respect and regard for all living beings interdependent

Edgar Cayce And The Eternal Feminine

upon the earth, cooperation between genders in accordance with a balanced androgynous ideal of Oneness, as well as the belief that humanity inception is in original blessing.

The overturn of the matrifocal religions and way of life, by invasions of patriarchal warrior cults who either ruthlessly destroyed or slowly co-opted the Goddess worshipping cultures, is then discussed. Finally, it is shown how patrifocal ideologies have become established over the last 3,500 years with the resulting turning away from the Way of the Mother to the Way of the Father.

Facilitated communication can be accomplished with computers, as well as handwriting.

Joe Haddox represents the eternal masculine compassionate father. Shown with his autistic step daughter, Vanessa whom he loves as his own. (Drawn by Lynn Rogers for Venture Inward Magazine 1996)

CHAPTER THREE
FUTURE HORIZONS

CHAPTER THREE

FUTURE HORIZONS

In this chapter the resurgence of the Eternal Feminine in the modern world is discussed. Although the Edgar Cayce materials do not explicitly address this resurgence, it is implied. This resurgence will be demonstrated as follows: through prophesies of the upcoming Aquarian Age of peace and fellowship; through new revelations related to Mary's role through time; through new myths, including the green myth, women's liberation and planetism; through androgynous trends encouraging thinking and feeling in both genders; through the incorporation of and reevaluation of women's traditional skills to enhance planetary stability; and through new religious forms which are springing up in answer to the earth's call for a new holistic and humane agenda. The traditions associated with the Goddess religion, such as integration of spirit and nature, appreciation for the cyclical patterns of life, and personal honor with respect for others are being revived and recreated.

The Reemergence of the Eternal Feminine

Today one hears increasingly expressions like Father/Mother God; or God, Goddess and All That Is. (Lazaris Material, Pursel, 1988) Is this an awkward exercise or is it an exciting invocation to a new era of integration of two great principles that transcend time?

The idea of God as Divine Mother is bubbling up into the mainstream. For example, in February 1983 the conservative Catholic Digest reprinted an article by Anne Bowne Follis entitled "The Mother Love of God." In summary, Follis states that our narrow perception of God as a man is inadequate. Follis further states that the Mother Love of God and the Father Love of God are really one and the same. (Follis, 1981)

The 14th century English mystic, Julian of Norwich, whose works are currently being revived, anticipated this insight many centuries ago. She spoke with disarming simplicity of God Almighty who is our kindly Father and God all Wisdom who is our kindly Mother (Doyle, 1983). Further, modern Indian Holy Mother, Mata Amritanandamayi, or "Ammachi," states:

> "A woman is looked upon as a sister by her brother, as a wife by her husband, and as a daughter by her father. No matter who looks at her with what viewpoint, she remains one and the same. Likewise, God is only one. Each person sees God in a different way according to his attitude." (Amritanandamayi, 1986)

Sources such as Norwich and Ammachi revive the ancient awareness of Father/Mother God, or God, Goddess and All That Is—One.

Madigan (In Press) further commented regarding the Oneness underlying twin souls and the cyclic patterns of feminine and masculine ascendancy through time:

> 'HE'—'SHE'—have been one from the Beginning. It is the two aspects of the *same* Soul. The Ages in the Earth also reflect this duality, since shortly after the Time of the worship of Isis, the Masculine aspect of the soul began its domination.
>
> The Feminine Goddesses and their teaching, many of them holy teachings, were torn from the temples. The influence of Women was degraded.
>
> This was also karmic because the Masculine Forces in Mankind had lived through the later centuries of Atlantis where the Feminine aspect of the souls had *long been in ascendancy*. Prayer to the Mother Goddess was the basis of worship of the latter day Atlanteans.
>
> Whatever is repressed within the consciousness—individual or collective, must one day *rise up again*. (Madigan, In Press)

Graves (1948) stated that in our time, the Goddess is on the rise. The Cayce sources suggest that by the end of this century the records of Atlantis may be discovered. One of the truths of Atlantis is the Divine Feminine. Today humanity stands on the threshold of the Aquarian Age, which follows the 2,000 year Piscean Age. Edgar Cayce, Nostradamus, the Hopi Indians, Mother Shipton and other prophets described the upcoming Aquarian Age as an age of peace and fellowship in the earth. The Aquarian Age is the age of remembrance. The Cayce readings emphasize that it's hard to know where one is going until one knows where one has been—therefore the importance of past life study. Not only are we recovering personal, past life memories but also the lost truths of previous epochs, including that of the Eternal Feminine. Astrologers state that the last constellation of Pisces is that of Andromeda—a woman breaking her chains.

Mary, according to the Edgar Cayce sources, was an Aquarian. One individual was told, "Remember thou art in the same signs, omens, as the Mother of Him; that [who] gave to the earth the physical man, Jesus— Aquarius in its *perception*, perfection..." (1222-1) To understand Mary esoterically is to understand the saga of the Eternal Feminine in the earth.

Esoteric Mariology and Marion Appearances

Around the world, Mary has become a non-sectarian symbol for the call to world peace. The Edgar Cayce sources foretold this development by describing Mary as the companion or twin soul to the Master throughout time. Mary has been one of the few representations for westerners of the feminine in religion. Both Catholics and many non-Catholics believe that her current "appearances" bring hope for planetary peace and a return to the Christ message.

Whereas the exoteric Catholic Church has traditionally viewed Mary as the human vehicle for "God's birth", in the esoteric Catholic teachings and in the hearts of simple worshippers, she is experienced as the Mother of God or as a human reflection of God-Our-Mother. Writings published by the retired sisters of the Order of the Sacred Heart in Menlo Park, California, for example, reflect this theme. (RSCJ, 1988)

Edgar Cayce described Mary as the twin soul of Jesus, even closer to him in the Palestine experience, else she would not have entered earth embodiment. "Neither Mary nor Jesus had a human father. They were *one soul* as far as the earth was concerned; because (otherwise) she would not be incarnated in flesh, you see." (5749-8) On August 3, 1987, a group of women and men from my "E.S.P. Evening" class series approached the historic landmark statue at Our Lady of Peace Church in the heart of Silicon Valley in Santa Clara, California. Five individuals experienced a similar vision: The statue assumed an androgynous appearance as if Mary was reflected by its right side and Jesus, its left. An instant "understanding" came to one meditator and she "knew" that in Palestine the two had, as Cayce said, been closer in consciousness than twin souls—"Yes... rather they are ONE..."—almost flowing in and out of each other's awareness.

Three women from the group, each coincidentally representative of a different generation, felt impelled to approach the steel feet of the huge outdoor statue. Catholic parishioners traditionally bring only flowers to the windy shrine, but this night as the women drew nearer they found three slim, unlit candles among the flowers. Each of the three lit "her" candle with a quiet prayer that an awareness of the Divine Feminine might again live in the earth. Despite the wind, the flames flickered brightly and the women saw themselves for an instant as priestesses of the Triple Goddess of Old.

Madigan (1970) speculated before her death in 1986 that Mary may have attained to Christ consciousness in the Atlantean era. As stated previously, the Edgar Cayce readings gave an Aquarian birth date for Mary, the Mother. Madigan sometimes referred to the Aquarian Age as "The Age of Mary".

Esoteric author Chew (1977) writes that there is every likelihood that Mary could become the Aquastor for the Aquarian Age and that "Mary, as the latest representation of the Great Goddess, continues to hold her time-honored place in the hearts of the common people. All that she lacks to come into her own is an honest and devoted following, under good leadership, which will not permit euphemisms, rationalizations, and substitutions to occlude her sovereignty." (Chew, 1977, p. 66)

As Carl Jung stated, the archetype is a living idea that constantly produces new interpretations. Moreover, this Marion tradition is continued in the unfolding of ecclesiastical dogma. "An example . . . concerning the Virgin . . . refers . . . to the mother goddess who was constantly associated with the young dying son . . . she was very distinctly prefigured in the Sophia of the Old Testament . . . (thus) the mother goddess is naturally implied in the archetype of the divine son." (Jung, 1963, p. 522)

Starhawk (1979) says that perhaps humanity will see a new cult of the Virgin Mary. In the fall of 1989 at the Common Boundaries seminar held in Washington, D.C., Jungian analyst Marion Woodman, introduced the Black Madonna as the new myth. Male and female audience members alike reported that She is now suddenly emerging in their dreams with increasing frequency. J. Holcombe (personal communication, 1991). What greater joy and comfort for women who have lost faith in the Judeo-Christian Father God of their childhood than to discover Mary as a link to God as Divine Mother and the recovery of their own tradition.

Personal past life regression experiences at the 1987 "ReSearch" Series, which I presented with hypnotherapist Alexi MacKinnon, gave possible experiential insight into an Atlantean Mary. In what appeared to be the Poseidian "Hall of Flowers", she appeared as a Christ like being revered as the Master Teacher—much as we regard Jesus today.

Further, on April 19, 1991, I offered intuitive material in an altered state of consciousness at the request of Northern California Regional Coordinator Suzanne Keehn and Judith Martin.

> She who was written about at the time of the Mists of Avalon, is an archetype of the Atlantean Mary. It is She who faded into the mist at the time of the temple closing, and it is She who is being reborn into the Earth, not Mary as She has been understood in the Piscean age, but the

> Aquarian Mary... just as the lives of Jesus were understood and uncovered through what is known as the Edgar Cayce material primarily—and the offsetting or augmenting of others—so there must be further work as to completing the understanding of the Atlantean Mary in the Earth, as She was not only a loving nurturer, she was empowered with the Violet light of truth. Her wisdom must touch the Earth, will touch the Earth again, and that which faded into the mists is reemerging; hence the Edgar Cayce readings, in part, about the submerged lands. For the submerged Atlantean land is a land of consciousness as well, that is reemerging into the light of day.

Moreover, this material further stated that the movement toward revivification of the Divine Feminine, expressed through the archetype of the Atlantean Mary in this century, began before the close of the last.

> At the turn of the last century, there was a decision on a soul level to bring forth in this century the flowering that would become even greater than the Little Flower. For this, on a soul level, was a mission—to bring back into Earth's expression the feminine energy. The Little Flower was, in a sense, what John the Baptist was to Christ, in that she—and we say SHE in capital letters, for it is a soul group energy, it did occur in other ways in other parts of the world... What we wish you to understand was that there was a decision made by many in and out of the body, to bring forth in this century, before the turn of the century on whose doorstep you now stand—that is the twenty-first century— to bring a turn in the awareness of men and women in the Earth toward a reunion with the energy of the Mother, as expressed by the Atlantean Mary.

One nineteenth century movement, forerunner for the resurgence in awareness of the Eternal Feminine in the 20th century, is described by Reuther (1983). The American Shakers believed that there must be a new stage of redemption in female form.

> The Shakers based their belief in a dual Christ, male and female, on their doctrine of the androgyny of God. God is both Father and Mother, and humanity as male and female is made in the image of an androgynous God. Redemption, having taken place so far only in the 'male line', is, therefore, incomplete. The female side of

God, Holy Wisdom, has not yet been disclosed.... This new and final stage of redemption must be disclosed through a female. A male Christ alone cannot disclose the fullness of human possibility and divine nature as male and female. (Reuther, 1983, p. 133)

Numerous Edgar Cayce readings stated that Jesus the man became the Christ. For example, one reading refers to "the Law of One as manifested in the man Jesus, as signified in the Christ consciousness. (Please gain the difference of these!)" (1010-12) Further, reading #2533-7 stated that, "Jesus is the man ... the power then is in the Christ. The pattern is in Jesus."

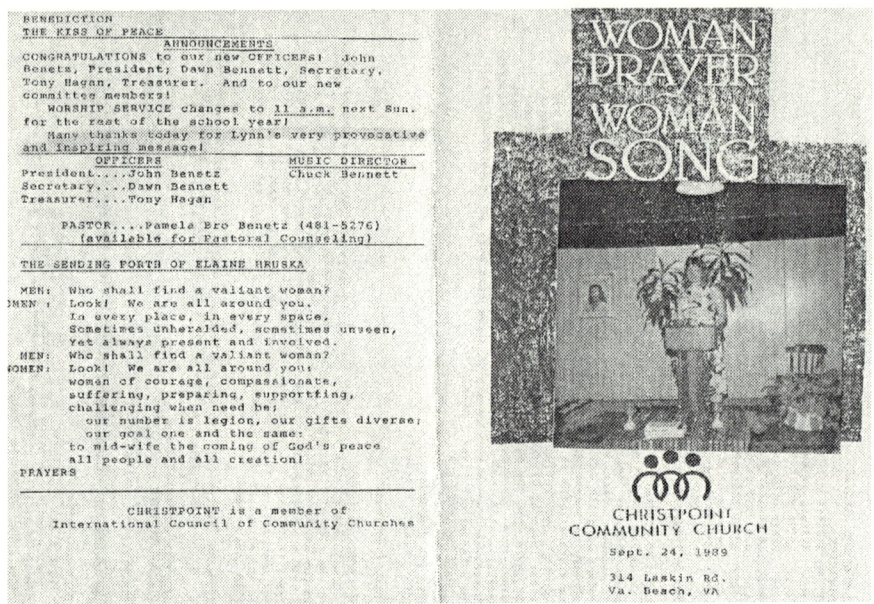

**Lynn Rogers presenting at Dr. Bro's Christ Point Church.
Theme: The Feminine Side of Christ**

In becoming the Christ, the man Jesus came to embody many traditionally "feminine" characteristics, i.e. gentleness, compassion, suffering the little children to come unto Him, etc. It appears to me that Mary, as the feminine Christ model, may come to embody, too, the qualities of empowerment, vitality and creativity most recently appropriated as "masculine" characteristics, but once a hallmark of the Goddess.

Mary Daly comments upon the "functioning of the confusing and complex 'Mary' symbol within Christianity." (Daly, 1975, p. 36) Through it, Daly suggests, the power of the Great Goddess symbol is enchained, captured, used, tokenized, domesticated, and tranquilized. In spite of this, Daly believes that:

> ". . . many women and at least some men, when they have heard of or imaged the 'Mother of God', have, by something like a selective perception process, screened out the standardized, lobotomized, dull derivative and dwarfed Christian reflection of a more ancient symbol."

Daly suggests that they have perceived something that might be described as the Great Goddess, which translates in human terms as the strong woman who can relate because she can stand alone. (Daly, 1975, p. 36-7) These are strong words.

Reuther (1983) asks whether there is any Biblical basis for an alternative Mariology which doesn't scapegoat female sexuality for sin and death, which names sexism as a sin, and which would liberate women and men from the dualisms of carnal femaleness and spiritual femininity. She believes there is such a Biblical basis for an alternative Mariology, particularly in the Lucan identification of Mary with humanity or the Church. The Edgar Cayce material implied that one of Edgar Cayce's grandsons, Charles Thomas Cayce—current president of the Cayce organizations—had a past incarnation as Luke. "To be sure it was a physician in the period of the Master,—and a writer." 2824-1 This is of particular note as Reuther gives Luke's writings as the Biblical basis for inclusion of the Eternal Feminine. Mary's motherhood, to Luke, is a free choice and symbolizes the co-creatorship of God and humanity. The Edgar Cayce readings state that it is our destiny to become co-creators with the Father/Mother God, or the Creative Forces.

Today it is from the realms of Esoteric Mariology that we find fresh, alternative images of Mary, twin soul of the Master, according to the Cayce material. For example, personal psychic experience at the time of this writing indicates that Mary is manifesting her presence both in terms of her model of motherly loving-kindness and in terms of spurring feminine self-sufficiency and fulfillment. It seems to me that through her Sophia-like wisdom, opposites may be reconciled and the fragmented goddess archetypes that Jean Bolen (1984) described in *Goddesses in Every Woman*, integrated within the psyche. For example, the Eternal Feminine, symbolized by Mary, helps unify the goddess archetypes—or sub personalities—within a woman's psyche so that Athena may harmonize with inner Aphrodite, or Hestia, or Hera.

Today Mary, as an immanent and transcendent archetype, is further unfolding in the collective consciousness. Gadon quotes the French novelist, Roland Barthes, "The symbol of (the Virgin) is so powerful it has a dynamic and irrepressible life of its own." Further, Gadon asserts, "not just the Catholic Church believes that Mary existed from all time." (Gadon,

1989, p. 222) Many non-Catholic women and men in transpersonal circles appear to be becoming increasingly receptive to this archetype in our times.

For example, Suzanne Keehn had the following dream experience in early 1991: Keehn dreamed she was on the beach looking at the sand with a few others. She looked at the ground and told the others, "Look, the sand is forming Mary." And then an oval shape appeared in the alive, moving sand. The sand formed her gown covered with sea grass. In the next scene the dreamer was given a small, gold-framed, impressionistic—not stylized—painting of Mary. Keehn interpreted the dream to mean that the Mary energy is in the earth and is being formed by each one of us (because it was impressionistic); so we each add to the whole understanding of Her. (S. Keehn (personal communication, 1991))

Thus the image of Mary and the Divine Feminine may become the hub—the Way—through which such integration may be made possible, just as the image of Jesus, who became the Christ, emerged from the Piscean age as the Wayshower. In our times, the influence of Mary is electrifying the spiritual world.

Through the child visionaries of Medjugorge, Yugoslavia on August 30, 1984, Mary offered a message of peace and unity. "In God there are no divisions and there are no religions. You in the world have made the divisions. The one mediator is Christ." (Ashton, 1989, p. 9) Long before this message, the Cayce sources stated that only in Christ do extremes meet. (J. Madigan (personal communication, 1972))

On April 25, 1985, the Blessed Mother told the children to "begin to work in your hearts as you would work in the fields". (Hancock, 1988, p. 73) Interestingly, Ashton states that the followers of St. Francis have shepherded the Roman Catholic flock in Medjugorge since the fourteenth century. Mary's message, to work in the field of the heart to prepare it for the influx of spirit, is similar to the message St. Francis received hundreds of years earlier—"to rebuild God's church".

Hancock (1988) describes the apparition of the word "Mir" in large letters across the sky above Mt. Krizevak in Medjugorge. Hancock likens this phenomenon of sky writing to "a mirror of peace in the sky". (p. 61) How similar the image to the "ancient mirrors of womanhood" that reflected the light of the Goddess of old. Madigan (1965) described the young priestesses of the Temple of Diana in ancient Greece who gazed into the waters of Lake Nemo to heighten intuition.

Hancock (l988) states that the most recurrent phenomena in Medjugorge have also been observed near Mt. Krizevak. Not only have globes of brilliant white and colored lights been seen in the heavens, but also the Krizevak Cross has radiated and become transformed into a 'woman of light'. (Hancock, 1988, p. 61) The Edgar Cayce readings predicted that in our time, in "the times of the end", His light again would be seen in the heavens. "These will begin in those periods in '58 to '98, when these will be proclaimed as the periods when His light will be seen again in the clouds . . . " (3976-15). And is not His light, Her light?

From the above, the conclusion can be drawn that Mary is becoming an esoteric symbol for world peace and God as Mother. The Edgar Cayce material clarifies Mary's role through time as the human embodiment of the Eternal Feminine in full co-creative expression—including both Her love and empowerment.

New Ideologies

Transpersonal psychologists David Feinstein and Stanley Krippner wrote in 1988 that the costs of having placed the male individual's heroic journey above caring and connectedness continue to mount. Rollo May stated in 1981 that we have reached a mythoclasm, a time when a guiding truth has gone bankrupt and people reckon with the shortcomings of principles they once venerated. From the new transpersonal "psychology with a soul", called Psychosynthesis by its founder Roberto Assagioli, it is learned that the Self can influx higher energies to the personality to correct an imbalance. (Assagioli, 1965) This influx can be experienced as a spiritual crisis. Mircea Eliade, the historian of religion, wrote in 1959 that "the sacred bursts into the profane at the darkest hour". (Feinstein and Krippner, 1988, p. 16)

Today there is a resurgence of interest in the ancient Goddess archetype. Why might this be so? Mythologist Joseph Campbell stated in 1968 that "Myth is the secret opening through which inexhaustible energies of the cosmos pour into human cultural manifestations". (Campbell, 1968, p. 3) For example, in many consciousness circles, messages have apparently been received recently regarding a new incoming "silver ray". (Essene, 1986) This ray represents the "inpouring" of the pure energy essence of the Eternal Feminine. If myth, as Eleanor Wilner asserted, is the first step in alignment of social order, (Wilner, 1975) what archetypes are (re)emerging within esoteric traditions that reflect what Wilber calls "the growing tip of human consciousness?" (Wilber, 1981) And, if myths have reflected this current dilemma, it is our potential for the formulation of new myths that can, as Houston (1982) suggests, become the stimulus, the lure of becoming that prepares the ground for society's transformation. What myths can help us find our place in the new gylanic partnership age that is emerging?

Rollo May (in press) said that there are three new myths necessary for our survival: *The green myth* (showing our proper relationship with nature), *women's liberation* (which would ensure the rights and draw upon the talents of all people) and *planetism* (which shows the world as a place which transcends political boundaries).

In the early 1970's, Dr. Henry Reed of Atlantic University posed a question to a group collecting and studying their dreams: "What will the new myths be?" One of the dreams Reed collected was about a UFO. The pilot was a woman. She appeared to be the Virgin Mary. She was holding a plant. H. Reed (personal communication, 1989) Here it appears to me that all three of Rollo May's myths can be seen: the plant—the greening myth, the woman pilot—women's liberation, the UFO—planetism. However, the dreamer's vision of the Virgin Mary suggests a fourth theme. That of the Divine Feminine, which would break through as the counter myth necessary to balance understanding of Creative Forces.

Carl Jung departed from Freud by postulating the masculine and feminine psychical structures as two sides of the same coin. However, in my opinion, some of his initial associations regarding masculine and feminine qualities are temporal archetypes. In 1931 Jung advanced a typal schema in which he concluded that an individual possesses two attitudes (introversion and extroversion) and four functions (thinking, feeling, intuition and sensation) but tends to be dominant in only one of the attitudes and two of the functions.

Rouse (1985) addresses these typologies in terms of Jung's thoughts on gender dominance related to the typologies. According to Rouse (1985) Jung initially "advanced the hypothesis that thinking dominance is more often a male function and feeling dominance a female function." Rouse states that Jung later discarded this hypothesis, finding no significant gender difference in such typologies. In fact, Jung concluded, "Thinking could be the primary function of either sex and vice versa." Rouse believes that "current androgynous cultural trends encourage the strengthening and development of thinking and feeling in both sexes." (Rouse, 1985, p. 285)

Edward C. Whitmont, a Jungian analyst and Chairman of the Board for the C. G. Jung Training Center, further comments on Jung's statements regarding female and male predispositions. In this light Whitmont presented the following in a paper to the International Jungian Congress for Analytical Psychology in 1980:

> During the early Thirties, Jung made an initial attempt at what he then called a preliminary characterization of the female and male predispositions. He termed Eros the tendency to relatedness, which he deemed fundamentally expressive of the feminine; Logos, spirit, creative and ordering intelligence, and meaning typified in the male attitude. Unfortunately, this first preliminary attempt has been treated in much Jungian literature as though it were the final word for the intervening forty years. Unfortunately, because in the light

of women's increasing awareness of themselves, more and more evidence has been accumulating that the Eros-Logos concept is inadequate for covering the wide range of feminine and masculine dynamics. Moreover, it is also terminologically and psychologically inappropriate. (Whitmont, 1980, p. 119)

Whitmont expands upon this theme. Relationship and relatedness, he states, are "by no means typical or exclusive characteristics of the feminine any more than spirit is to be considered an exclusively male property." (Interestingly, Eros is a male mythological deity. He expresses outgoing libido, the urge to connect, to possess and to penetrate.) He also states:

> Spirituality as a predominantly male characteristic and woman as the embodiment of soul are heirlooms of 19th century romanticism, still dominant in Jung's day but no longer valid in our generation. Women can and always should be deeply involved with and psychologically determined in their conscious outlook by Logos and out of touch with their affects; men can be immensely sensitive to instinct, feeling, and affect and quite at loss in respect to Logos . . . (Whitmont, 1980, p. 119)

Further, Whitmont explores the concepts of anima and animus. They shouldn't be necessarily limited to one sex, he asserts. Bolen further expands this theme in her best selling book, *Goddesses In Every Woman*.

> Subjective feelings and dream figures help differentiate whether a woman's active focus is associated with a masculine animus or with a feminine goddess pattern . . . when Athena and Artemis are well developed aspects of her personality, a woman may be *naturally* assertive, think well, know what she wants to achieve, or compete comfortably. These qualities, far from being alien, feel like inherent expressions of who she is *as a woman*, and not like the qualities of masculine animus that does it 'for her'. (Bolen, 1984 p. 43)

Michael E. Tyson, LMFCC, (1990) writes about the new hero's journey. Even the psychological expression, he states, of a man getting in touch with his feminine side, useful though it may be at times, is inherently oppressive to both men and women. Feeling deeply, Tyson believes, is being deeply masculine. And for women, he asserts, being feminine is certainly more than just having a lot of feeling. (Tyson, 1990) Christian and feminist theologian Rosemary Reuther (1983) states: "there is no biological basis for labeling certain psychic capacities, such as reason, 'masculine' and others, such as intuition, 'feminine'". (Reuther, 1983, p. 111)

Lynn Rogers above the Bay 1999
Goddess energy can be active and free.

Recent medical research overturns gender stereotypes. Severe epileptics who required the surgical severing of the brain hemispheres to control severe seizure activity were studied. In such patients, a slightly greater number of post-surgical male patients came to use the right— "intuitive"—hemisphere, and a greater number of females, the left— "logical, linear"—hemisphere. Brain researchers believe that it is too soon to draw gender-related conclusions about brain functioning, but initial research defies previous gender stereotypes. (Rosser, 1983)

Reuther also questions the idea of an "androgyny" constellated around stereotypic (and possibly fallacious) notions of masculine and feminine psychic attributes. Such stereotypical thinking "suggests that males should integrate their androgynous identity around a 'masculine' core of psychic capacities and females should integrate their androgyny around a 'feminine' core. We need to affirm . . . that all humans possess a full and equivalent human nature and personhood *as male and female*." (Reuther, 1983, p. 111)

Whitmont conceives of the constellation of what I would call "the temporal masculine and feminine archetypes" as something like a zodiacal wheel in which any section can be accentuated to different degrees in different people. He states that Jung once complained that theories and terminologies are "the very devil" (Whitmont, 1980, p. 121) in psychology and that, while we cannot do without them, we should not hang on to them beyond the limit of their usefulness. He was an empiricist who did not hesitate to revise theories in the face of new evidence.

> We are discovering that many gender patterns, which even thirty years ago were considered *a priori* genetically or archetypally prefigurated, have been the result of cultural repressive limitations. Femininity and masculinity are archetypal *a priori* structural patterns of psychic, no less than biological, functioning. But in respect to identifying their specific contents, we still need to retain open minds and be prepared to revise our views. (Whitmont, 1980, p. 121)

Before her death, Madigan shared insights received through inspirational writing about *a priori* masculine and feminine psychic structures in regard to twin souls:

Jessica Madigan 1911-1986 (Photo Courtesy of Jery Stier)

> The twin soul is not a half-soul, my Daughter. In entering the body, the *polarities were set* as to the choosing of the physical body—*masculine* or *feminine*. The blending of the heart and mind and spirit is shared by each ... (Each) twin soul may build up its personal attributes over the ages ... the attributes of Self are built up by the entity—by the individual expressing Self

throughout the ages ... Even with twin souls—there is a blending of mind and emotions. It is as if each *drinks* from the same cup of life; each *eats* at the same Table of Life. Each chooses that portion which it wants as its own. ... You (have) shared the same soul throughout the ages ... From your own table—your MUTUAL Spirit—you make choices. (The concept of twin souls) ... is an *eternal archetype*, which existed even *before* the Beginning of Time. But the attributes—Feminine qualities—Masculine qualities—attributed by Man to these archetypes are not irrefutable. (Madigan, in press)

On a more practical level, Muriel Schiffman, innovative educator who devised the Self-Therapy and Gestalt Self-Therapy processes, stated that she originally attempted to people her therapeutic workshops with equal numbers of women and men. Over time, Schiffman concluded that it was more important to balance personality types for group cohesiveness—and that such types did not necessarily correspond to gender. M. Schiffman (personal communication, 1989)

The transpersonal "psychology with a soul"—Psychosynthesis, holds similar precepts. Roberto Assagioli, the father of Psychosynthesis, states that there can't be a general psycho synthesis of women—or of men. There is only, for each individual, or either sex, a personal, unique journey toward the development of one's emotional, mental and spiritual faculties. (Assagioli, 1974)

Assagioli states that the human being today is no longer defined by any of his or her roles. Assagioli believes that the primacy of a human being is not conditioned by his or her sex. (Assagioli and Servan-Schreiber, 1974) Thus, Psychosynthesis distinguishes the essential transpersonal Self from gender roles and functions. Psychosynthesis postulates the personality as an egg shape, which brings to mind Hildegarde of Bingen's conceptualization of the egg-shaped universe created by Father/Mother God. The egg shape is a feminine form, and the return of this image to this modern psychological domain suggests to me that future ideologies will be more gender inclusive. Further, the psycho synthesis concept of the Transpersonal Self parallels the Edgar Cayce sources' description of persons as "entities" or souls, which concept transcends gender.

In summary, at this point in human unfoldment, unique opportunities exist to lift the veil of temporal archetypes and glimpse the Eternal Feminine through more inclusive new ideologies, which are emerging.

Future Horizons

Lynn Rogers with a group of A.U. students after a Moon Cycle Process on a Virginia Beach rooftop 1990. Men and Women sharing spiritual partnership and joy.
Larry VanHoose, Stase Michaels, Peppy Mocko, Lynn Rogers Ellen Hylton and Denise Tisker

Gylanic Partnership Ideals

In *The Chalice and the Blade*, Riane Eisler (1987) coined the term "gylany" to refer to the linking of both halves of humanity—female and male in a partnership—"power with", rather than a dominator—"power over"—model. The Edgar Cayce material contains many suggestions of such "power with" ideals for spiritualizing human relationships. This idea of gylanic partnership seems to be struggling to the surface of mass consciousness today.

Pogrebin (1983) theorized that current upheavals in gender and family structure may be the seismic reverberations of increasingly democratic notions pushing their way to family and individual levels. She says that the "traditional patriarchal family is democracy's 'original sin'; it is an elemental flaw in an otherwise perfectible political system." (Pogrebin, 1983, pp. 18–19) I believe that basic democratic goals cannot be achieved as long as the family is unfree. The democratization of marriage and equalization of gender and race relations are the next required steps for democracy's continued evolution.

Feinstein and Krippner (1988) cite studies by Gray, Little and Burks in 1983 as showing the happiest marriages as egalitarian; whereas marriages where one partner dominates correlated with marital dissatisfaction. Mansbridge (1980) calls for a new vision of democracy that can support the individual and at the same time promote a greater sense of community and more harmonious relations.

The call for gylanic partnership is not new. In 1792, English writer Mary Wollstonecraft was compelled to write *A Vindication of the Rights of*

Woman. Although eighteenth century seminal thinkers, such as Rousseau, were defining human liberty in the milieu of the American and French revolutions, such thinkers were inconsistent where women were concerned.

Rousseau shared a fundamental assumption about women, which has persisted since the time of the great gender polar axis shift from matrifocal "power with" to patrifocal "power over" models of human interaction. Rousseau stated a belief still prevalent today:

> For this reason, the education of women should always be relative to men. To please, to be useful to us, to make us love and esteem them, to educate us when young, and take care of us when grown up, to advise us, to console us, to render our lives easy and agreeable—these are the duties of women at all times, and what they should be taught in their infancy. (Flexner, 1972, p. 164)

In answer to Freud's question, "What do women want?" Modern British psychologists Orbach and Eichenbaum (1983) state that from the cradle to the grave, males experience an uninterrupted stream of female nurturing. Rather than being dependent, these authors maintain that the young girl child is often pushed to be emotionally independent. She's expected to nurture to others—before her own childhood-dependency needs are met.

Chesler states that "female children are, quite literally, starved for ... physical nurturance and a legacy of power and humanity from adults of their own sex ('mothers')." Moreover, Chesler further suggested (in 1972) "most mothers prefer sons to daughters and are more physically nurturant to them." This unmet need for maternal nurturance may propel daughters toward adult males who may experience the young girl's need for affection as "sexual". (Chesler, 1972, p. 18)

Starhawk asserts that the abuser, rapist or molester, does so because he does not see the young girl as having an independent and valid existence of her own. She is a servant, like other females in his life; someone to meet his needs. (Starhawk, 1987) Such incest and sexual abuse occurs against the backdrop of what Chesler calls an Olympian sexuality. When the Goddess was submerged and Zeus figures predominated, when a hierarchical dominance model prevailed—immature maidens were sexualized. (Chesler, 1972)

Even today, although society is beginning to "grow up", many pornographic magazines exploit the "virginal" baby doll. This phenomenon exists alongside a society in which mature women, in the prime of their sexual expression, are frequently devalued. Why? Perhaps, in part, because daughter (or handmaiden) doesn't threaten the "power over" model. The

Mother and the Wise Woman challenge for equality and "power with"—as defined by Eisler, (1987).

Not only can this Olympian model affect personal relationships and sexual expression, but sometimes employment opportunities as well. For example, in Buffalo, New York, nine competent waitresses and restaurant employees between the ages of 41 and 58 filed a complaint to the New York State Attorney General that they had been fired because of age discrimination. Attorney General Robert Abrams voiced a new wave of support for mature women in our country. "It is untenable that these women, some of whom have been successful at their jobs for close to twenty years, were fired simply because they do not conform with the youthful stereotypes demanded by the hotels." (Kash, 1983)

A further example can be drawn from current uproar surrounding male and female news casting groupings. Typically today, older middle-aged male newscasters are paired with female newscasters who are in their earlier childbearing years. When these younger women seek maternity leaves they are often fired and replaced with other (sometimes pregnant) young female newscasters. At the same time, more "mature" women of later or post-childbearing years are often forced to institute lawsuits when fired because of age discrimination.

An obvious solution to one aspect of this overall problem might be to pair male and female newscasters of similar age and experience. Thus, younger personnel might work out more flexible schedules together to accommodate parenting responsibilities, and more mature women and men could be paired in similar settings requiring greater experience and more availability.

With fuller models of feminine expression derived from the timeless Goddess tradition, eternal archetypes of feminine wisdom and beauty at all life states may emerge. Perhaps a signal that the Eternal Feminine is abroad is the reintroduction of full-flowering, popular, mature role models for women through the medium of film and screen. Today's more mature actresses model feminine competence, talent and beauty: to wit, the heightened popularity of images like Fonda, Evans, Hepburn, Collins and "Cher".

And today, also, sister spirit is being revitalized. I presented talks and facilitated ritual processes (The Circle of Light/Moon Cycle Process described below in Chapter Four) regarding the Eternal Feminine to women in various parts of the country. Small groups of women searching for the Goddess are springing up. The Edgar Cayce material frequently referred to the power inherent in small groups searching to better understand their relationship to the Creative Forces. 262-1 through 262-5 Individuals who study their relationship to the Creative Forces together in Edgar Cayce Study Groups find that meditating, praying and cooperating together enhances their spiritual unfoldment. Similarly, gathering together to discover their relationship to the Divine Mother—the neglected aspect of the Creative Forces, strengthens women. Author Kim Chernin states in *Reinventing Eve* that "The Goddess returns to a culture when women need an empowering image to guide their development." (Chernin, 1987, p. xx)

One such mainstream group in California comprised a cross-section of Silicon Valley electronics professionals and homemakers who drew together spontaneously to sort out early religious training and its impact upon them as women. They included former Catholics, Protestants, and one Jewish woman. This mainstream group voiced a yearning for some new form of women's spirituality. Similarly, a Virginia group found themselves drawn to Mary from a more esoteric viewpoint. Six Protestant women had begun to pray the rosary together for peace. In Idaho, a blue-collar woman had convened a small group in her basement to discuss and apply new readings about women's spirituality. From coast to coast, it seems to me, the Atlantean priestesses are awakening. In unexpected environments, the Goddess is on the rise. Mother/daughter relationships are strengthening as Demeter rescues her beloved Persephone from over 3,000 years submergence in the patrifocal underworld in Pluto's grasp. Men are also responding to this new trend. For example, recent studies suggest that girls are slightly favored by fathers and mothers in American adoptions. Perhaps one day any religious "Trinity" (or quaternity) will include Mother and Daughter—and the Divine Family will be rounded out with Father/Daughter and Mother/Daughter, in addition to Father/Son and Mother/Son relationships.

Ultimately, Chesler believes that the girl-child's deprivation stems from not being experienced as "divine" by father or mother. And, tragically, such deprivations and early sexual exploitation set the stage—in some cases, according to Chesler—for mental imbalance or "madness". (Chesler, 1972)

Authors Orbach and Eichenbaum (1983) contend that, by contrast, males seldom experience their own dependency needs, as female nurturing of males is seldom withdrawn. "Can I get you anything to eat? Are you feeling sad?" I suggest that early parenting and nurturing of young male and female children by men, as well as women, would begin to bring healing for both sexes.

Interestingly, young pre-school children in day nurseries have been reported to seek and respond to—even crave—the caring attentions of male, as well as female, caretakers when available. Today, a new breed of fathers is making its influence known. The tender sight of a strong man cradling a newborn, scooping up a toddler, or advising an older child in the parks and supermarkets of the country is not uncommon. Such practices have obvious benefits to both father and children.

Future Horizons

John Benetz and Daughter – Father and Child of the Future 1990
"What I know about myself is, my wife and my children are the most important part of my life. That's what drives me.
That's what I'm about." 2004

Acclaimed psychological author and educator John Bradshaw (1991) speaks of modern society's collective issue of the lost father. The industrial revolution took fathers away from children, Bradshaw states, causing deep psychological wounds (perhaps the greatest to males), and God has become overmasculinized as a result of idealizing the missing father. (Bradshaw, 1991) Shared parenting brings the lost father home.

In addition, such shared parenting enables mothers to actualize their full potential in terms of intellectual and creative accomplishments offered to society as a whole. Communities are increasingly benefited by women's fuller participation and leadership styles. Recently, San Jose, California, Mayor Susan Hammer was sworn into office. She celebrated the ethnic diversity of her city, and stated that such interrelationships would be more significant than new buildings. This is Goddess spirituality in action.

Perhaps modern society is at last ready to respond to the impassioned plea for equality, which Mary Wollstonecraft uttered two centuries ago:

> Glorious Creator of the whole human race! Hast Thou created such a woman, who can trace Thy wisdom in Thy works, and feel that Thou alone art by Thy nature exalted far above her, and for no better purpose? Can she believe that she was only made to submit to man, her equal—a being who, like her, was sent into the world to acquire virtue? Can she consent to be occupied merely to please him—merely to adorn the earth—when her soul is capable of rising to thee? And can she rest supinely dependent on man for reason, when she ought to mount with him the arduous steps of knowledge? (Flexner, 1972, p. 160)

Although Wollstonecraft asserted that reason is "the sign of an immortal quality in us", the flip side of this can also be stated. Whereas opportunities to exercise reason have historically been denied to women, other intrinsically valuable traits, such as intuition and compassion, have been developed by women through default or by necessity. Chesler (1972) refers to the overall price exacted by sexism for such female "talents".

Newer authors are helping frame such developed abilities in a new light. Budapest, (1980) for example, encouraged women to go against social conditioning and use the intuitive, nurturing, inventive, sensitive aspects of personality that society has encouraged in woman —toward her own empowerment. In her heralded book, *In A Different Voice*, Harvard professor Carol Gilligan asserted that women's social status, cultural conditioning, and biology give rise "to experiences which illuminate a reality common to both of the sexes." (Gilligan, 1982, p. 172)

Thus the "different voice" of women's experience calls to humanity as a whole to address the neglected human values of maturity through interdependence and the fusion of love and justice. Further, clarification of a different voice parallels Fox's (1983) description of the "anawim"—those voiceless ones who now must be heard. Similarly, it parallels Eisler's (1987) peaceful concept of "power with" versus the aggressive patrifocal "power over" model. In regard to aggression and anger, human potential author Muriel Schiffman's work on "cover emotions" suggests that anger is often the mask for fear and vulnerability. (Schiffman, 1967) Perhaps, called by women, a new movement for peace will ensue as aggression will come to be seen as the failure to connect.

According to Gilligan:

> ...women's development delineates the path not only to a less violent life, but also to a maturity realized

through interdependence and taking care." The reevaluation of women's life experience and contributions may contribute to more balanced spiritual models for men and women alike. (Gilligan, 1982, p. 171)

Through such gylanic partnership models and reclaimed values, persons may stretch toward self-transcendence as well as self-realization, or what transpersonal psychologist Abraham Maslow calls the "Z path" of transcendent self-realization. (Maslow, 1971) This is compatible with the philosophy expressed through the Cayce readings. For the Edgar Cayce material recommended to "Know thyself", but stated that Jesus' prayer was ever, "Others, Lord, others." G. Tedrich (personal communication, July 15, 1991)

New Religious Forms

Fox states that the earth is calling to us with a new agenda. (Fox, 1990) Goddess spirituality speaks to us today through the voices of what he calls the "anawim" or those excluded from recent patrifocal traditions. Certain of the Edgar Cayce readings imply that this country must listen fairly to its voiceless ones. (Stern, 1967, p. 88) Moreover, according to Madigan (1970) Cayce dreamed he would be reborn with the purpose of showing the Oneness of world religion. Matthew Fox suggests that, in answer to this call for a new agenda, new forms of ritual will spring forth, drawn from ethnic roots, which will give voice to the anawin amongst whom the Christ must walk.

New ritual celebrations reflect this trend. These new religious forms help to integrate experiences springing forth in our collective awareness and to actualize the potential for gender partnership and balance. They help recover the wisdom of the past and birth it anew for the age to come.

If spirit inspiration precedes manifestation, then such forms will spring up in the form of new celebrations and rituals. Matthew Fox (1990) suggests that humanity is called to move away from hierarchical religion where the authority is outside of self, and to draw from personal experience again. At this time of psychic axis shift one must ultimately draw from one's own experience, then come together in such processes as help humanity create new religious forms. The Edgar Cayce philosophy offers a solid foundation for this shift in emphasis toward inner authority. A consistent theme throughout the readings is that the Divine maybe discovered within each person.

New forms and practices of women's spirituality answer that call. As we have noted, many of the readings Edgar Cayce gave on Atlantis, particularly its latter era, referred to women of the present era as priestesses and leaders of the past. In my opinion based upon intuitive research, more than ever before since the closing of the last Temple of the Living Flame in the Atlantean lands, those priestesses are becoming empowered and enabling humanity to part the veil that separates them—women and men alike—from glimpsing again the face of the Divine Feminine.

Interest in the Goddess and those traditions connected to her continue to grow. Although there is a great deal of diversity in goddess worship, there are a few basic beliefs and practices shared by all who invite Her to manifest through them. She is seen as having three aspects: Mother, Maiden, and Crone, which manifest themselves according to the lunar new, full and dark moon cycles, respectively. She dances with the god or masculine principle to create the seasons. Through the seasonal and lunar cycles the cyclical nature of life and death is observed, honored and incorporated within the self. Another universally held tenet is that the Goddess is immanent in the world and in its myriad forms of life, including people. There is no split between spirit and nature; nonetheless, the balance between these aspects of divinity is not automatic. It must be constantly renewed through both personal, inner work and work directed out into the universe. This is a large part of the function of Goddess rituals.

Lynn Rogers with Young Priestesses – Bree and Chelsea 1990

There is no traditional concept of sin in Goddess worship; no external set of rules defines sin. In general, personal honor and respect for the individual are hallmarks of this religious system in which the Goddess is honored within self and others. However, this does not mean that instances of evil, such as rape or child molestation, may not be recognized. Budapest (1979) states that, as in the early nature religions, the determination of evil is made from within. Only if one knows, not just thinks, that personal integrity has been violated, can evil be redressed.

The use of magic is another element shared by the various traditions of Goddess worship. Many women have sought experience of ancient Goddess traditions in pagan forms. I believe that these "pagan" (which originally meant peasant) practices are the surviving, "root chakra" remnants of a more complex antediluvian religious system.

When the Greek Goddess-worshipping oracles had closed their last temple, this religious form went underground to reemerge at the time of the medieval genocide of the so-called "witches" (originally derived from "wiccan" which meant wise). Starhawk (1979) wrote that the Goddess Religion is experiencing not only an electrifying reawakening—but a re-creation.

Today the Eternal Feminine is being expressed through the reemergence of the Divine Feminine—or Goddess tradition. Mary is seen in a new light as a symbol for the upcoming Aquarian age, prophesied to be one of peace and fellowship on earth. New myths are arising regarding humanity's proper relationship with nature, gender equality, and a global view of the world as transcending political boundaries. New religious forms are developing. The Universal Feminine emerges through women's unique experience calling to humanity to live according to the values of maturity through interdependence and the fusion of love and justice.

In summary, this literature review provides an historical overview of the role of the Eternal Feminine principle through time. In the Beginning, the Eternal Feminine was one of two co-creative energy essences that comprised the Divine. She was known from Atlantis through Goddess-worshipping times as "associated with life-giving powers, renewal, rebirth, transformation and the mystery of death." (Chernin, 1987, p. xx) After the gender polar axis shift, She was lost in the world's awareness for the last 3,500 years.

Submergence of the Eternal Feminine has contributed to a worldview of human dominance over nature and hierarchical social structures. This has resulted in life on a planet at risk from pollution and war. I agree with Budapest, (1980) that if you oppress the life carriers, you oppress all life. In addition, societies have been relatively deprived of the talents and contributions of one gender in many regards. Also, women and men both have suffered from this ideological gender polarization in that they have lacked opportunities to express all of themselves.

However, today the Goddess is on the rise as we step over the threshold into a new consciousness paradigm. This is expressed through new rituals and ideologies. The Edgar Cayce material can provide a bridge of understanding for humanity in the reawakening and reconnecting with the Eternal Feminine. In regard to the study of Atlantean androgyny, for example, A.R.E. author Mark Thurston asked recently, "What is the spiritual underpinning for gender, if at one time souls had not yet separated themselves during incarnation in to male or female?" (Thurston, 1991, p.34) Further, the Cayce material offers healing ideals of compassion, co-creativity with the Divine and partnership motifs through time, which ideals parallel the Eternal Feminine.

The fabled New Age has dawned and we are still in the War of Armageddon. There's a backlash against women's rights worldwide. On TV news we see Middle Eastern women beaten with sticks by the Taliban and even in our country outside family planning clinics. Recently, I spoke with African American Pulitzer Prize Winning Author Alice Walker. At a local lecture, Walker underscored the important world movement to stop genital mutilation of female children—brutalized by this horrifying practice in the year 2004! Because of all this, fear of an ignorant patriarchal backlash threatening women's physical safety is still in our unconscious. Women are still being hurt. Thus it's scary to reach for the Goddess part of the Creator, even if we feel Her call.

For example, at the time of the medieval plagues in Europe, women healers survived by drinking Rose hips tea. These wise women offered their healing remedies to any who would accept their wisdom. Those who did not listen to this holistic wisdom—including many men—perished. Thus many healing women were widowed and left in charge of land. Then these women were brought to 'witch trials' and made to pay for the trial with their land.

Like these foremothers, women of today who espouse Goddess wisdom may be subject to patriarchal backlash on physical and psychic levels. Lynn Andrews wrote about a woman initiate affected by a force called "Red Dog." Working on this recently, I felt Red Dog bark at the gate. For example, an uniformed male associate called the ancient Sumerian Goddess who gave birth to the stars and all life an "arrogant bitch." This happens when glimpses of a new order shine through. A backlash at the same time new archetypes abound.

In March, 2004, Reverend Richard Smith of the Center for Eternal Life in Florida stated, "This is the age of the Holy Spirit. The feminine aspect of God is manifesting everywhere in our lives." I agree. A few examples. Mary Magdalene is reemerging as Christ's closest apostle teaching compassion and trusting the spirit within: "If the Savior has made her worthy, who are you to reject her?" (Coptic Gospel of Mary). Oprah Winfrey frees women of all colors to soar above oppression. The Mystical Life (2004) describes Jessica Madigan as "the female Edgar Cayce."

Jessica said the "sixth root race" of this new millennium, would come into body with an instinctive awareness of their true purpose and twin soul. Many such younger women have joined our diverse circle of light seeking wisdom from the more mature. Dale Aycock, author of She Who Is, heralds a female Aquastar born far in the future. We need Her now.

**Lynn Rogers, Fifth Root Race
and her daughter Megan, Sixth Root Race**

Lynnhaven Bay, named for the "Witch of Lynnhaven." Grace Sherwood was a tall, attractive, outspoken holistic healer of 17th Century Virginia Beach. The herb Rosemary grew to the right of her door. Her neighbors said she flew to England at night in an eggshell to fetch the flower. They tied Grace up and threw her into the ocean. She survived.

SECTION II

DIRECT RESEARCH

Section Two

Direct Research

This section includes two studies, which explore the relationship between the Eternal Feminine and the Edgar Cayce material. The first study deals with a new religious form: The Circle of Light/Moon Cycle Process. The comments of the participants in the process are examined to identify connections with the Eternal Feminine and the Edgar Cayce concepts. The second study deals with women connected with the Edgar Cayce work through interviews that elicit data in the following areas: excitement regarding knowing Edgar Cayce and/or the Work; challenges or difficulties; sense of personal contribution; and hopes for women in the future of this Work.

Lynn Rogers facilitates a Moon Circle for Atlantic University students in Virginia Beach 1991

Lynn Rogers facilitates another Moon Circle for Atlantic University students in Virginia Beach 1991

CHAPTER FOUR

THE CIRCLE OF LIGHT/MOON CYCLE PROCESS

Lynn Rogers leading a Circle of Light in front of the old Cayce Hospital building in Virginia Beach 1990

Lynn Rogers leads Solstice Celebration before A.R.E. Congress 1990

CHAPTER FOUR

THE CIRCLE OF LIGHT/MOON CYCLE PROCESS

Definitions

Intuition

Intuition is the faculty of knowing without use of rational processes. Intuition is described by a Latin translation of the word, as "the teacher within", which implies accessing an inner source. Thus intuition, for purposes of this study, means psychic phenomenon anchored in the soul rather than merely mental faculties, as opposed to the more commonly used definition of psychic as relating to extraordinary and nonphysical, mental processes. (Intuition is often associated with the feminine in the Edgar Cayce material.)

Scrying

Scrying is the exercise of intuitive or extrasensory abilities in the setting of the Moon Circle.

Ideal Setting

Ideal setting refers to determining one's spiritual ideal. Thurston (1984) relates the spiritual ideal described by the Cayce material to the sense of one's purpose for incarnating. For the purposes of this study, ideal setting is making this sense of purpose or intent conscious by focusing and articulating this ideal in a word or phrase. Thurston states: "The word or statement you will . . . choose to represent your spiritual ideal is both a statement of aspiration and a reminder of something you have experienced, however, briefly." (Thurston, 1984, p. 88)

The Problem

The stated intention of this book has been to discover the points of relationship between two systems of discourse—the Edgar Cayce material and the emerging body of literature regarding the Eternal Feminine—is herein addressed through an experiential process. The framework of this process includes concepts common to both systems of thought (the Edgar Cayce and the Eternal Feminine traditions) such as: the power of a small group gathering regularly to enhance spiritual unfoldment; the understanding of the Creative Forces found through attunement with nature; the discovery of the Divine Within through meditation and guided imagery; prayer for others as an application of the spiritual ideal; visualization and affirmations in keeping with one's ideals; and acceptance and development of psychic ability as emanating from the Divine Within.

This experiential ritual pattern draws from Divine Feminine (Goddess) traditions, which are for the first time here anchored in the Edgar Cayce concepts. The Cayce material often implies the Divine is Feminine but this has not been fully elucidated. The Divine Feminine traditions encourage expression of psychic unfoldment but lack anchoring in spiritual ideals. This process seeks to translate the language of each system into that of the other.

My expectation that participation in the Circle of Light/Moon Cycle Process would lead to greater understanding and integration of the Eternal Feminine with the Edgar Cayce concepts is explored. Such integration and understanding can be demonstrated through the appearance of heightened intuition and feminine imagery in the comments of participants. Both traditions teach that the Divine is within each person. Most religious forms today use male imagery only for God. This is oftentimes, though not always true (as has been demonstrated) in portions of the Cayce material. This ritual incorporates some elements from the ancient Goddess tradition to invite gender balance. As a result, participants would experience increased feminine imagery. Further, anchoring Goddess scrying techniques for psychic unfoldment with Cayce concepts for spiritual development, like ideal setting, would increase intuitive phenomena.

This is demonstrated through examination of data yielded from records of participation, which include comments in response to questions such as: "What did you experience in the exercise?" "Is there anything you would like to share?"—as well as spontaneous reports of feelings and impressions by participants. Various themes which become readily apparent in this examination are categorized by grouping quotes of participants' comments—as reported by the process developer (myself) and three student teachers—in response to the following: "State participants' most typical or frequent responses." Finally, the appearance of intuitive phenomena and the perception of feminine imagery is discussed in regard to the original problem, to determine the points of intersection between the Eternal Feminine and the Edgar Cayce traditions. These two systems of discourse are connected through the experiential process I developed.

Background

I have developed a new religious form, The Circle of Light/Moon Cycle Process, for the purpose of integrating the Divine Feminine (Goddess) tradition with the Edgar Cayce material through the training of intuition. In August of 1987 after extensive research and much trial and error, I began to recreate portions of extant ritual patterns within a transpersonal framework. After working with women (and later women and men) three times monthly for over two years, a new process began to emerge. (The developmental sequence is detailed in Appendix A.)

Thus the Circle of Light/ Moon Cycle Process that emerged synthesized Divine Feminine traditions—including surviving Goddess practices and esoteric Mariology—and anchored them into the conceptual framework outlined by the Edgar Cayce readings for the purpose of training intuition in a gender-balanced way. I first drew ideas from some previous Goddess tradition sources (such as Starhawk and her teacher, Budapest). These ideas include the creation of sacred space by a group gathered in a circle, celebration of nature's cycles through natural settings and imagery, recognition of the Divine Feminine and gender balance, and psychic expression through scrying. These concepts were then grounded in my 20-year experience as a student and teacher of the Edgar Cayce and transpersonal traditions.

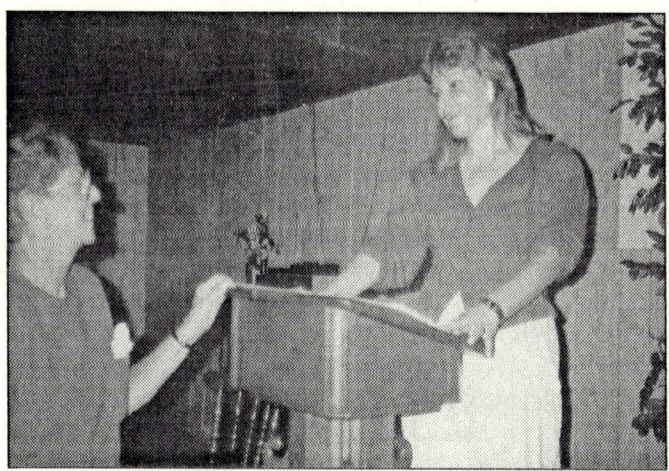

**Christ Point Church talk by Lynn Rogers on
Edgar Cayce and Transpersonal Traditions 1990**

The Cayce material links intuition to the Divine Within. The readings state that each person is "made a co-creator with the Godhead." (5163-1) Moreover, the readings encouraged a number of individuals to develop intuition and "begin to study all phases of psychic phenomena . . . " (5124-1) "Write such visions—keep them, they will be helpful to many."

(2073-2) "For this is an intuition which ye need to cultivate. For this is, not as an omen, but as an influence that would be ever present." (5163-1) Edgar Cayce gave a talk in 1931 about the misuse of the mind forces by the Atlanteans for self-gratification at the expense of others in which clear warnings are given about such selfishness and the domination of others:

> Many of you who have studied something of the history of Atlantis know that these mental forces were highly developed there. Many individuals were able to think with such concentration that they brought material things into existence by the mere power of their thought. But to use such a force, as they did, for selfish interests can result in evil. The greatest sin in the world today is selfishness, and the domination of one individual will by another. (Cayce, 1946)

Here Cayce was stating that mind power can be exercised, but – beware— as:

> ... the very thing that you would control in another will become the thing that will destroy you—it will become your Frankenstein! (Cayce, 1946 p. 43)

Thus the readings tie intuition inexorably to soul, rather than just mental forces.

Once the process was established, elements from other religious and transpersonal traditions were incorporated. Eclectic religious and ethnic elements, which reflected gender balance, were also chosen from such traditions as the Native American Medicine Wheel, Jewish Kabala, mystical Catholicism, and especially the Hindu tradition, which incorporates feminine and masculine imagery in the descriptions of the seven chakras. (Chakras are the energy centers corresponding to the glands in the human body.)

The Edgar Cayce sources linked the seven chakras to the Book of Revelation. Moreover, like other esoteric sources through time, Cayce related the chakras to planets, musical notes, and colors. (Cayce, 1945) An archetypal link between the colors, metals, and musical notes has persisted throughout the ages, but I conclude that when there is a shift in the masculine or feminine emphasis or yin or yang principle of ascendancy, such systems shift also. For example, Edgar Cayce gave two sets of planets in connection with the chakras. It is evident to me that the Cayce sources were attuned to historic systems that reflected different gender ascendancies. (See Table 2).

CHAKRA	GLAND	COLOR	GODDESS SYSTEM	GOD SYSTEM
ROOT		Red	Mars	Saturn
SACRAL	Leydig	Orange	Sun	Neptune
SOLAR PLEXUS	Adrenal	Yellow	Mercury	Mars
HEART	Thymus	Green	Saturn	Venus
THROAT	Thyroid	Blue	Jupiter	Uranus
BROW	Pineal	Indigo	Venus	Mercury
CROWN	Pituitary	Violet	Moon	Jupiter

Table 2. **Correlations of Alternate Cayce Planetary Associations with Goddess and God Systems**

Note: This table is derived from comparing Cayce material including portions of the Color Chart from Cayce 1945

Moreover, Stier, who witnessed my process in a Philosophical Roundtable Conference in 1985, noted that this effort to research and recreate ancient Goddess rituals for a modern age appears to have yielded a ritual similar to late Atlantean religious rite

The Circle of Light/Moon Cycle Process exemplifies a new religious form drawing from ancient patterns to give rise to integrative new myths. The 17th century philosopher Liebnitz wrote that human life is sharing integrally in a greater order of process, that it is an aspect as well as an agent of universal evolution. Grof (1985) says that society should assume a mythic, rather than mechanistic posture in confronting the developmental crisis of its members. Joseph Campbell believes new myths must be more intellectually (as well as emotionally) grounded and attuned to deeper psychological processes. (Campbell, 1972) By grounding this Divine Feminine ritual in the secure framework of the Edgar Cayce philosophy, an inclusive transpersonal process evolves merging old myths with new ones. It is my opinion that concepts from both systems were once integrated in Atlantis and in early civilizations and are now reintegrating in ritual forms such as the Circle of Light/Moon Cycle Process, as the Eternal Feminine reemerges in the modern world.

Overall, it became apparent that the process I developed could be summarized qualitatively as a prelude to further quantitative research. Thus the following survey study delineates further areas of research possibilities to be undertaken.

Methodology

A group of subjects participated in the Circle of Light/ Moon Cycle Process under my direction subsequently with three student teachers. (see Appendix B). Comments regarding subjective effects were solicited from the participants. These responses were recorded, later sampled, and emerging themes were determined.

Subjects

Between August 1987 and May 1991, a total of approximately 2,216 individuals participated in the Circle of Light/Moon Cycle Process; 1,431 of these came to sessions conducted by myself. In addition, approximately 4OO individuals attended sessions conducted by student teacher and research assistant A; approximately 250 individuals attended the sessions conducted by student teacher B and related personnel, and approximately 135 sessions were conducted by student teacher C. All the student teachers were women, a mixture of race and age.

**Lynn Rogers leads A Moon Cycle Process at Atlantic University 1989
Henry Reed, Barry Mack, Register Nancy Reiner and Dick Daley**

Apparatus

A tape recorder was used to record responses during all of the process developer's sessions and in most student teacher's sessions when open-ended questions were asked.

A sign-in sheet for names, addresses and phone numbers was provided for all of the process developer's sessions and in most of the student teacher's sessions. Respondents almost always completed these.

Standardized materials consistently used in the process included: a square cloth approximately 3' x 2'; a central candle in a holder; an image of

The Circle Of Light/Moon Cycle Process

the Divine Feminine—such as a statue of Mary; other candles and their containers; matches; other objects—such as a crystal wand, feather, or knife used to gesture toward the Four Directions; and natural material—such as greenery, sand, water, shells or flowers.

Other materials often used included: incense, sage or sweet grass or other American Indian mixtures for a smudge, or cleansing smoke, stick; further statuary or miscellaneous representational imagery; music provided by tape-recorded cassettes; further cloths or draperies; pieces of mirror, and objects provided spontaneously by participants for temporary inclusion in the circle, such as jewelry, stones, crystals, photographs or feathers.

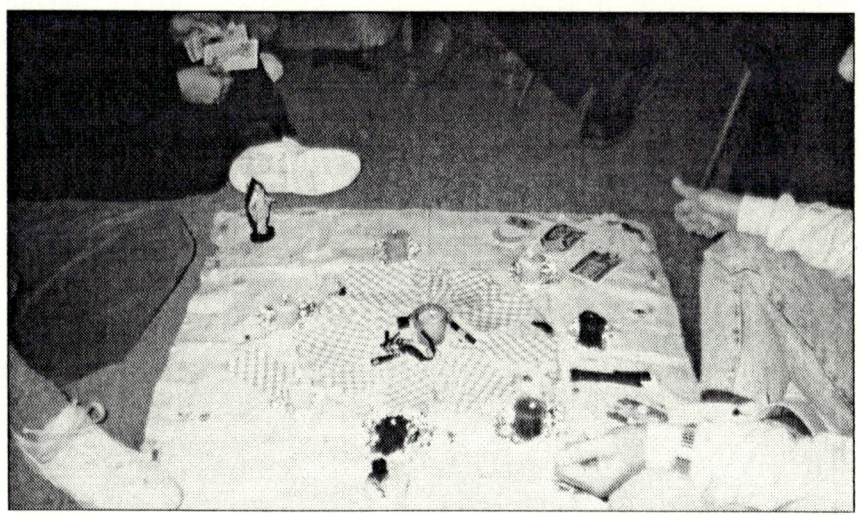

Creating Sacred Space on the floor with Mary, an image of the Divine Feminine (located on the back left corner of the cloth)

Procedure

Subjects participated in the Circle of Light/Moon Cycle Process (described below) under my direction or that of my student teachers. Typical responses of the participants were culled from a preliminary sampling of my taped sessions. Further, I interviewed the student teachers and correlated the typical responses of their participants with those of my own participants.

The following represents the standard procedure for the Circle of Light/Moon Cycle Process I developed and administered for this study.

Step one

Placing a central cloth and light in the center of an area where a circle of people will sit creates a circular, sacred space. The facilitator places an image of the Divine Feminine and other sacred symbols on the cloth around a central light—often a white candle. (Earth symbols such as fallen leaves, Air symbols such as incense, Water and Fire symbols such as a floating candle can be used.)

Participants sit on the ground, sand or floor. They are invited to place objects sacred to them in the circle. Then deep breathing exercises are begun as participants "empty" themselves in the womblike darkness. Next, Mother/Father, "God, Goddess and All That Is", Source, is imbued in the preliminary prayer for the light of protection.

The leader or an assistant (called priestess or priest in the ancient Goddess tradition) calls to the "Grandmothers and Grandfathers" of the Four Directions while gesturing with wand or feather. The Four Directions are associated with typologies that are mentioned during this calling, as the facilitator sees fit. For example, "I call to the Guardians of the Watchtowers of the North—realm of midnight, winter, earth, our bodies, and the sensate." (See Tables 3 and 4).

TYPOLOGY	NORTH	EAST	SOUTH	WEST
ELEMENT	Earth	Air	Fire	Water
HERMETIC GENDER	Female	Female	Male	Male
FOUR BODIES	Physical	Mental	Spiritual	Emotional
JUNGIAN TYPOLOGY	Sensate	Intellect	Intuition	Feeling
SEASON	Winter	Spring	Summer	Autumn
TIME	Midnight	Dawn	Noon	Dusk
GODDESS	Gaia	Aurora	Brigit	Aphrodite
ANGEL	Raphael	Gabriel	Michael	Uriel
MYSTIC	Mechtilde	Hildegarde	Francis	St. John of the Cross
FRANCISCAN CANTICLE	Mother Earth	Brother Wind	Brother Fire	Sister Water
NATIVE AMERICAN HERB	Tobacco	Sweet Grass	Cedar	Sage
NATIVE AMERICAN COLOR	White	Yellow	Black	Red

Table 3.   The Four Directions and Typologies
Note: This table derived by synthesizing eclectic sources

ELEMENT	INTERPRETATIVE ASSOCIATION
Water	Emotion, Intuition and Dreams
Fire	Inspiration and Activation
Earth	Integrity, Perseverance and Strength
Air	Intellectuality, Ideation and Imagination

Table 4.   The Four Elements in the Circle of Light/Moon Cycle Process   Note: I received this table through a dream

The Circle Of Light/Moon Cycle Process

Lynn Rogers A.R.E. Survey Lecture on Dreams

**Circle of Light on the beach in Virginia 1990
(It rained everywhere, but on us!)**

Step two

The leader uses a crystal wand or an ornate metal knife to "part the veil that separates the worlds" of our "left-brain" vs. "right brain" awareness. Participants imagine light surrounding each of them and circling to the left to form a complete Circle of Light.

Facilitator leads a brief visualization reverie keyed to the phase of the moon (See Table 5) and sometimes to the current point in the wheel of the year. Meditators now "meet the Goddess within" in one of her three aspects: New Moon—Maiden of new beginnings, Full Moon—Mother of creative ideas, and Dark Moon—Wise Woman who sees beyond the veil.

ASPECT	LUNAR CYCLE	MEANING	NAMES	APPLICATIONS
MAIDEN	New Moon (Waxing)	New beginning	Artemis, Nimue	Plant seeds for next 28 days (e.g. in work relationships). Develop new Intuitive skills.
MOTHER	Full Moon	Creativity Heightened	Diana, Mary	Offer healing Prayers. Practice intuitive Skills.
WISE WOMAN	Dark Moon (Waning)	Power. Part the Veil of Perception	Hecate, Anna	Release and transmute unwanted conditions (e.g. fears that hinder spiritual growth). Exercise advanced intuitive skills.

Table 5.   The Three Aspects of the Eternal Feminine and Cyclicity

Note: This table is primarily derived from the my experiences facilitating this process, (with resource material from sources such as Starhawk, 1979, and Budapest, 1980)

Step three

A crystal or candle is passed around the circle and individuals make affirmations clarifying their true nature in order to, for example, attract better working conditions, stabilize relationships with others, or overcome fears that hinder the spiritual path.

At the close of the individual's spoken or silent affirmation, she or he says "Blessed Be", or any other closure of choice, such as "Let It Be", "Amen", etc. Then the group energizes the individual's affirmations or prayers by repeating the individual's closure in unison.

Step four

A second round of prayers is made for others. Now the affirmations and prayers are released without attachment to "be realized for the highest good of all"—as hands are raised upwards towards the moon. Participants "draw down the moon".

Step five

A chant is selected and repeated three to seven times.

Step six

Now participants are given instructions to "scry" or attempt to train and exercise clairvoyant and extrasensory abilities (as in the Temple of Diana as suggested by Madigan, 1965). Participants first define spiritual ideals and pray to be of service, as per the Cayce readings' suggestion that intuition must be associated with soul rather than merely mental origins. Next, participants train and practice intuitive gifts as a group and later in pairs. A variety of psychic tools or "left-brain" anchors are implemented to anchor these impressions. Then participants share their responses with the group. (See Table 6).

SUBJECT	SCRYER	IMPRESSIONS
Randi	John	Light, lost horizon, old ancient wise man
	Lynn	Easygoing sea priestess—"it's time now— take it up and go"
	Bill	Dark purple and blue aura—spiritual, Himalayas, monastery, walking up in snow
	Gwen	"Also about take wing"—hard time letting go
	Nancy	Like Cleopatra—the way the candle hit your eyes
	Virginia	"End of struggle'"—enormous amount of growth—"woman emerging"
Virginia	Randi	Intense blue shadow saw as shaman in a cave, something to do with Indians
	John	Triangle with light—triangle pointed down
	Lynn	Ancient Greece, Atlantis—This birthday is going to be really good for you—positive monetary changes
	Bill	Green and blue, England—old
	Gwen	Glow of Aura—but saw no color— leadership coming out later this decade
	Nancy	Bird soaring through canyon—bird means freedom, etc.
Lynn	Bill	Purple—very strong hard effect around your head and a lot of blue and white spike right above your head
	Gwen	Young girl in garden, maiden – goddess— strong medicine woman
	Nancy	Inner strength—bold light
	Virginia	Earth mother—giver of life
	Randi	At first—girls at 12 or 13—then saw plaster death mask of a saint martyrdom

Table 6.   Sample Scrying/September 11, 1990/Moon Circle/84th Street Beach/Virginia Beach/Facilitator: Lynn Rogers

Step seven

Now participants offer final prayer for each other and the planet. When this is done the priestess closes the veil that parts the worlds, the Four Guardians are thankfully released, and healing energies gathered are lovingly grounded back into the earth. The circle is complete. The Moon Circle Ritual concludes.

For a more complete description of this process and its conceptual correlation to the Hindu chakra progression as described by Johari, (1987) see Appendix C.

Circle of Light participants share the results of "Scrying" by moonlight in Virginia Beach 1990

Lynn Rogers "Scrying" with Moon Cycle student, actress P. Renee Blakes, California 2002

Limitations

This is a preliminary qualitative, phenomenological study using participants' written or spoken words and observable behavior. Although the process is well developed and standardized and the data is extensive, I am at this time only suggesting themes for further qualitative and quantitative study. Until such further study is completed, this initial research can only yield typologies and qualitative estimates of heightened intuition and feminine imagery which the proceeding Tables represent.

Further limitations include the following: supervision of student teacher's administration of the process was impeded by student teachers' individual levels of willingness to report and consult consistently and to keep accurate records; varied settings were used, including indoor (homes, offices, colleges, community facilities including churches and conference centers) and outdoor (yards, beach and mountains). (See Table 7).

SETTING	PROCESS DEVELOPER	STUDENT TEACHER A	STUDENT TEACHER B	STUDENT TEACHER C
Private Office (Classes)	354		190	
Community Facility (Church, YWCA, etc.)	380			
Outdoor Setting	205	160	60	
Homes	175			135
Retreat Facility (Asilomar, etc.)	185			
Colleges	172	240		
Total (2,216)	1,471	400	250	135

Table 7. Correlations of Approximate Number of Participants per Facilitator in Varied Settings

Findings and Discussion

Typical responses that emerged were culled from a preliminary sampling of taped responses. I interviewed the student teachers and correlated the typical responses of their participants with those of my own participants. Trends appeared through the survey of participants' comments that suggested preliminary core themes.

Main themes as identified by the process developer and the three student teachers are summarized in the following Tables: (See Tables 8, 9, 10 and 11). These themes are ranked by frequency. (See Table 12). Although content analysis of these themes is beyond the scope of this particular study, it would be useful to undertake this at a later time for more in-depth understanding.

The following anecdotal experiences highlight and illustrate the findings:

"For me the moon circle is the necessary touch for me to truly acknowledge and experience the feminine side of divinity, rather than just reading about it."

"It's like going to church without the dogma."

"It's like experiencing a high, or altered state, without drugs."

"The Cayce material is presented with the Goddess tradition in the moon circle in a more lively fashion."

THEMES	FACILITATOR'S COMMENTS
Eternal Feminine Imagery	Non-intrusive imagery of Divine Feminine accepted well—women feel empowered—men find new respect for feminine.
Benefits or Patterns of Participants Prayers and Affirmation	Empowering to define one's own needs for affirmations—uplifting to make affirmations for others.
Noticing Cyclic Patterns	Some women who had monthly period difficulties reported easier periods—some regular participants in all women's sessions reported period synchronizing with moon phases and/or with each other's cycles.
Sense of Oneness	About 80% of participants linger after the sessions are complete and seem reluctant to go home.
Sense of Sacred Space	No comment
Heightened Intuitive Phenomena	Setting ideals of being of service to each other before scrying creates more meaningful material or intuitive impressions.
Inner Clarification	No comment

Table 8. Summary of Main Themes as Noted by Process Developer

THEMES	FACILITATOR'S COMMENTS
Eternal Feminine Imagery	Connection with Universal Feminine made through rituals which repattern similar to Catholic Church rituals to Father God—Dance enhances this.
Benefits or Patterns of Participants Prayers and Affirmation	Most common affirmations participants make are about 1) Relationships, e.g. the twin soul and/or "divine loneliness" 2) Healing people and Mother Earth 3) For job or life direction.
Noticing Cyclic Patterns	No comment
Sense of Oneness	Overall sense of Oneness—connections are made in the paired exercises—bonds.
Sense of Sacred Space	No comment
Heightened Intuitive Phenomena	Synchronicity.
Inner Clarification	Increased awareness of the inner critic which impedes intuitive perceptions.

Table 9. Summary of Main Themes as Noted by Student Teacher A

The Circle Of Light/Moon Cycle Process

THEMES	FACILITATOR'S COMMENTS
Eternal Feminine Imagery	A calm energy entering, like a Mother – about 50% female guides are seen in meditation [without previous suggestion].
Benefits or Patterns of Participants Prayers and Affirmation	No comment.
Noticing Cyclic Patterns	No comment.
Sense of Oneness	No comment.
Sense of Sacred Space	No comment.
Heightened Intuitive Phenomena	More dreams and perceptions of communication with spirit guides afterwards
Inner Clarification	Self-counseling—Touch down to core emotions.

Table 10. Summary of Main Themes as Noted by Student Teacher B

THEMES	FACILITATOR'S COMMENTS
Eternal Feminine Imagery	Increased Goddess awareness.
Benefits or Patterns of Participants Prayers and Affirmation	No comment
Noticing Cyclic Patterns	Adds to rhythm of life.
Sense of Oneness	No comment
Sense of Sacred Space	Creating sacred space helps to manifest reality better.
Heightened Intuitive Phenomena	Greater sense of synchronistic experiences after the process. Communication with those "in Spirit" in meditation.
Inner Clarification	No comment.

Table 11. Summary of Main Themes as Noted by Student Teacher C

THEMES	PROCESS DEVELOPER	STUDENT TEACHER A	STUDENT TEACHER B	STUDENT TEACHER C
Eternal Feminine Imagery	X	X	X	X
Benefits or Patterns of Participants Prayers and Affirmation	X	X		
Noticing Cyclic Patterns	X			X
Sense of Oneness	X	X		
Sense of Sacred Space				X
Heightened Intuitive Phenomena	X	X	X	X
Inner Clarification		X	X	

Table 12.   Themes Ranked by Frequency

Wise Women's Circle

This class will review women's spiritual roots, acquire tools to create sacred space, attune your body to natural rhythms, train your intuition and manifest your goals.

Fee:
Dates: — ONGOING SESSIONS —
Time:
Where:
    San Jose

Instructor: Lynn Rogers, M.A.

For registration information, call 723-6703 or 723-6553. Call:
(For additional information about the course call the Instructor at (408) 559-5995.)

Check, Cash, Visa or Master Card accepted.

Lynn Rogers' Wise Women's Circle class

**Lynn Rogers with "Moon Men." The Guardians are released.
Virginia Beach 1990**

Recommendations and Conclusions

Recommendations for Future Study

This study represents a beginning exploration and a glimpse into the extensive research possibilities regarding the Circle of Light/Moon Cycle process which seeks to experientially integrate the Edgar Cayce material with the emerging body of knowledge regarding the Eternal Feminine.

As this project began to unfold, a large body of information was better defined which offers great promise for continuing research. Ideas for future research that would derive from a more in-depth study of the tapes could include: Responses by gender, previous transpersonal background, indoor vs. outdoor settings.

Conclusions

The Circle of Light/Moon Cycle Process experientially integrates the emerging body of knowledge related to the Eternal Feminine with the Edgar Cayce material through: a framework using common elements from both traditions; inclusion of the Divine Feminine and gender balance; and psychic unfoldment anchored in spiritual ideals. The process seeks to complete both traditions by elucidating the Divine Feminine implied by the Cayce material, and by
grounding the intuitive and psychic practices of the Divine Feminine traditions in conscious spiritual ideal setting. The incorporation of these factors helps balance each tradition. This process illustrates the underlying premise of both systems—that the Divine is within each person. As expected, the preliminary study of the process indicated that participants experienced increased feminine imagery and heightened intuition.

This process translates the concepts of each system into language of the other. For example, the Cayce concept of ideal setting becomes the anchor for the intuitive work of scrying, which was an ancient Goddess traditional practice. Feminine representations, such as a statue of Mary in the circle, link the Christ focus of the Cayce readings with such Goddess traditions, so that God and Goddess and Father/Mother God are linked to provide gender inclusive imagery for the Creative Forces.

It is my opinion that core concepts from both systems were once integrated in Atlantis and in early civilizations and may now reintegrate in ritual forms, such as the Circle of Light/Moon Cycle Process, as the Eternal Feminine reemerges in the modern world. The Circle of Light/Moon Cycle Process integrates concepts from the Eternal Feminine and the Edgar Cayce traditions in that common elements are established, Divine Feminine imagery is incorporated, and psychic unfoldment is anchored in spiritual ideals.

Joline Swain and Georgia McCoy Paterson

Dr. Kathy Derby, P. Renee Blakes and Lynn Rogers 2002

The Circle Of Light/Moon Cycle Process

Lynn Rogers and daughter Megan

Marcel Stuckey and granddaughter

Gail Sanchez and Joline Swain celebrate after a circle

California Adult Education, Wise Women's Circle Class

Lynn Rogers leading a Moon Circle in California for members of UCM Church 2003

Lynn Rogers, Janet Childs and Nancy Payne

SOLAR & LUNAR CYCLES

The Wheel of the Year: Celebrating Earth's Holy Days

by Reverend Lynn Rogers

In the ancient Goddess tradition, as it has survived in the form of nature religions, the Wheel of the Year is created when god and goddess dance together to make the seasons. The creative forces are seen as a dyad that work together to create life.

The expression "Father/Mother God" well describes this tradition, where the male and female forces are the same force flowing in opposite, not opposed, directions.

According to Starhawk, author of *The Spiral Dance*, the goddess is seen as the life-giving force, the power of manifestation, the energy flowing into the world to become form. The god is seen as the death force, in a positive, not a negative sense – the force of limitation that is the necessary balance to unbridled creation, the force of dissolution, of return to formlessness.

God and goddess are part of a cycle, each dependent upon the other. Thus, life is a circle or spiral; each ending paves the way for a new beginning. Each phase is sacred, significant and to be celebrated. Here are the highlights of the solar cycle, or the Wheel of the Year:

Yule/Winter Solstice (Dec. 20 - 23)

On this longest night of the year, the Great Mother now gives birth to the Divine Sun Child, dispersing all darkness. We sense the stillness behind motion, and turn the wheel to bring the light, calling the Sun Child from the womb of night Mother. At the Festival of Lights, winter's introspection mends the psyche for new creation.

Eostar Ritual/Spring or Vernal Equinox (March 20 - 22)

The life force perpetuates and renews all nature at this time. Persephone returns from the underworld to reunite with her mother Demeter. The Prince of the Sun stretches out his hand, and Kore, the Dark Maiden, returns from the land of the dead, clothed in fresh rain. Where they step, flowers appear.

Midsummer Night/Lithia/Summer Solstice (June 20 - 23)

This is the longest day of the year; light triumphs, yet begins its decline into dark. The Sun King embraces the Queen of Summer in the love that is death, because it is so complete, that all dissolves into the song of ecstasy that moves the worlds. Like the Lord of Light, who sails away on the dark sea toward rebirth, we too must accept changes and the passing of the sun.

Mabon/Fall Equinox (Sept. 20 - 23)

Day and night are in perfect balance. It is a time of thanksgiving

One can celebrate Earth's sacred days with a moon circle as illustrated by Reverend Lynn Rogers.

and joy, of leavetaking and sorrow. The Sun King has become the Lord of Shadows. Life declines, and we give thanks for what we have harvested. We give thought to the balance in our own lives; we meet to turn the wheel and weave the cord of life that will sustain us through the dark.

The lunar cycle

The feminine force of the creator—the Triple Goddess—is experienced in her three aspects: as the *Maiden of New Beginnings* celebrated at the new moon; as the *Mother of Life* in full expression, celebrated at the full moon; and as the *Wise Woman*, or crone, who understands the mysteries of life and death, celebrated at the waning moon.

Thus, at the new moon, we plant seeds of endeavor for the coming month. At the full moon, projects and psychic and healing energies are heightened. And at the waning moon, our ability to "scry," or use intuition and ESP to see behind the facade of things, to the deeper reality, is sharpened. Further, we have increased power now, to transform or release from ourselves and our lives those elements and conditions that no longer serve our destiny.

Flowing in greater harmony

Many Goddess traditions are the silent undergirding for contemporary religious practices. In Christianity, for example, Christ is resurrected at the Eostar point in the wheel.

By becoming aware of these points and experimenting with their applications in our lives, we can enhance our personal empowerment and well-being. And by understanding earth's sacred days, it is possible to flow in greater harmony with nature and with the balanced creative forces that are mother and father to us all. ■

Universal Church of The Master Quarterly, article by Lynn Rogers

CHAPTER 5
WOMEN IN THE WORK:
MULTIGENERATIONAL INTERVIEWS

CHAPTER FIVE

WOMEN IN THE WORK: MULTIGENERATIONAL INTERVIEWS

Definition of The Work

The Work includes the Edgar Cayce material and all activity surrounding that material in terms of its research and dissemination, as well as efforts to live the deeper ideals of the philosophy it contains. For the purposes of this study, the material and all efforts applied to compiling, researching, disseminating, and living in accordance with the philosophy it contains—and all related activities—will be referred to as the Work. Thus, such activity is not limited to that of the official organizations set up for this purpose, (A.R.E., the Edgar Cayce Foundation and Atlantic University, the A.R.E. Clinic), but includes the independent effort of other individuals and groups who share this purpose (such as the Scottsdale Holistic Medical Group and the Philosophical Roundtable Society).

The Problem

As previously stated, there is an emerging body of literature regarding the Eternal Feminine that points to the need for a more gender-balanced understanding of ourselves, our world, and the Creative Forces. The problem I sought to solve in both the literary review portions of this thesis that became a book, in the previous study, and in the following study, was that this body of knowledge had not yet been related to the Edgar Cayce readings.

The stated intention of my book was to discover the points of relationship between two systems of discourse: The Edgar Cayce material and the emerging body of literature regarding the Eternal Feminine. It was my expectation to find that the relationship between the Eternal Feminine and the Edgar Cayce materials would be elucidated through the lives of individual women in this important work in terms of points of connection or disconnection.

Background

Decades ago, I was inspired to explore the Edgar Cayce philosophy through a woman mentor named Jessica Madigan. Very young at the time, I quickened to answers found to life's fundamental questions and to the high ideals represented by the philosophy as expressed by this dynamic teacher. However, I did sense that some conflict had occurred long ago between Madigan and the official establishment surrounding the Work she loved so much. As a result of perceiving my teacher's disappointment with that establishment, I became an A.R.E. member for self-study purposes but did not explore a fuller role in ARE until after Jessica Madigan's death in 1986.

In the meantime, while very active studying and teaching Cayce and intuitive philosophies, my interests turned in the mid-1980's to the emerging field of women's spirituality. This field seemed to eventually complement and enhance m philosophical framework derived from the Cayce material. However, there were instances of crisis in terms of disconnection from the portions of the Cayce material that seemed to exclude the Eternal Feminine. It was my teacher, Jessica Madigan, then close to her passing from this plane, who helped me understand the discrepancies through her intuitive and psychological approach to Edgar Cayce—the man—and the readings. Thus, Jessica Madigan again helped translate this material into the language of the Eternal Feminine.

Because of all of the above, I first came to Virginia Beach—to A.R.E. Headquarters and to Atlantic University—in 1989. I was deeply and pleasantly surprised at the spiritual beauty of the entire established effort surrounding the Edgar Cayce work in Virginia Beach. As with many others, I had a feeling of "coming home".

Later, however, when studying with he charming, acclaimed author of the *Sleeping Prophet*, and in other circumstances as well, a painful and disappointing element of sexism inspired me to search for connections between women's spirituality and the Edgar Cayce material, in light of current transpersonal studies at Atlantic University. This resulted in the present research with women of varying chronological generations and "generations in the Work".

Part of the women's spirituality tradition is the emphasis on women's own experience and their connections together. In light of my own experience of both connection and disconnection between the Edgar Cayce Work and women's spirituality, it seemed particularly appropriate to explore other women's experiences in this regard.

Methodology

A group of women were identified who had participated in the Work surrounding the Edgar Cayce material. Women were chosen who represented various chronological generations and levels of exposure and involvement in the Work. I interviewed these woman in order o clarify heir experience *as women* in the Work. Questions focused on areas of excitement, challenge or difficulty, personal contribution and hopes for the women of tomorrow.

The interviews yielded a great deal of information from which I selected significant passages and organized these according to question and the subject's chronological generation, as well as generation in the Work. From these, repeated themes of connection and disconnection between the Eternal Feminine and the Edgar Cayce work emerged. Further, these were analyzed based on chronological generation and generation in the Work.

Subjects

The subjects for this study were twenty-five women of various generations and socioeconomic and educational backgrounds who had participated in the Work surrounding the Edgar Cayce material. Interviews were conducted with twenty-two women (on both coasts) representing nine generations ranging in age from 14 to 102 years of age. Three sets of interviews were conducted with the family and friends of three women who were deceased from this plane. The subjects are further described in greater detail in the Definitions section above. Also see Tables 13, 14, 15 and 16 below. Subjects were connected with the Edgar Cayce Work by generation, as follows:

Chronological Generations

Chronological generations were established starting with teenagers, then in 10-year increments beginning at age 20.

Generations in the Work

Generations in the Work were delineated by a woman's status in the waves of the Edgar Cayce Work, as defined by myself and for the purposes of this study, into the following subsections:

First Generation

These women knew Edgar Cayce personally.

First Generation—Part One.

This category included women who knew Edgar Cayce personally as family members. They include 1) Gertrude Cayce, wife of Edgar Cayce and conductor of the readings, also mother of Hugh Lynn Cayce and Edgar Evans Cayce, and 2) Sally Cayce, daughter-in-law of Edgar Cayce, wife of Hugh Lynn Cayce, mother of Charles Thomas Cayce and Greg Cayce.

First Generation—Part Two.

Four women knew Edgar Cayce personally but were not relatives.

Edgar Cayce And The Eternal Feminine

Gladys Davis Turner was Edgar Cayce's secretary and worked closely with both Mr. and Mrs. Cayce in the Cayce home. Mae Gimbert St. Clair received readings and was a friend of the family. Irene Seiberling Harrison opened her home in New York to Mr. and Mrs. Cayce, Miss Davis, and Hugh Lynn Cayce so that readings could be given to individuals in that area. Irene Harrison's daughter, Gertrude (Trudy) Faith Harrison, knew Edgar Cayce as a child in her mother's home; there she witnessed readings and came to know Mr. Cayce as a trusted friend.

#	SUBJECT	CHRONOLOGICAL GENERATION	GENERATION IN THE WORK
1	Gertrude Cayce	Deceased	1-1/E
2	Gladys Davis Turner	Deceased	1-2/E
3	Jessica Madigan	Deceased	2-1/E
4	Irene S. Harrison	Centenarian	1-2/E
5	Sally Cayce	80's	1-1/E
6	Mae Gimbert St. Clair	80's	1-2/E
7	Nell Clairmonte	80's	2-1/E
8	Dr. Gladys McGarey	70's	2-2/W
9	Trudy Ketchel	60's	4-2/W
10	Grethe Tedrick	60's	2-2/W
11	Trudy Harrison Clawson	60's	1-2/W
12	Rev. Mary Garry	50's	4-1/W
13	Suzanne Keehn	50's	3-3/W
14	Gail Cayce Schwartzer	40's	3-1/E
15	Marsha Hunter Mossman	40's	3-2/W
16	Lyn Costaldo	40's	3-3/E
17	Rev. Pamela Bro-Benetz	40's	3-1/E
18	Jean Holcombe, PhD	40's	3-2/E
19	Mary Chacon	30's	3-2/W
20	Linda Hagen	30's	4-1/E
21	Teresa Lott	30's	4-1/E
22	Carol Robertson	20's	5/E
23	Becky Sias	20's	4-2/W
24	Megan Flautt	Teens	5/W
25	Deja Elizabeth Howard	Teens	5/E

Table 13.   Multigenerational Interview Subjects

Author Elsie Sechrist who received a reading from Edgar Cayce and worked with Hugh Lynn Cayce. Virginia Beach 1991

Women in the Work: Multigenerational Interviews

Mae Gimbert St. Clare who was associated with the Cayce Family. Virginia Beach 1991

SUBJECT	CHRONO-LOGICAL GENERATION	GENERATION IN THE WORK									
		1st		2nd		3rd			4th		5th
		1	2	1	2	1	2	3	1	2	
1	Deceased	E									
2	Deceased		E								
3	Deceased			E							
4	Centenarian		E								
5	80's	E									
6	80's		E								
7	80's			E							
8	70's				W						
9	60's								W		
10	60's				W						
11	60's		W								
12	50's								W		
13	50's						W				
14	40's					E					
15	40's						W				
16	40's							E			
17	40's					E					
18	40's						E				
19	30's						W				
20	30's								E		
21	30's								E		
22	20's										E
23	20's									W	
24	Teens										W
25	Teens										E

Table 14.   Subjects Sorted by Chronological Generations

SUBJECT	CHRONO-LOGICAL GENERATION	GENERATION IN THE WORK								
		1st		2nd		3rd			4th		5th
		1	2	1	2	1	2	3	1	2	
1	Deceased	E									
5	80's	E									
2	Deceased		E								
4	Centenarian		E								
6	80's		E								
11	60's		W								
3	Deceased			E							
7	80's			E							
8	70's				W						
10	60's				W						
14	40's					E					
17	40's					E					
15	40's						W				
18	40's						E				
19	30's						W				
13	50's							W			
16	40's							E			
12	50's								W		
20	30's								E		
21	30's								E		
9	60's									W	
23	20's									W	
22	20's										E
24	Teens										W
25	Teens										E

Table 15.   Subjects Sorted by Generations in the Work

GENERATION IN THE WORK									GRAND TOTAL
1st		2nd		3rd			4th		5th	
1	2	1	2	1	2	3	1	2	
2	4	2	2	2	3	2	3	2	3	25

Table 16A.   Total Subjects by Generations in the Work

CHRONOLOGICAL GENERATION	TOTALS
Deceased	3
100's	1
80's	3
70's	1
60's	3
50's	2
40's	5
30's	3
20's	2
Teens	2
Grand Total	25

Table 16B.   Total Subjects by Chronological Generations

EAST	WEST	GRAND TOTAL
15	10	25

Table 16C.   Total Subjects by East vs. West

Second Generation

These women entered the Work between about 1950 and 1960 and participated in efforts to disseminate it to a wider audience.

Second Generation—Part One.

Two women who did not know Edgar Cayce personally but came into the Work by 1950, became part of the movement at that time to disseminate the information to a wider audience: 1) Nell Clairmonte, on the staff of Venture Inward Magazine and formerly active traveling throughout the country to develop Study Groups 2) the late Jessica Madigan, instrumental in developing A.R.E. programs in Southern California beginning in the early 1950's and later an author and founder of the Philosophical Roundtable Society.

Second Generation—Part Two.

Two women came into the Work by about 1960 at a time when it was becoming more widely disseminated; they have played key roles in regard to further outreaching and establishing the Work. They include 1) Dr. Gladys McGarey of the Scottsdale Holistic Medical Group in Arizona who came into contact with the Work in 1957. McGarey is an author, lecturer and co-founder of the A.R.E. Clinic in Phoenix, Arizona where she worked to apply and integrate the Edgar Cayce medical material as a prototype for holistic physicians, and 2) Grethe Tedrick, A.R.E. Northern California Regional Coordinator who came into the work in 1961 and who has made extensive contributions in the field, including the development of youth programs.

Dr. Gladys McGarey, Second Generation Part 2

Third Generation
These women became involved with the Work around 1970.

Third Generation—Part One.
These women came into association with the Edgar Cayce work before 1950 because their parents were involved with the Cayce material, and were personally involved in the Work by 1970. They are the daughters of first generation (male or female) parents—who may or may not be mentioned in this study. They include Gail Cayce Schwartzer, daughter of Edgar Evans Cayce and former director of the Edgar Cayce Foundation, and Reverend Pamela Bro-Benetz, (granddaughter of Marguerite Harmon Bro) daughter of Revs. June and Harmon Bro.

Third Generation—Part Two.
Five women came into association with the Edgar Cayce Work by 1970, through association with (male or female) first or second generation mentors, and participated either in the East Coast Atlantic University experimental sessions or the parallel West Coast Philosophical Roundtable experimental sessions in the 1970's. They include Jean Holcombe, PhD, Marsha Hunter Mossman, and Mary Chacon.

**Marsha Hunter Mossman
now known as Sonshine Freedom.**

Third Generation—Part Three.
Two women came into association with the Edgar Cayce Work around 1970 through association with (male or female) first or second generation mentors. They include Suzanne Keehn and A.R.E. Field Service Director Lyn Costaldo.

Fourth Generation
These women came into the Work after 1970 through the present.

Fourth Generation—Part One.
Three women came into association with the Edgar Cayce Work after 1970 and before 1980 and were exposed to First or Second Generation—Part One (female or male) mentors. They include homemaker and holistic researcher Linda Hagen; A.R.E. Headquarters employee Teresa Lott, and Rev. Mary Garry.

Fourth Generation—Part Two.
Two women came into association with the Edgar Cayce Work after 1980 and did not have direct exposure to First or Second Generation—Part One mentors. They include study group leader Trudy Ketchel, M.A., and Becky Sias, my student assistant.

Fifth Generation
Three young women were coming into the Work at the present time. They are the daughters of Second Generation—Part Two or Third Generation parents who may or may not be mentioned in this study. They include Carol Robertson, daughter of Dr. and Mrs. Robertson, Megan Flautt, daughter of Lynn Rogers, and Deja Elizabeth Howard, daughter of Gail Myers. Carol Robertson was exposed to the Work as a child and was pursuing self-study of the material; however, at the time of the study, the teen-aged girls' primary exposure to the Edgar Cayce Work was, through their mothers.

Apparatus
A questionnaire was developed to use in the face-to-face interviews. (See Table 17 below) A tape recorder was used to collect the subjects' responses.

Limitations
This study was limited in size, and to women (or their family and friends) who were at the time of the interview, currently within the interviewer's geographic localities—East and West coasts.

The sample was not randomly chosen. There was a subjective bias on the part of myself in choosing subjects. Some of the subjects are contemporaries of myself and so shared comparable developmental experiences. Further, the study was limited to women who were associated with the Edgar Cayce Work in the following ways: 1) women who knew Edgar Cayce in his lifetime, and 2) women who had investigated the Edgar Cayce material or who had participated in the A.R.E., the Edgar Cayce Foundation and Atlantic University, or other independent Cayce philosophy-oriented groups such as the Philosophical Roundtable Society.

NUMBER	QUESTION
One	What has been most exciting about your association with Edgar Cayce and the Work?
Two	What has challenged you or been difficult in regard to knowing Edgar Cayce and the Work?
Three	How do you feel you've been able to contribute to the Work?
Four	How do you see the Woman of Tomorrow contributing to the Edgar Cayce Work?

Table 17.   Interview Questions

    The information was gained through interviews, and thus subjected to the variability of the interviewing technique. Variables included the length of the interview and the number of previous contacts between the interviewer and the subject. Questions for the interviews were selected subjectively and reflected m bias. Some persons who were interviewed adhered closely to the questions; others chose to digress to matters of interest to them.

    Definitions of "Generations in the Work" were derived subjectively and also reflected the bias of myself. Moreover, "Generations in the Work" did not necessarily correspond to chronological age or to a familial relationship with the Cayce family. Moreover, it appeared that there were women who could have been categorized in more than one Generation in the Work.

    A companion group of males was not assessed, as this study focused specifically on women in light of the book topic: Edgar Cayce and the Eternal Feminine. It was not this author's intention to compare women's with men's experiences in the Work, but to offer a descriptive multigenerational survey study of women's experiences in the Work.

Findings and Discussion

Findings: Highlights of Questionnaire Responses

    The following is a sample of representative highlights from the response passages to the interview questions, as given fully in Appendix E.

Question One: **What has been most exciting about your association with Edgar Cayce and the Work?**

"It was the fact that he saved my younger brother's life by my husband and myself following the advice we gained through the Edgar Cayce readings." Age: Centenarian/GW: 1-2/E

"As a child, he told me he saw a pink fairy on my shoulder. I could never doubt it because I totally trusted him, though I never saw it for myself." G: 60's/GW: 1-2/W

". . . the feeling of 'coming home' that this Work and these people have brought me. . . . I have needed to be a part of something bigger, that I can believe in, and to make my contribution there." G: 60's/GW: 2-2/W

"I remember good times; we'd all eat up on the hill together with lunches of gelatin and almonds [Cayce stuff] and it was just really special in a lot of ways." G: 40's/GW: 3-1/E

"Everything about Edgar Cayce—his life and his work—opens for the individual a need to know, pursue and investigate greater concepts of living and greater principles of being." G: 40's/GW: 3-2/W

"I think bringing past-life consciousness to the foreground, and as a young woman assuring me that I was not unusual. I was validated by his works, his philosophies." G: 30's/GW: 3-2W

"I had been around several spiritual groups . . . these people impressed me with their integrity; they seemed to live what they spoke. I knew that I had found my soul group . . ." G: 50's/GW: 3-3/W

"Thinking of God as my friend—being co-Creators with God. Finding a God that wasn't punishing; a God of Love. . . .That moved me."
G: 40's GW: 3-3/E

"It's very much family [working at Headquarters in Virginia Beach]. Everybody looks out for each other." G: 30's/GW: 4-1/E

"I think it's great to have such a big organization to turn to; it gives credibility. . . . Here is a foundation based on the study of psychic readings." G: 20's/GW: 4-2/W

"I'm excited about the resource of the library." G: 20's/GW: 5

"His life, how he was ostracized by his peers [if he had any] how he channeled basic tips for the human race, spiritually, physically, etc." G: Teens/GW: 5/W

Question Two: What has challenged you or been difficult in regard to knowing Edgar Cayce and the Work?

[Regarding Gertrude Cayce] "To me that was remarkable . . . to get up and serve nine people and then go to the grocery store and buy all the groceries, come home and do a reading, then give a lunch. Not only that, her attitude was so important. . . . It was so hard for her to let people sit there and watch her and him when he gave a reading." G: Deceased/GW: 1-1/E

"Jessica [Madigan's] story itself is heartbreaking. . . . Perhaps she seemed too eccentric for staid and solid and firm (unbudging) foundations—but she came from the heart. A 13th century mystic, Meister Eckhart says, 'Where do we begin? We begin with the heart . . .' Rather than ostracizing those that appear to be in disagreement with you, it is always wise to listen to what this seeming shadow has to say. As dreams prove—it is Shadow that holds your gift." G: Deceased/GW: 2-1/W

"I feel I've been treated very fairly as a woman. What's been hard is knowing that I'm responsible for trying to live the principles that I believe." G: 80's/GW: 2-2/E

". . . there are times when he gave incredible truths that are true for all time and times when I feel he was not able to transcend the limits of the culture and the sexism." G: 40's/GW: 3-1/E

"I'm looking at women traditionally being the handmaidens, being willing to work for nothing. Men who work for nothing are not respected. Men who are not in a high position are not respected. They have constantly tried to put women in key positions. But they keep choosing women who are . . . the father's daughter." G: 40's/GW: 3-2/E

"The difficult part is the conservative approach to Spirit and the masculine language connoting that God is a 'he'. There's a strong current of fundamentalism in the people who've explored this Work, perhaps more than in the readings themselves . . . It continues to be a problem, and I think the wisdom of the readings has to be understood as having filtered through the mind-set of the belief system of the man Edgar Cayce." G: 40's/GW: 3-3/E

Question Three: How do you feel you've been able to contribute to the Work?

"She [his mother, Gertrude Cayce] held the family together. She purposely kept in the background. . . . Talking to Dad and keeping the family going—in the household, the budget—I think she was a strong person." G: Deceased/GW: 1-1/E

"This Work would not have happened without women like Gertrude Cayce or Gladys Davis." G: Deceased/GW: 1-1/E, and G: Deceased/GW: 1-2/E

"When I met Mrs. Sally Cayce I learned in her presence [about the] Cayce work of yesterday. It was sweet and spiritual and warm and gentle."
G: Deceased/80's/GW: 1-2/E

"For years my job was to travel—over 100,000 miles—to encourage people to set up Study Groups. I gave pep talks wherever they had a little group. My chief job was to visit the small towns that couldn't afford to pay to have somebody come. . . . Almost invariably, I'd have an enthusiastic response. I remember one—'It's beyond our wildest dreams that anyone from The Beach would visit York, Pennsylvania.'" G: 80's/GW: 2-1/E

"Edgar Cayce would want us to continue to pursue, question, challenge, seek. In this way I feel I have helped the Work." G: 40's/GW: 3-2/W

"By continuing the growth of this work, by sharing it and giving it to my children, not only to my physical children, but to the children of the earth. By sharing as I go through everyday life. For example, at work there's always a little piece to give out." G: 30's/GW: 3-2/W

Question Four: How do you see the woman of tomorrow contributing to the Edgar Cayce Work?

"I think Cayce is one of dozens of movements that women are interested in that lean toward the goal of helping to educate the present peoples of the earth planet to get a new focus, a new perspective on what life is all about." G: Centenarian/GW: 1-2/E

"This is where again I see the women's role [in medicine]. Healing has to do with accepting . . . the whole life process and working with it. . . . There's a painting, which a friend of mine is giving me for our office, and it's magnificent. It shows Jesus and his female counterpart nose-to-nose, face-to-face . . . we're co-creators . . . I think the 90's is when this is going to happen." G: 70's/GW: 2-1/W

"Leslie Cayce is a real neat woman and very strong and very gifted. There could be a pattern of co-partnership there in very exciting ways for women." G: 40's/GW: 3-1/E

"Women of tomorrow as women of today will always have a strong and vital role in 'the work of spiritual enlightenment'. They are the Mothers. Nurturing (a great act of love) brings powerful revelations. The woman of tomorrow will be freer to reveal these . . . than those that have gone before . . . Christianity, per se, has not been kind or accepting to equality of vision and awareness . . . But through *the Edgar Cayce work—a gentle gift to woman*—the freedom [is given] to accept their own inner knowing, their dreams, their revelations, until the bonds of restrictions are broken and she can take her wisdom's flight, release her plight and know her co-heritage with the divine principles of being." G: 40's/GW: 3-2/W (Author's italics)

"Better pay scale." G: 30's/GW: 4-1/E

"There's still a few unsaid things for women, but I think that everyday it will get better. You know, like, my daughters will have things that I didn't have, and it will be just totally different than today. I think it's a very good time to be a woman". G: Teen/GW: 5/E

Dr. Gladys McGarey in her office in Arizona

Discussion of Findings

The preliminary descriptive data presented in Appendix E based on survey research indicates that the Edgar Cayce material connects and disconnects with the emerging body of knowledge regarding the Eternal Feminine through the following *main themes* that emerged:

Main Themes of Connection

Answers to Life's Fundamental Questions.

The Cayce material answered deep fundamental questions about life for virtually all the women in the study—why we're here, why there is suffering, etc. For example, one woman said the readings shaped her life in terms of ideals and purpose.

Relatedness, Connection and Community.

Relationships in terms of warm personal contact were important to women in every grouping irrespective of Chronological Generation or Generation in the Work.

One A.R.E. employee described the working environment as providing a sense of family, people looking out for each other, loving you for what's inside of you. This emphasis on relatedness suggested a need for warmer, personal contact in the Work, perhaps through emphasis on regional and community activity to personalize the Work. One woman stated that salvation is not a "me" thing and hoped there would be more emphasis on service in the community in future.

Lynn Rogers connecting with Dr. Jean Holcombe

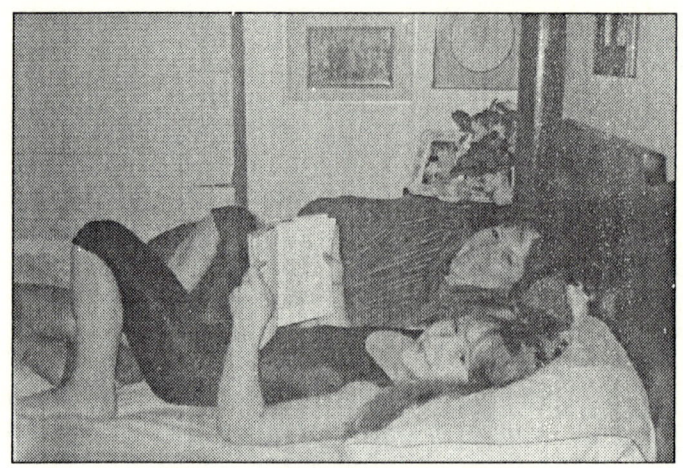

**Dr. Jean Holcombe and her nine year
old daughter Bree sharing a story**

No Separate Issues or Discrimination as Women in Material or Work.

A number of women did not perceive disparity by gender in regard to the material or the Work. This was especially true of older women in the study. In general, these women believed that the readings indicated gender equality as souls had lived as male and female before. It appears to me that a relevant factor for these women was the fact that at their time the Work opened doors for women relative to the prevailing societal gender norms.

Even the younger and generally more critical women recognized the androgynous potential contained in much of the Edgar Cayce material. They wanted themes of spiritual androgyny, [i.e., twin souls and gender partnership] better articulated and incorporated into the actual practice of the Work.

Unique Female Attributes Complement the Work.

Some women believed that they had a special contribution to make in areas complementary to the Edgar Cayce philosophy, specifically in terms of: 1) nurturing skills with people; 2) an inclusive style of leadership; 3) the holistic approach to healing; 4) ability to acknowledge both negative and positive feelings honestly; 5) flexibility and independent-mindedness in terms of trusting their own intuition and direct experience, thereby being freer from hierarchical constraints and outside authority. In my opinion, (and the opinion of some of the subjects) these attributes are not necessarily the domain of women; however, cultural experience had fostered the development of these attributes in the female.

Main Themes of Disconnection

There was, however, a perception of areas of sexism in the material and in the Work for many women.

Masculine Language in the Readings.

Subjects in the study reported feeling disconnected from masculine God language in the readings. Women felt though, that such language reflected the man's—Edgar Cayce's—outer personality and his times. As stated above, they felt that the concepts regarding the Eternal Feminine, such as androgyny in Atlantis, gender partnership, and twin souls were underrepresented in the subsequent material and work through the A.R.E.

Women As Handmaidens/Unrecognized/Underpaid.

There was the complaint of not using women's talents and keeping them in subordinate roles as handmaidens or Athenas. There was a sense of a double standard. The earliest women models surrounding Edgar Cayce seemed either invisible or extolled for self-sacrifice and staying in the background without recognition for the full scope of their contribution. Their role seemed to be to nurture and support the man's creative efforts. Many felt that it was time for women to come forth now to use their full potentiality as creative leaders as well as nurturers.

Thus many women at the time of the study felt disconnected from the model of early self-sacrificing women and the double standard between these women and their partners, in terms of opportunity for recognition and personal growth. For example, some younger creative women did not feel that they had been equally mentored or offered opportunity to the degree their male contemporaries had. One woman described these male contemporaries as "Hugh Lynn's boys." Also, women workers often felt they served idealistically but for low pay or no pay.

Almost all subjects in the study—across all groups—felt that it was time for women to come forth now to use their full potentiality as creative leaders, as well as nurturers, and to receive commensurate pay for these efforts.

Lack of Dealing with the "Shadow".

Some women felt that because the Work at the time of its inception may have been controversial in the world, conventional values of conformity to prevailing patriarchal mores of credibility, religiosity and conservatism may have been over-emphasized. Thus, this patriarchal tendency may have led to the following: 1) denial of feelings; 2) projection of the shadow onto women of spontaneous, independent and feeling types, thus splitting off a certain kind of creativity and mature feminine wisdom from the whole. Such splitting tends to create rigidity and the fear of change.

Perceived Ostracism or Exile of Non-Conforming Individuals.

There was a repeated complaint by some women that if one did not fit into the image the official organizations appear to have wanted to project, and then there was ostracism. This is epitomized by the story of Jessica Madigan, one of a group of creative individuals who contributed greatly to the early A.R.E. efforts but later experienced a kind of exile when their creative efforts exceeded and appeared to threaten the status quo. (In the fifties and sixties, Jessica Madigan lectured and wrote articles for the A.R.E., in addition to developing its west coast membership.) This creative group may well have served as scapegoats for the establishment, as they represented the shadow or unintegrated element. Yet they continued to be productive in the Work in unique ways.

After her separation from the Work she loved, Madigan continued serving the overall Cayce philosophy independently as an author, lecturer and psychic counselor. (For an example of her intuitive work, see Appendix F). On the West Coast, Madigan inspired a large group of young people to explore the Cayce philosophy. Here she turned away from dogma to personal accessibility and connection—which is central to the Eternal Feminine. Thus she may have represented elements traditionally associated with feminine wisdom—especially the heart element—interpreting the material through one's own intuition and feminine styles of empowerment and leadership.

Jessica Madigan was not alone. Many women in this study, regardless of generation, felt that they experienced personal crucifixion when they went against the prevailing concept of a woman in the Work. There was a sense that a fully empowered woman is threatening to some, not only in this Work but also in the world, despite great areas of progress where women are concerned.

However, women who felt a part of the Work—but not necessarily of the A.R.E. because of these factors—sensed that this had pushed them into a fuller understanding of the place of the Work in the larger human community. Therefore, they feel the "silver lining" of exclusion, in some sense, was opportunity to be on the cutting edge of the Christ work in the world.

In summary, there were areas of connection and disconnection that emerged from the subjects' reports. The areas of connection were numerous. Almost all women found answers to life questions, a sense of relatedness and community, and potential gender equity within the material.

However, there were areas of disconnection that showed how he Eternal Feminine was left out of the Work. These included the perception of sexism in regard to: masculine language in the readings; women as handmaidens; lack of dealing with the shadow; and perceived exile of non-conforming individuals.

Overall, women remained hopeful for change in terms of greater opportunity and equality in terms of freedom from sexism and almost universally were committed to the Work.

Generational Comparisons

Areas of connection and disconnection can be described as they relate to the different generations of women in the following ways:

First Generation.

First generation women, such as Gertrude and Sally Cayce, seemed to have lived their dedication to the purposes of the Work through unfailing personal service to their husbands and children and to have enjoyed the stimulation expressed through people in their lives through the Work. Others, such as Gladys Davis Turner, were dedicated to the continuity of the Work through their tireless efforts to record and organize the readings for future study. In general, first generation women did seem to have great difficulty discussing any areas of challenge or difficulty for them as women in the Work.

Second Generation.

Second generation women seemed to have a great love for sharing the ideas expressed in the work. For example, for one woman, connectedness focused on answers to the question of human suffering in the Cayce concepts of reincarnation, karma and grace, as well as on the breadth of esoteric material on dreams, twin souls, Atlantis, astrology, colors, health and world prophesy. For another, the connection was the application of spiritual ideals of service; where for another, connectedness was enhanced by the wealth of medical information. For example, Dr. Gladys McGarey found the readings freeing from her early religious upbringing into a more universal worldview and a more holistic view of medicine, which is her great love. Grethe Tedrich felt a deep commitment towards service and application of the principles contained in the readings.

In regard to pointing out areas of difficulty, the majority of Second Generation women reported few challenges to expression as a woman in the Work. For example, Nell Clairmonte felt there were equal opportunities for her as a woman in the early work when she traveled to different parts of the country to set up the study group program. Even Jessica Madigan seldom spoke to others about the difficulties she had experienced; moreover, I doubt that she would have associated these difficulties with her gender.

Nell Clairmonte

Third Generation.

Third Generation—Part One women were able to identify individual challenge areas perhaps because they were so close to the earlier proponents of the Work through family relationships. Third Generation—Part Two women were well able to articulate general challenge areas, perhaps because these women spent some years in the 1970's in group experiential process settings relative to the Edgar Cayce themes. Third Generation—Part Three women were also able to identify some areas of challenge, although they identified fewer areas of difficulty proportionately than Third Generation—Part Two women. Additionally, most of the members of this group are part of the "sixties" generation as a whole; therefore, criticism of the established comes most naturally to them.

**Lyn Costaldo in her office at A.R.E.
Virginia Beach 1989**

Despite these perceived areas of challenge, these women were deeply connected and committed to the Work and incorporated the material that they found in keeping with their own idealism in every sense, including religious ministries, private therapeutic practice, and homebuilding.

Fourth Generation.

Fourth Generation women have made contact with and incorporated the Work in various ways. Although Fourth Generation—Part One women had greater contact with individuals from the earliest groups, while Fourth Generation—Part Two individuals did not; however, no clear pattern to distinguish the two groups emerged. Thus each individual woman seemed to represent a unique style of participating in the Work. For example, one minister used portions of the material in her talks and workshops; a homemaker incorporated the ideals in her child rearing and conducted private research; a third assisted another woman in her teaching efforts regarding the Edgar Cayce material. However, the women's approach and critiques of the Work seemed more in keeping with other women of a similar Chronological Generation listed elsewhere in the study. For example, one-Fourth Generation—Part Two woman made very similar comments to a Second Generation—Part Two woman of similar age. This pattern was repeated.

Fifth Generation.

This generation had a unique vision of the Work in the future. They wanted o see it in the mainstream. Also, perhaps due to their youth, they had a strong sense of individuality. They didn't want to be joiners: they didn't find authority outside of themselves. One-teen age girl thought that some adults were seeing Cayce as a deity or guru; this perspective she questioned. In some ways these young women already seemed to embody the woman of the Work of tomorrow in that they trusted their own judgement and inner authority and they wanted to see the Cayce philosophy reach the masses.

Geographical Comparisons

Some women reflected that the Work in the east seemed to have a more stereotypically masculine orientation in that it was more intellectualized and organized along hierarchical lines, with an emphasis on credibility; whereas the Work in the west seemed to express the feminine component in that intuitive development, sisterhood, independent operation (i. e., grass roots, community-based style) and individual empowerment has unfolded. (For example, women who came into contact with the Work through the Jessica Madigan line of outreach seemed to see the Cayce philosophy as an incitement to further individual seeking and growth and trusted their own potential.)

Girls in the Work of Tomorrow

Recommendations and Conclusions

Recommendations

This descriptive data could become the basis for more extensive quantitative study. Recommendations for further areas of research could include a quantum content analysis of typical themes—in terms of frequency—according to Chronological Generations, Generations in the Work and Geographical factors.

Conclusions

This study implied that the direct experience of Women in the Work elucidates the points of relationship between the Emerging Eternal Feminine and the Edgar Cayce material.

The Multigenerational Interviews helped clarify the connection between the emerging body of knowledge about the Eternal Feminine and the Edgar Cayce work, as illustrated through the lives of individual Women in the Work.

Evaluation and Reflection

Evaluation

This book provides an overview of the connection between the emerging body of knowledge regarding Eternal Feminine and the Edgar Cayce material. This overview was accomplished through an extensive review of literature in the areas of creation, the Goddess tradition, and future trends regarding the Eternal Feminine. In addition, direct research was undertaken regarding a new religious form, The Circle of Light/Moon Cycle Process, involving the Divine Feminine and a study of the Universal Feminine through study of the life experiences of women in the Work.

It is my conclusion that despite areas of apparent disconnection there are many areas of connection between these two significant, and heretofore unrelated, bodies of knowledge: the material related to the Eternal Feminine and the Edgar Cayce material.

This book provides a framework through which individuals can further explore the areas of intersection between the Edgar Cayce readings and women's spirituality and the reemergence of the Divine Feminine. I hope that continued explorations in this field will further our collective progress toward entry into an age of balance and synergy in harmony with the Creative Forces.

Reflection: The Union of Forces

Today we may be approaching a synthesis of the earliest matrifocal thesis and its more recent patrifocal antithesis. Eisler (1987) describes this phenomenon as the gylanic partnership between the feminine chalice and the masculine blade.

"With this ye touch upon delicate subjects, upon which much might be said respecting that union of influences or forces that are divided in the earth in sex, in which all must become what? As He gave in answer to the question, 'Whose wife will she be?' In the heavenly kingdom ye are neither married nor given in marriage; neither is there any such thing as sex; ye become as one—in the union of that from which, of which, ye have been the portion from the beginning." (262-86)

Lynn Rogers returning west from Virginia Beach

APPENDIX A

DEVELOPMENTAL SEQUENCE: CIRCLE OF LIGHT/MOON CYCLE PROCESS

The developmental sequence for the creation of The Circle of Light/Moon Cycle Process was as follows:

1. Existential crisis.
2. Influx of Divine Feminine yearning and consciousness.
3. Researching extant information about Goddess rituals and integrating these within a conceptual framework provided by the Edgar Cayce philosophy.
4. Development of new rituals with a woman partner (through trial and error in an attitude of receptivity, to intuitive input and feedback via synchronistic events, telepathic exchanges, subjective feelings of congruity and universal resonance).
5. (Once a pattern has suggested itself and been enacted for one or two complete lunar cycles) inclusion of a third woman participant, as power seems more available when maiden, mother, and wise woman aspects are all symbolically represented.
6. Continued tracking and recognition of benefits manifesting in the inner and outer lives of participants, including:
    a) The training of intuition during the "scrying" portion of the ceremony as anchored through ideal setting.
    b) Goddess tradition archetypes as keys to new views of the human life cycle and as manifestations of the Creative Forces.
    c) Sense of greater physical wellbeing and ecological responsibility through attuning to lunar and seasonal cycles of nature.
7. Expansion to a larger group of women and men (acknowledging the role each new person may wish to play; clarifying and observing the healing potential for men, also, as they recognize in the threefold archetype the essential dignity and power inherent in the "priestesses" or women in their own lives, as well as in themselves).

8. Unification of these rituals with other traditions (exploring new senses of the underlying meaning of global cyclic religious and secular celebrations).
9. Receptivity to the emergence of "daughter" groups as this organic process unfolds.

Role of Leader

The role of the leader of such a ritual process can be seen as threefold: as new moon maiden-initiator, playfully innovating a fresh new process; as full moon mother-leader, pushing forth and nourishing its unfoldment in gentleness and strength; as dark moon crone—wise woman parting the veil of the mysteries, knowing when to retain power and demand the respect of wisdom, and knowing when letting go is the necessary death which leads to new birth.

The particular importance of knowing when to retain power was illustrated for this researcher by the following instance:

Student Teacher B prematurely, without permission, attempted to take the process elsewhere to be used in service of ideals other than those that had been specifically stated. On the other hand, Student Teacher A used a form of the process in appropriate contexts with permission and continuing consultation by myself, author/developer. This was not only more ethical, but also more appropriate to the Emerging Eternal Feminine tradition which emphasizes connection, communication, and mutual respect, as well as to the Edgar Cayce tradition material which advises anchoring intuitive development processes in the stable ground of spiritual ideals. (See Appendix B).

Process Leader Lynn Rogers

APPENDIX B

PROCESS LEADERS

Process Developer:
Rev. Lynn Rogers

Student Teacher A:
Nancy Payne R.N.

Student Teacher B:
Iona Serrano

Student Teacher C:
Lisa Miletich

Nancy Payne creates a circle

Another of Nancy's circles

Night Moon Circle

APPENDIX C

CIRCLE OF LIGHT PROCESS CORRELATED TO THE SEVEN CHAKRAS

Introduction

The following represents a journey through the "Circle of Light" Moon Cycle Process from the perspective of the study of the seven human energy centers, or chakras (as described by Johari (1987).

Step One/The Root Chakra

The first chakra is represented by a square made up of the four dimensions of earth itself, the four directions. These can be represented as a circle with four petals. Here the vital life force, Kundalini Shakti, is in the form of a coiled serpent, a lingam (male generative symbol) or a triangle (female generative symbol). The deity Brahma sees in four directions at once, towards the four aspects of physical consciousness: The physical self, the rational self, the emotional self and the intuitive self. Behind the physical reality of this instinctual, survival-oriented chakra represented by the elephant headed ruler, Ganesh, can be seen the union of love and wisdom, of Shakti and Shiva. This foundation chakra is the root of all growth and awareness of human divinity.

The Circle of Light moon cycle process begins when the priestess or priest calls to the Guardians of the Four Directions: North—Earth, East—Air, South—Fire, West—Water. We are seated on the ground or floor (the earth). The underlying reality of the Father/Mother Source is imbued in the preliminary prayer for the light of protection. An image of the Divine Feminine is present (such as a statue of Mary). Often, participants will collect and place in the circle. Earth symbols such as fallen leaves, Air symbols such as incense, Water and Fire symbols such as a floating candle.

Step Two/The Sacral Chakra

This chakra is represented by a moon-shaped crescent and its water element is circular. This center of procreation is directly related to the moon (which the Edgar Cayce astrology readings described as pertaining to relations with the opposite sex). Vishnu holds four implements: The conch shell, a ring of light, a wheel and a metal club. Here the male/female energy splits into duality, bringing a creative interplay and longing for reunion.

The moon circle is set when the priestess or priest uses a crystal wand or an ornate metal knife to part the veil that separates the worlds. Participants now imagine light surrounding them and circling to the left to form a complete Circle of Light. A brief visualization reverie is keyed to the phase of the moon and sometimes to the current point in the wheel of the year, is conducted. The moon, symbolizing the Goddess archetype, is seen in her three aspects: New Moon—Maiden of new beginnings, Full Moon—Mother of creative ideas, and Dark Moon—Wise Woman who sees beyond the veil. As participants work to synchronize with natural rhythms, greater physiological and esoteric balance is gained.

Step Three/Solar Plexus Chakra

This chakra is the seat of fire within the body. The inverted triangle (a yonic, or female genital organ, symbol) is its yantra form. Group effort toward a desired aim is highlighted. All that exists returns to Lord Braddha Rudra, who also represents the power of destruction. Lakine Shakti holds the thunderbolt of vajra, a wand indicating electrical energy and heat emanating from her body. She also holds the arrow shot by Kama, the Lord of Sex, in the second chakra. Her third hand holds fire; her fourth forms the mudra of granting fearlessness. By remaining true to one's nature, relationships with others will be more stable and clear.

At this point in the moon circle ritual, a wand or candle is passed around the circle and individuals make affirmations, clarifying their true nature in order to (1) attract better work conditions (2) stabilize relationships with others, or (3) overcome fears that hinder the spiritual path. The group energizes these affirmations or prayers toward manifestation by saying in unison, "Blessed Be." Sometimes many individual candles are lit, increasing the glowing fiery light of group energy.

Step Four/The Heart Chakra

The yantra form of the heart chakra is two overlapping triangles. Shiva, facing upward, is the male principle. Shakti, facing downward, is the female principle. "A balance is attained when these two forces are joined in harmony". (Johari, 1987, p. 63) Red lotus petals fold outward, representing expansion of energy that is not linear (first chakra), circular (second chakra) or triangular (third chakra) but which expands in all direction as a six-pointed star. It is the seat of balance in the body, the spiritual heart where one mediates and listens to pure sound. In this spiritual heart one listens to pure sound. Desires cease to be a problem. Blockages are released for upward energy movement. Moon-faced Shakti appears for the first time as a beautiful goddess, no longer coiled around the lingam but sitting independently in a yogic posture. Meditation brings a further balance of male and female energies, power of Vaju, the air element, clarity of conscience and the ability to give without attachment.

In the moon circle, a second round of prayers is made for others. The affirmations and prayers are released without attachment to "be realized for the highest good of all". Hands are raised upwards towards the moon. Prayers are released. Energy is sent in all directions at once. We "draw down the moon". Music may be played as participants experience a deep, meditative journey. Imagery is selected to help heal heart blockages. Perhaps one "meets the Goddess" within. Upon returning from meditation, individuals share experiences of inner clarification.

Step Five/The Throat Chakra

This chakra is represented by a silver crescent within a white circle shining as a full moon surrounded by sixteen petals. "The silver crescent is the lunar symbol of nada, pure cosmic sound." (Johari, 1987, p. 71) (The flower petals are classic yonic symbols.) Spoken words come from the fifth chakra, giving voice to the emotions within the heart. The voice of the fifth-chakra person penetrates to the heart of the listener, changing his or her space of mind and being. The camphor-blue skinned deity, Shiva, has five aspects including the nature of Akasha.

Shakina has pale rose skin and one of the four objects she holds is an ankush, an elephant staff to control Gaja, the elephant of intellect, who can become overly intoxicated by knowledge. Memory, wit, intuition and improvisation are related to Shakti. Many of her teachings are revealed to aspirants through dreams. This plane gives psychic energy, clairvoyance and communication without words.

At this point in the moon circle, individuals are invited to share inspired messages. A stream of words from the akashic level might unfold, a waking dream of guidance, or other manifestations of psychic energy emerging from the heart. A lunar priestess (or priest) may become the vehicle for these inspired messages of benefit to the group.

Janet Childs sings, tuning the throat chakra.

Step Six/The Brow Chakra

The yantra form of this chakra is a white circle with two luminescent petals. Its seat is the pineal gland. A lingam, or genital organ, appears in the center of the circle. The half-male, half-female deity, Shiva-Shakti, is symbolic of basic polarity. The third eye of Shiva is called her organ of clairvoyance, giving her command of all aspects of the self in this plane of liberation. She is the granter of knowledge. The aspirant now becomes one-pointed, knower of past, present and future, because of a non-dual consciousness. Ida and Pingala end her, and the third eye is the unified conscience. The two physical eyes see the past and the present, while the third eye reveals the insight of the future. All experiences and ideas only serve to clarify one's perceptions in Ajna chakra.

Now within the moon circle we begin to "scry". Scrying was the exercise of clairvoyant and extrasensory abilities in ancient times. Moon maidens at the Temple of Diana in ancient Greece would gaze at the moonlight rippling over the waters of Lake Nemo and attune to third eye images. (Madigan, 1969) Here we train and practice intuitive gifts in pairs and as a group. We use a variety of psychic tools to anchor these impressions.

Step Seven/Crown Chakra/Soma or Moon Chakra

This chakra is the most resplendent of all, on the whole predominantly violet. Cayce also gave violet as the crown color and the moon or Jupiter as its planet. (Cayce 1946) This chakra can become a channel of radiation outward from the realized individual. In Christian symbology this radiation is depicted as a gold crown. The Soma chakra is a minor chakra within the crown, located above the "third eye" in the center of the forehead. The Soma chakra is the seat of the moon. In twelve petals rests the crescent moon. The deities, Kameshvara and Kameshvari, are in eternal embrace. Here the essence of the male energy spiritualized unifies with the lunar female energy and the interior and exterior union become tantra or expanded consciousness in enjoyment and detachment. Kameshvari is now at peace with her beloved. She is no more the furious (kundalini) serpent who breathes out fire, as she was when suddenly awakened from her sleep. Eternal bliss has been realized through the union of Shiva and Shakti. "Negative and positive, the complements of duality become equalized in Sarasvati."(Johari 1987,p.79)

Summary

The moon circle ritual concludes. Since it has begun, participants have: Invoked the four earth guardians, parted the veil, attuned to the lunar and natural cycles, lit brightly the candles of group power for manifestation, raised this force through prayer for others, released affirmations and prayers to the highest good of all, meditated to music, spoken inspired messages from the heart center, and shared clairvoyant scrying. Now this energy is radiated outward through final prayer for each other and the planet. When this is done, the priestess closes the veil that parts the worlds, the Four Guardians are thankfully released, and energy is lovingly grounded back into the earth. The circle is complete. The Triple Goddess as Maiden, Mother and Wise Woman with the moon of new beginnings in the second chakra, the full moon of the brow chakra and the resting crescent of the soma chakra within the crown.

APPENDIX D

SALLY CAYCE INTERVIEW
Interview with Mrs. Sally Cayce—December 5, 1989

**Lynn Rogers interviews Sally Cayce
at Mrs. Cayce's home in Virginia Beach 1989**

Sally: Shall I tell you a story while you are sitting in that chair?

Lynn: Yes, I would like to hear about it.

Sally: It was during the war years, and both of Edgar Cayce and Gertrude's sons were in the service... Hugh Lynn and Edgar both were in the service. One day Gertrude went to Edgar and said, "I'm tired and I want to go to my home in Kentucky just for a change and to rest some. I'm very tired." And he said, "Gertrude, I can't do without you right now—the house is just full of people asking for information; But here's some money; go to a furniture store and go and buy you a comfortable chair and put it up in the window in our bedroom, and sit in the sunshine, and look at the ocean—but I can't let you leave." And that's the chair.

Lynn: My goodness, I feel honored.

Sally: She did get a comfortable one.

Lynn: Well, gee, that made up for being tired.

Sally: When they were closing up the Cayce house, I asked for that chair.

Lynn: I don't blame you.

Sally: Well, do you want me to tell you something about humor? Then we'll get to business. One day two or three men who had an apartment with Edgar Cayce came from New York. The door was open, so they walked in the living room, and this voice said, "Come in and sit down". There wasn't anybody in the room at all, and they heard the voice again, saying "Come in", and they started to run out of the door. Nobody in the room. Hugh Lynn got them before they got out, and he said it was just the parrot in the corner.

Lynn: They must have thought it was some psychic house.

Sally: They didn't know what it was. They thought it was kind of a ghost.

Lynn: I guess [your son] Greg told you that I'm a student at Atlantic University and I've had a lot of interest for a long time as a woman in what might be the special contributions and challenges that special women might have faced in relation to the Edgar Cayce work. I guess that's an issue to younger women today; it's kind of in the air. I felt very honored, in a way, when I got the opportunity to chat with you. Please tell me your thoughts and ideas.

Sally: Please let me tell you two things that I think will show you what kind of person Gertrude Cayce is. I want something written about her, Gertrude Cayce, wife of Edgar Cayce.

Lynn: I'd love to.

Sally: See, that would put his name on the book, too. I want a booklet or book written "Gertrude Cayce, Wife of Edgar Cayce".

Lynn: Maybe, I'm the one. That would be a good title for it.

Sally: It would be her book, but his name would be on it too, and that would sell.

Lynn: Yes.

Sally: You know, she used to entertain people constantly. Gladys Turner was always there, and Gladys had a brother too. Tom Sugrue and his wife Mary was there. They had a little girl, and she used to have to go upstairs to take Tom's meals to him upstairs while Mary was feeding the little girl.

Lynn: It's very tiring to have people in your house, I know that. They had so many guests all the time.

Sally: She was so wonderful with people. And Mary put the little girl, she could just walk, and Mary put Patsy in the playpen in the middle of the living room so she could get up to Tom and so she could go around. And Mother Cayce said to me, "Why don't you ask Mary to take that child out of that playpen—it's not fair to shut that little girl up." Now she was thinking about the little girl, rather than Mary and herself. When everyone else was going around, she didn't want to see the little girl in the playpen. I thought that was a very unselfish thing.

Lynn: I have two children, and one of them is disabled, and one of the things they've said is that you shouldn't put a child in a playpen, because their mind won't develop well. It sounds like she had the Christ attitude and ideal very much.

Sally: Another thing that I thought was beautiful. Christmas I went down there, and there was a girl sitting by the fireplace in the living room with a table in front of her and she was writing on that table. When I went in the kitchen, I asked her who was that girl writing in the living room? She said she's a young lady who came down here to see her husband, and his ship is out, and she can't see him, and she left her two children with her mother. So she come down here to see her husband and that's why she's crying, because she doesn't know whether she's going to see him or not, and I've tried to stop her from crying by asking her to sit down by the fireplace and address my Christmas cards. I thought that was a very unselfish way to help. She was always thinking of the other person.

Lynn: How do you think Gertrude made a difference in the work of Edgar Cayce?

Sally: He couldn't have done it all without her.

Lynn: I tend to agree with you. (Pause) In what way do you think he couldn't have done it without her?

Sally: He would have given it up. A young couple with two little boys. He had to make a living; and if she had insisted that he give it up to make money and buy a home, he wouldn't have carried on his psychic work. She had enough love and interest in him to talk to him, and I suppose, for them to decide that he had a very unusual talent and that he should use it. And I asked her one time why he didn't give it up—he was a very good photographer. She said, "People wouldn't let him alone." They kept coming to him for readings and help, and they just decided that this should be his life's work. And he couldn't do it at all if she hadn't have helped him. She not only helped him, but sitting by him taking the readings and encouraging him and being friendly and helpful to the people who came— and they would send other people. So the number of readings that he gave increased a lot. His attitude toward each person was very important.

Lynn: Then she was having many people in her home most of the time? Giving up certain things too.

Sally: Tom, Mary, and the little girl, and two of Gladys's brothers, that's five. She had her own two sons, which made seven and herself and Edgar made nine. There was always as many as nine people and sometimes one or two more. So she was keeping house, buying groceries and cooking, taking readings two times a day. To me that was most remarkable.

Lynn: That was true, too. I hadn't thought of it.

Sally: Get up and serve nine people and then go to the grocery store and buy all the groceries, come home and do a reading, then give a lunch.

Lynn: She was doing both the reading part and the practical part. It's like a lot of working mothers today, they go out and work and then they come and clean the house until all hours. She was kind of like the working mother of today.

Sally: Not only that, her attitude was so important as she sat down by him, with two or three people watching him give a reading. You see, if you had to clean up a room, and there wasn't anybody here but you, it wouldn't be so hard. It was so hard for her to let people sit there and watch her and him when he gave a reading.

Lynn: Did you see the two of them give the readings sometimes?

Sally: Oh sure, but we didn't live in the home, we had our own little home.

Lynn: I had no idea how much she contributed, what a big part Gertrude was.

Sally: I don't think the A.R.E. would be here at all if it wasn't for Gertrude.

Lynn: Very good point.

Sally: Mr. Kahn and, who were the other two men from New York that started the A.R.E. and built it?

Lynn: Blumenthal and . . .

Sally: I don't think Hugh Lynn would have worked with the wealthy men who started the A.R.E. if it hadn't been for her.

Lynn: Why was that? She was the one that encouraged him the most?

Sally: Sure.

Lynn: And he wasn't sure about doing it?

Sally: Well, I imagine they just talked, like we are talking and she would say this is a good way to increase the number of people.

Lynn: They were partners; they talked it over and shared decisions.

Sally: It was a hospital they started, and then it developed into the A.R.E. And you know, for awhile, they had to close it. David Kahn, that's who it was.

Lynn: What circumstances did Gertrude have to work on, or struggle with, related to the work of Edgar Cayce?

Sally: People who came to their home, and people who asked for a reading but who didn't quite have confidence and understand the work. They didn't know anything about psychic ability. The people would come, and her quiet and sincere attitude as they came into the house—they were very much influenced by her attitude toward everything that was going on.

Lynn: Thinking myself, as a mother, and as someone trying to study, it's hard for me sometimes to keep a sincere, cheerful attitude. Sometimes I lose my temper, and I wonder if she felt like that too.

Sally: I don't know, I never did see her lose her temper or complain. Maybe she just went off by herself in the corner of the bedroom or something. I never did see her show any temper. Now, I didn't live down there, but I would go down there.

Lynn: You seem to admire her very much, and love her. When did you first meet her?

Sally: I can't remember. You know Hugh Lynn was very active in Scouts, and he would ask me to come to his house and help him with Scouts—giving them little cookies or something—that's when I really met Gertrude.

I can't remember really what the circumstances were. And she used to play bridge with us.

Lynn: Oh, she liked bridge.

Sally: No, she didn't like it, but she'd take a hand and play with us when we needed her.

Lynn: Did Edgar Cayce, like today's husbands, take a hand in the home with the cooking or anything?

Sally: Oh, yes.

Lynn: Cooking and cleaning, and getting things ready.

Sally: I never saw him do anything, but in the kitchen he did a lot of canning. I used to have a lot of applesauce that he made and he used to do a lot in the kitchen. I remember one time—you know we lived right on the lake—and he had a pier out there, and he used to always have two or three little children out there fishing. And one time he was in the kitchen with me and I was fixing Charles Thomas's bottle of milk, and he said "Oh, listen to those children out there on the pier, they've caught something real big and they don't know what to do with it. And here's the man who brought me my two chickens, and I have to pay him for my two chickens, and I've got to go out there and see about that big fish. Here, you take over and help me in this kitchen." She was somewhere, but there he was—he always bought chickens. He didn't want to buy store chickens, he wanted to buy . . . chickens.

Lynn: That's like couples today. They were sharing more. It sounds as if she helped him with the readings and he helped in the home. They were more partners than people might know.

Sally: I never did see him do anything more in the home, except in the kitchen. I never did see him do any cleaning or change a bed or vacuum. I never did see him do anything other than cook in the kitchen.

Lynn: Did he help put the meals out for the guests sometimes?

Sally: Gladys Turner was there and Gladys would help.

Lynn: In those days, men and women didn't help as much in the household chores, but today that's changing as women work more. She sounds like some gal, someone really worth knowing.

Sally: It was always her sincerity, her desire to be helpful to everybody, whether it was to him or to Gladys or to me or to Mary or Tom. She always had the attitude to be helpful.

Appendix D

Lynn: Was it difficult for Gladys and her family to be living there all the time, or did she adapt to it pretty well?

Sally: Gladys lived in the house, and then she lived in the little house out in the yard where the Catholic Church was, and she had T.J., who was Gladys's brother's little boy.

Lynn: It was a very busy household she had, very busy. Any more thoughts that you had about Gertrude I'd love to hear. Also I'd like to ask you about your husband's work. What you particularly enjoyed and looked forward to and what you think you might have helped accomplish.

Sally: Are you talking about Hugh Lynn?

Lynn: Yes.

Sally: Well, you see, I never did have the readings in our home like she did, but I enjoyed the people who came and listening to the conversations. I enjoyed the people. It was very interesting the different types of people who would come here and visit. For a good many years we had a study group of about forty people.

Lynn: That's a huge study group. Most of them are about 18—or 12, maybe.

Sally: Well, Hugh Lynn put them in four rooms; one in each room. Ten on the porch, ten in that living room, and ten in here and ten in there. So they would all come together and get to know one another and then he would divide them into groups of ten and put a leader in each group.

Lynn: So each of them was a small group?

Sally: Each of them was ten, approximately.

Lynn: On the same evening you'd have this?

Sally: Yes.

Lynn: So you enjoyed the stimulation of the visitors and the study groups were intellectually interesting to you?

Sally: Yes, I enjoyed it.

Lynn: I imagine you made quite a contribution to Hugh Lynn's work, much like Gertrude made a contribution to Edgar's?

Sally: No, not nearly. See, she had it in her home, and I never had it in my home. You see Hugh Lynn had the A.R.E.

Lynn: Yes, now that's different.

Sally: Yes, we just had them here one night a week.

Lynn: Did you two work together to help the A.R.E.? Helping at home to ease the responsibilities for him.

Sally: I always went to every meeting up there. I don't think I ever missed any one of his lectures.

Lynn: Oh, was he quite a lecturer?

Sally: Yes.

Lynn: I hear that he was very lively and warm and that they enjoyed him very much and miss him.

Sally: He really was a remarkable person. He would sit here and take a little nap, and then he would wake up and give a good lecture.

Lynn: He didn't lie down, or anything?

Sally: Oh, I'm just joking about him sitting up here in front of 150 people, and he'd be completely relaxed. He'd sit right there in front of a nice long fire and be fast asleep and the study group would come and I'd wake him up. His relaxation ability was excellent, even on the buses around the World.

Lynn: There's not many people who can fall asleep, wake up, and keep working. Was he traveling a lot, building up the A.R.E.?

Sally: Yeah.

Lynn: Was that difficult? I know when a husband's gone, the wife has extra responsibility, with the children and you miss him too, I imagine?

Sally: Yes, he was gone a lot.

Lynn: Related to Hugh Lynn's work, what took special energy or time for you?

Sally: I think maybe the Study Group of 40 people or more, knowing every Wednesday night they would be here.

Lynn: I can imagine. Did you have groups of your own, any guests of your own, or any special friends or colleagues that you had?

Sally: I enjoyed the Study Groups a lot. You know, Birley used to sit over here in this chair, and that was Hugh Lynn's chair. And now when I walk around the block, this Navy wife over here, he's a retired Admiral, she'd come beside me and say "I still remember those Study Groups that Hugh Lynn and Birley, getting up in the middle of the room trying to convince each other what they thought."

Lynn: Is that Birley who used to work in the library?

Sally: Yes.

Lynn: Yes, he's quite a gentleman. Birley had a lot to say, I like him.

Sally: The room would be full of people, and from here to here, they really would argue.

Lynn: Did he help you get ready for all those people, tidy up or cook or anything?

Sally: No, I just kind of got used to people coming in and out of the house. I'm not a very good housekeeper. Some of the people that were here were very interesting, and I think the man from Australia, Raynard Johnson, was one of the most interesting people we ever had. Are you familiar with him? You really should read his book, The Spiritual Ladder. I have my own autographed copy of his lectures. There were fifty of us who went to Australia. We were on the island of Fiji. We were on a World trip, and we went to Australia to hear Raynard Johnson to hear his lecture, "The Spiritual Ladder". If you do the very best you can, next incarnation, go up the ladder. If not you go down. You can get it at the A.R.E.

Lynn: You know I get the feeling, when I hear about people like Lynn and Edgar Cayce, and Gertrude and yourself and some people I knew in California who passed away, that there was a special magic at the A.R.E. at that time. It is wonderful at the A.R.E. and Atlantic University, but it's a little more scientific, and I don't get the sense of that warmth.

Sally: It's not quite as spiritual.

Lynn: This is the feeling I get, and you agree with that? That there's some spark, or some magic of the heart that's missing. I like the scientific and the way that we're studying things is very up to date, but it just seems that there's a special charisma and warmth and spirituality that I just feel is different. Someday, it would be nice if that could come back again.

Sally: I think the A.R.E. is working on that. Bringing that spirituality back.

Lynn: Well, things have to go in cycles.

Sally: Well—you know—what you was thinking about—how you could be warm and friendly with 100,000 people around the World.

Lynn: Gosh, that's true, you know. Maybe the trick is for the people out in the field is to make little groups that can be warmer like that.

Sally: Well, like you coming from California to Atlantic University and coming here to talk with me—that's a warm and friendly thing to do. But, you can't approach and touch 100,000 people.

Lynn: No, not really.

Sally: It just has to be done just by two and two, and one and one.

Lynn: I wonder if that's true. Maybe that's something that Gertrude understood, and that's why she was so warm to each one that came in her home, because she must have touched them in a way that you can't have in a big bookstore, or a big lecture hall.

Sally: To her, she was seeing people in comparison to 100,000. She was seeing people who came in for readings, trying to help Gladys with the mail. During the war, this is very interesting, he got so much mail that the post office put on an extra truck, just to take Edgar Cayce's mail to him.

Lynn: In a way, she managed to reach the multitudes, but one by one. She touched large numbers of people.

Sally: And through the office, she had Gladys answering the letters.

Lynn: These women gave the warmth, one on one that was needed.

Sally: Not necessarily warmth, but information.

Lynn: Well, intelligent information and personal attention. I wonder what women today, who are interested in the Edgar Cayce information can make their contributions and what challenges they might find. Today the world has changed so much. I think of Ellen, for example, who I have met. She seems like a special gal who's trying to find her opportunity in the Work. I imagine she faces challenges today that are a little different than you did or Gertrude did, because the world has changed.

Sally: Well, It's all in contact with people, like the Admiral's wife over here, seeing the type of person she would admire from the A.R.E. Not long ago, I went to the beauty parlor, and the woman who was doing my hair said, "You're connected with the A.R.E., aren't you?" I said, "Yes", and the girl over next to me said, "Oh, there's nothing unusual about that, we are all psychic to a certain degree". I thought that was an interesting comment from a young girl in the beauty parlor.

Lynn: It really is. It says quite a lot. Today, that she would accept this and know this. She wasn't intimidated and felt that it didn't just belong to just a few, that it could belong to her too.

Appendix D

Sally: We all have psychic abilities, and I was somewhere, and this young teenage girl came up to me and said "You know, I enjoy reading and talking about the A.R.E. I think it makes living so much more practical". You ought to put that down somewhere.

Lynn: I will, because I want to have something from a very young girl.

Sally: It was a beautiful thing to say about the A.R.E.

Lynn: That it makes living more practical.

Sally: She said, I am glad to meet you, and glad to talk with you, because reading, thinking and studying about the A.R.E. makes living so much more practical.

Lynn: About how old was she would you say?

Sally: Well, I don't know, she was not old at all.

Lynn: Like a teenager or in her early twenties?

Sally: Something like that.

Lynn: I brought my own daughter, who is fifteen, here this summer. At home it was hard to interest her in this, because we don't know that many people who are interested in the Edgar Cayce work. I made her agree to come to at least one lecture a day, because she was only going to be here for a short time—and boy, I had to drag her away from the T.V. and the V.C.R. and the music and everything else. But after the first lecture she said, "Mom, you know, I have to admit it, it was pretty interesting." She has quite a lot more respect for me and what I'm interested in. She sees the A.R.E. and what it is, and how much it does mean to so many people. I think someday—I have kind of a feeling now—she may become quite interested herself.

What I like about today, is that this is a time where women have lots of choices how they'll go about the Work. They can entertain people in their home, or they can get up as Ellen does and give a lecture or a talk. They have lots of options. Sometimes the wife or at other times the husband may be the one to be interested. There's just more freedom, I think, to choose what you like to do, and if a man likes to do canning, he could do a lot more of it today—or if a woman enjoys giving talks. If you were coming into a future life, way in the 21st century, what things might you enjoy doing in the Work?

Sally: You want me to imagine a future life.

Lynn: Yes, if you could imagine, what would be most interesting to you?

Sally: Work with people, and maybe teach school. I used to teach school, and I really enjoyed it, and of course, work in Sunday school. I have to say, work with the children—not too young of children, but maybe between 10 to 14, that age when children are beginning the think, and beginning to make decisions. I think to work with children, teaching.

Lynn: I wish we had something around the country in the A.R.E., that teaches children at that age, because it's very hard. A child, so often, does not want to listen to their parents, but if somebody else would say it and see other young people together. There's a gal in California, Grethe Tedrick, who teaches young people. You would be a great person to teach young kids. Not everyone has the right patience or aptitude. I don't, but that sounds like that is a special area of interest of yours to reach young people and teach them.

Sally: I used to be a den mother for Greg and his Cub Scouts, and one day I had several of them in the car, and I drove through the city. There was a lady over walking on the sidewalk, and I knew she worked in the library at the A.R.E., and that she wanted to go up there, and I thought it would be more convenient if I took her, than if she waited for a bus. So I stopped and got her in the car and told I'd take her up to the A.R.E. I had three or four boys, including Greg, in the car, and when we turned to go up the hill, one of the little boys said "Don't stop here, there's ghosts up here".

Lynn: [Laughter]

Sally: I looked at Greg, and Greg was horrified. That was his dad's business. His little friends were talking about ghosts, and I thought, oh, what can I do for Greg in this awful moment. One of the best teachers who ever was here, Bob Clapp, had an apartment right in the back of the building and as we turned to the back of the building, we heard this one little boy say, "Well, I can tell you something, my teacher lives right there, and he ain't no ghost". And Greg smiled and everything was all right.

Lynn: Anything else that comes to your mind?

Sally: . . .

Lynn: It's going to be hard in a way to go back to California. This a special place. You make so many friends, that you'd never believe you'd make, there still is a warmth here around the A.R.E. that is special.

Sally: I think the library is wonderful. Many elderly women like me, work in there or volunteer in there.

Lynn: Oh, good point. They seem to enjoy what they're doing so much. I look at the gal that was working in there—I don't know her very well—Mae Gimbert St. Clair. Apparently she's in her eighties. I was telling a friend in California is that this place is a fountain of youth. If in later years people look alive, as you do, energetic, vivid and vigorous, there's something about the philosophy of life and in the health material that helps people.

Interview continued on December 8, 1989

Lynn: We're reviewing here about Gertrude and that whether she was cooking and running a vacuum or taking a reading, that she had a good sense of humor and she was good with little children.

Sally: The next thing—that's Number Three? Well, Number Four—you don't have to write yet, but Edgar Cayce never drove a car—she had a car and she had to do all the driving that involved the car, so she was an excellent driver.

Lynn: So he didn't drive?

Sally: He didn't drive at all, I never saw him in a car.

Lynn: Did everyone know how to drive, or was that unusual?

Sally: It was very unusual then—never would get in a car—never would have anything to do with a car. I don't think he ever had a car.

Greg [Cayce]: He wouldn't even ride as a passenger?

Sally: Yes, he would ride as a passenger, I suppose, 'cause they would take him up to where they were building the A.R.E.—he couldn't have walked that far. I don't remember that Hugh Lynn and I took him anywhere, but he used to come to see us. From their house to our house on 23rd street, but she would always bring him in the car. I don't think he ever drove a car. She did all the driving.

And Number Five, she didn't talk much. Always quiet and let everybody else do all the talking. I have as Number Six, she was a good listener. She would listen to anybody who was talking who came in, whether it was Mary Sugrue, or Lucille Kahn or whether it was Hugh Lynn or Edgar or me, or anybody. She listened very well. Strangers and friends or anybody. She listened to every type of person.

Now her hours—heard her say one time that Edgar got up very early and she never could go back to sleep after he got up, so her hours were from very early in the morning to very late at night. Well, this is very normal, but the only thing that I ever heard Gertrude complain about was about people staying so late at night. You see people would come all the way down here to the beach and they would want to sit and talk to ten, eleven, and twelve o'clock about the readings and about themselves and about his work, but she would never leave as long as there was company talking to him. So her late hours, she said she thought people should be more considerate of her and Edgar, than to stay so late at night. That's the only thing I can remember hearing her complain about.

Lynn: That is very normal, to get tired.

Sally: If you had come all the way across the United States to talk to Edgar Cayce, you wouldn't want to stop either. It was a very unfortunate situation. The people wanted to stay on and on and talk. Gertrude was sleepy and tired, and she wanted to go to bed.

Lynn: But, she didn't want to go to bed by herself?

Sally: No, I don't imagine she ever did. Those were the notes that I wrote down.

Lynn: Very good. That gives some details of her everyday life and that helps me understand her better.

Greg: Did she give Edgar advice at all, Mother?

Sally: No.

Greg: He wouldn't ask for advice?

Sally: No, I think you better put down that fishing—he loved to fish on the pier in the back yard. They lived on a lake, Lake Carla, and this is Crystal Lake—he used to take the children, Charles Thomas, and Patsy and all the children back there fishing. She was very unselfish about that. If he wanted to go out there in the morning and fish, she didn't object to it, but I don't think I ever saw her on the pier.

Lynn: What did she do to relax or to enjoy herself?

Sally: I don't believe she ever did anything, she was always busy. Cooking or running the vacuum or taking a reading or listening to people, I don't think I ever saw her do anything. I don't think I ever saw her reading a book.

Lynn: She didn't have time, it sounds like.

Sally: No, she was busy with all those things we've listed.

Lynn: It sounds like she accomplished a lot in any day. She got a lot of things accomplished in the home and in the readings.

Sally: Well, housekeeping and the readings, you can't do much more.

Lynn: No, you really can't.

Sally: Housekeeping, cooking, people and the readings: That's four things that keep her busy from early morning until late at night. She was not critical. I don't think I heard her criticize Edgar or Hugh Lynn or Edgar Evans or Gladys or anybody who ever came. I've never heard her criticize anybody and I've never heard her complain [that] they come too often, they stay too late, they talk too much.

Lynn: What gave her the strength to do so much, do you think? Many people couldn't be as strong as she.

Sally: I suppose she prayed, I don't know about that, but she must have. There must have been times when she thought she couldn't go on, or couldn't stand the circumstances like all the rest of us and she must have just prayed to give her the strength to go on. Her love and admiration of Edgar. I think that's what did it . . . and her sons. I think that's what did it.

Lynn: Was Edgar Cayce as much a practical business man as Gertrude was, or was he more the philosophical type person?

Sally: Philosophical, I would say.

Lynn: Somehow I had the idea he was very philosophical and not very practical.

Sally: Well, he was practical in a lot of ways, too. He knew that chickens that he bought out on a farm somewhere were a lot better than the chickens that you get in a store, and so he bought chickens from a farmer, and the farmer would bring the live chicken in and he would kill it, and dress it and cook it, so he was very practical in some ways.

Lynn: What ways was he not too practical?

Sally: Talking on the porch, or living room too long without saying "Good Night" to the people, and looking at her and seeing how tired she was and what a long busy day they had had. But, he had to be considerate to them too. They had come a long way and were here for a short time. I suppose he just tried to be as reasonable about his family and the visitors as he could be. He enjoyed children, too.

Greg: How about with money, Mama?

Lynn: Was he practical with money?

Sally: I don't think he was too practical with money, I think that he thought if he always spent what he had, that some more would come.

Greg: Some people would call that impractical.

Lynn: Was Gertrude more practical with money?

Sally: Oh, definitely.

Lynn: She had a better head with money. I know a man in California who was born at the time of Pisces, and he is very generous, but he'll spend what he has and doesn't think twice, and doesn't know where it went.
Sally: They both enjoyed children. That is something they both liked. She had three little children, and one little boy died when he was a baby.

Sally: Three sons, Hugh Lynn, Edgar and one son that died.

Lynn: Lynn was a lot older than Edgar?

Sally: I'd say five to ten years more or less.

Lynn: Did Gertrude ever miss having a little girl?

Sally: I'm sure she did, but she never said anything about it.

Lynn: Do you know much about her family? Her own family?

Sally: I don't know anything. What was her name . . . Gertrude Evans. I don't know, you could talk to Gail about that.

Lynn: What did you enjoy most about being with Gertrude? Did you two talk?

Sally: We usually just sat quietly and relaxed. We didn't talk, because we had talked to other people. Usually there were children around, Charles Thomas, Patsy and T.J.

Lynn: So Gertrude passed away before Greg was born, she didn't know Greg?

Sally: That's true, you know both Mr. and Mrs. Cayce died while Hugh Lynn was overseas.

Lynn: Were you here at that time?

Sally: Yes.

Lynn: Were they sick very long?

Sally: Well, that depends. I don't think they felt well for a long time, but I don't think anybody considered them dangerously ill for a very long time. Let's see, he went somewhere in the mountains, and he died very shortly after he got home. Have you talked to Mae St. Clair about this?

Lynn: I talked to Mae, but she talked more about the concepts in the readings, than she did about anything personal.

Sally: She can talk to you about life down there, about Gladys and Mr. and Mrs. Cayce. She might be helpful to give you some thoughts that no one else would.

Lynn: That's true too, she has some original thoughts. So, how long did you know Gertrude, was it a number of years?

Sally: Five years, more or less. It would be the time Hugh Lynn and I were having dates and after we were married, I would say five years.

Lynn: And you knew her during the war years when her sons were away. That was a trying time for her. Did people ask for readings from Edgar Cayce during those years?

Sally: Yes, the mail was enormous. The post office put on a special truck, just for the Cayce mail. People were writing him for psychic information and all that, so it was a very hard time. He and Gladys were very busy, and the one thing that bothered he and Gertrude very much was all the letters that came had a check in them.

Lynn: Really, that bothered them?

Sally: Certainly, they were so afraid the check would be misplaced and people would get the impression the A.R.E. was not honest. You see, this check had to be returned, and that meant that there was a lot of mailing, and he couldn't get very reliable help, so he had the wives of servicemen who wanted jobs and the place was just full of people trying to return checks and letters. It was a very, very hectic time.

Lynn: So, they had a lot on their mind during the war years, a lot worried them?

Sally: Greg, what kind of qualities did Gertrude Cayce have that made the difference in Edgar Cayce's work?

Lynn: Well, we've answered most of those, so we can think more. Could she just ever ask everyone to go home and take a rest? Did she ever take a holiday, or anything?

Sally: No.

Lynn: And yet she never complained. Most people would complain, and she didn't. Is that because she believed in the readings, and wanted to help people, do you know?

Sally: Yes, she wanted to help the people. It was a time of war, a time of sadness, fear and frightfulness, and she was hoping that the readings would help the people. She wanted to help Edgar and her family, and friends who came. She just wanted to help the people.

Lynn: She really cared for these people, their suffering, even though naturally she got tired sometimes with it. Do you think sometimes that what made her become so ill, being so tired?

Sally: Well, she had cancer.

Lynn: Oh, I didn't know that.

Sally: I don't think anybody knows what causes cancer. I assume it could be the wrong diet, it could be fatigue, it could be anything.
Lynn: Did it go through out her body?

Sally: I have no idea.

Lynn: Were there things, that if she'd had time, she would have liked to do, like did she like to sew or music?

Sally: I don't know, never heard her mention it.

Lynn: She had quite a life working all the time, you have to admire that.

Sally: He helped her a lot in the kitchen, I told you that, and she didn't enjoy fishing, and she didn't enjoy yard work, so he had a man that helped him plant flowers and plant the garden. It was people, it was housekeeping, cooking and people that she spent her time with.

Lynn: Did anyone give her a hand in the house?

Sally: I helped her, and I suppose Gladys helped her, and I found a black lady who would come in and helped her clean up. So I'd say yes.

Sally: I helped her, and I suppose Gladys helped her, and I found a black lady who would come in and helped her clean up. So I'd say yes.

Lynn: Were she and her husband kind to black people?

Sally: They were very kind to that girl, but I don't think that black people were around very much. He may have had a black person help in the yard, but I don't think the question of race came up.

Long before the sixties Civil Rights Movement brought positive changes in southern race relations "The Sleeping Prophet", Edgar Cayce, made a prediction. He warned, unless those who had built this country with the sweat of their brow were considered fairly, there would be rioting in the streets. From Jessica Madigan's World Prophesy, Volume Three*, 1965)*

Lynn: Did they enjoy going to church together?

Sally: No, he taught a Sunday school class, and she used to go to church with Hugh Lynn and me once in awhile, but he never did. Hugh Lynn used to insist that she go with us. She would once in a great while. But I wouldn't say either one were very much churchgoers.

Lynn: Was Hugh Lynn very close to his mother?

Sally: Very, she depended on him a lot.

Lynn: How did she depend on him?

Sally: Well, he worked in the office, of course, and he tried to help take care of the correspondence, and he was working with Edgar on the A.R.E., the building up there, and I'd say he helped her in every possible way.

Lynn: Was Hugh Lynn more practical than his father with money and things?

Sally: Yes.

Lynn: So he had a gift more like his mother to be a good head for practical things. Was Edgar Evans close to his mother?

Sally: Very close, because he tried very hard. He didn't like people as much as Hugh Lynn and his father did, and I think he tried to protect his mother a lot from people, and yes, I'd say he tried to help in every possible way he could.

Lynn: So, Edgar Evans and his mother were quieter, and they weren't as people oriented.

Sally: Yes.

Lynn: Did you have things in common with Gertrude?

Sally: Certainly, well we had Hugh Lynn and the baby Charles Thomas, and we had everything.

Lynn: Well, that's a good point. You both had similar life situations, you were both interested in the work, and you were working hard, both for the work and the family, so you had a great deal in common, and you could understand a lot of what she experienced. Did you have a lot of people in your life too? Did you have as many as Gertrude did?

Sally: Not exactly the same, no. A memorable family of seven or so, many brothers and sisters, and relatives and I taught school in five or six different towns, and I've taught school here in Virginia Beach, and I've worked in Sunday School for a long time so I did know a lot of people. Well, I think that's all I know about Edgar Cayce.

Lynn: That's fine, thanks a lot.

Judy Martin who transcribed this interview, made the following comment: "The overall feeling I received about this interview, was the deep sense of love that Sally seemed to have for Gertrude. I believe if Lynn had asked her who had been her hero in her life, she would have quickly answered 'Why it was Gertrude Cayce, of course.'"

**Portrait of Edgar and Gertrude Cayce
(Courtesy of Harriet Kornick)**

APPENDIX E

REPRESENTATIVE RESPONSES TO QUESTIONNAIRE

The following represents the my selection of significant passages from the total interview material organized according to question and identified with each subject's chronological generation as well as generation in the Work.

Only individual's deceased from this plane will be identified by name. All others will be identified by the following code: G: Chronological Generation; GW: Generation in the Work; E or W: Residence in the Eastern or Western United States.

**Question One:
What has been most exciting about
your association with Edgar Cayce and the Work?**

"She [Gertrude Cayce] was wonderful with people."
G:Deceased/GW: 1-1E

"Well, you see, I never did have the readings in our home like she [Gertrude Cayce] did, but I enjoyed the people who came and listening to the conversations. I enjoyed the people. It was very interesting the different types of people who would come here and visit. For a good many years we had a study group of about forty people. It's all in contact with people."
G: 80's/GW: 1-1/E

"It was the fact that he saved my younger brother's life by my husband and myself following the advice we gained through the Edgar Cayce readings." G: Centenarian/GW: 1- 2/E

"It goes back a lot to Gertrude being invisible for a lot of the years when I was growing up—she was totally invisible. Actually, who was visible was Gladys [Davis Turner], and she was alive when I was growing up and Gertrude wasn't, so we got to be really great friends and I just love her incredibly much . . .

"She felt fulfilled; now whether someone in my age group feels she was fooling herself is the trick—but she definitely felt fulfilled—and I definitely respect her for that . . .

"Well, she always talked with such reverence about Mr. Cayce, but I certainly feel . . . that she probably had a more realistic picture of Cayce than other people that we might know from the old Guard. She was really great on challenges and opportunities. Like when I was just despairing that I thought I would never get married and have a child—and that was my major thing I wanted to have in my life. She hadn't been married or hadn't had any children—she hadn't been married 'til she was in her 40's. I was about in my middle 30's then, and she was just great at giving me courage, telling me reading numbers that would help and she said that if your dreams don't come true, then God will replace your heart with a desire that He will fulfill. So she was just wonderful; and she wouldn't back away from life challenges. And then what was great was that she did end up getting married even twice in her later life.

"So she did things in a different way. She devoted her early life to Cayce, supporting him, but then she did get her own life—her own emotional life—when he died, so that was good." G: Deceased/GW: 1-2/E

At the age of 30 this individual met Edgar Cayce. She had been in a state of great despair. She had a reading by Edgar Cayce and came out with an excitement that "it's going to work, I have found an answer. I don't know what it is, I don't understand the reading, but there's an answer, which the doctors hadn't been able to come up with.

"I became like a member of the household for the rest of his natural life—and Mrs. Cayce's, the two of them. I lived only three miles from them, and I would go there and talk to him and ask him questions and ask him to explain what should I do in this situation and he would give some answer that was obviously very simple, and I would do that and come back perhaps with another question. He did a better job of that than anybody you'd ever know." G: 80's/GW: 1-2/E

"What I remember most about him [Edgar Cayce] is the feeling and the experience of him. I never looked at it as exciting, but his giving readings was very normal. As a child, he told me he saw a pink fairy on my shoulder. I could never doubt it because I totally trusted him, though I never saw it for myself." G: 60's/GW: 1-2/W

"Learning from the information in the material that we're responsible for what we are. We'd better stop blaming our parents or grandparents. We are the sum total of who and what we are. Hugh Lynn said, 'We can't get into any more trouble than we deserve.'"
G: 80's/GW: 2-2/E

"Clearly the most exciting thing about the A.R.E. for me has been the Work, the opportunity to participate in sharing these truths with others.

That has, of course, taken many forms. I have been grateful for the feeling of 'coming home' that this Work and these people have brought me. I have needed to be a part of something bigger, that I can believe in, and to make my contribution there." G: 60's/GW: 2-2/W

"Well, for me, the readings have been a freeing. I was raised in a very strict Presbyterian home, where my father was the authority and my mother brought humor and love and gentleness and everything. The Cayce readings really bring that out, that it is important to have both aspects—the gentleness that is important for a man and the strength that is important for a woman to manifest—these two things are brought out in the readings." G: 70's/GW: 2-2/W

"Just a little history . . . Even though we came here a lot of the summers during my growing up years, Mom and Dad never spoke to us about Cayce until I was about 13 years old and my little brother was born and they wanted to make his middle name Cayce. And I said, 'Who's that?' And they said that he was this man who had affected their lives in a very deep way. Shortly after that I got a copy of There is a River, and that is when the dialogue really started. Mom and Dad had done work with dreams and prayer and a little bit on meditation with us but tried to protect us from concepts like reincarnation or anything that might have burned us at the time in the culture. So my journey really began then and we had great feelings of community. We used to come down here when I was a baby and all the way through my teens . . . [there was] a great Spiritual community at the A.R.E.

"I remember good times. We'd all eat up on the hill together with lunches of gelatin and almonds (Cayce stuff) and it was just really special in a lot of ways. And then in the 60's when I had gone through my agnostic period in college and all that and I came back with a real understanding . . . I came back to the A.R.E. and it was all so exciting to be there. [There were] A lot of people! The most we had ever had—men as well as women. So it was just an exciting time.

"[Later] I had gone through my consciousness-raising phase in the 70's and my dad and I really knocked heads and parted ways because he couldn't hear a lot of the things that I really thought were important. So after that Marriage and Family thing I started challenging my mom on her reading where Cayce said that she should be in the home (she was headed for a concert pianist career) and that she should support Dad and all that, and I wondered if she ever regretted that or thought that some of that was Cayce's overlay of being from some patriarchal society.

"So, on the whole she said no, that it would have been too much a temptation for her ego if she had gone on to be professional. But there really was a question in my mind at the time. It [the reading] was especially for her. It might have been true. He said she could play in churches and keep grounded with her music, but there's part of me that thinks that maybe that was influenced by his own overlay of chauvinism at the time; but it was just cultural chauvinism.

"Things would have been so different if my dad had taken a greater part at home; but it took a very traditional split. So I remember that was the first time that I had the courage to raise—in front of an audience of a couple of hundred people—that maybe there was some patriarchal or chauvinistic overlay.

"This was in the 70's at a big lecture ... Panel discussion ... on Marriage and the Family. So then Mom and I—in 1981, I think it was—led a whole week (Mark wanted us to do it) on Women in the New Age. We were so excited. We only got about 20 people enrolled but we went ahead with it and it was just really exciting. But they didn't have the patience. It was right on the cutting edge, but they said, 'Well, this doesn't earn money, so ... and there doesn't seem to be enough interest ... ' Which basically they meant it was just a new thing—especially for A.R.E. ... they get many more women than men to come to the conferences. But the women are so unempowered—they're so powerless—that they themselves are threatened to come to something that would be empowering. I think it would have taken a while to build, but I think it could have been exciting. "G: 40's/GW: 3-1/W

"The most excitement was the potentialities Edgar Cayce himself explored. The whole idea opened realms of possibilities that would be exciting to explore and examine for years to come. For the truth seeker, a place to begin to quench their thirst. My first book was also my first living dream of a visit by the man. That itself was a mark that changed my life and my pursuits. My excitement was not however, found in the A.R.E. Much too confining to someone who wanted to explore it all—rather than accept his thoughts. Everything about Edgar Cayce—his life and his work—opens for the individual a need to know, pursue, and investigate greater concepts of living and greater principles of being."
G: 40's/GW: 3-2/W

This individual was most excited about having participated in what she described as the 'Golden Age' of Atlantic University in the 1970's "because the experiential sessions offered then 'dealt with the full, the whole; we used tools to be better people, to be who we were in that moment—real.'" G: 40's/GW: 3-2/E

"I think [by] bringing past-life consciousness to the foreground and as a young woman assuring me that I was not unusual. I was validated by his works, his philosophies." G: 30's/GW: 3-2W

"Cayce gave great understanding of the continuation of life, Oneness, meditation and prayer. [These] gave me great comfort. I was seeking. I got answers. I entered a service oriented field. Body/mind/spirit.

Appendix E

Jungian psychology fits with Cayce—mysteries, archetypes, the collective." G: 40's/GW: 3-2/E

"In 1978, I attended a day-long conference in San Francisco with my husband and several friends—one of who kept taking me to various A.R.E. meetings. I was impressed by the different speakers, which included Hugh Lynn Cayce, Elsie Sechrist, Shirley Winston and Charles Thomas Cayce. I had been around several spiritual groups, but for some reason these people impressed me with their integrity; they seemed to live what they spoke.

"In the afternoon, Shirley Winston was speaking on divine love and I was seated about three rows from her in the middle—so she was right in front of me. She was very passionate in her manner and delivery, and suddenly in my mind's eye I 'saw' a long line of people—many wide—all dressed in the clothes of many civilizations, and the words I 'heard' were from the beginning. (I normally do not see pictures and I saw this one right in front of my third eye.) I knew that I had found my soul group and that day I joined A.R.E.

"So the excitement was in reconnecting to a history—a pattern, a service that I have been involved with since the beginning of our journey into the earth—to manifest the Christ Spirit in the earth.

"Since that day, the work of the A.R.E. and my service within it has given purpose and focus to my life. Some of us started a study group in 1979 and that is still meeting even with four of the original members.

"I have held many jobs here in Northern California and am currently in my fourth year as one of the two coordinators for the Northern California Region for A.R.E. We have seen the community blossom during this time." G: 50's/GW: 3-3/W

"Thinking of God as my friend; being co-Creators with God. Finding a God that wasn't punishing—a God of Love. I may have heard it in churches before, but through the Cayce material it struck home with me. There's a reading that says, 'God misses us as companions.' That moved me." G: 40's GW: 3-3/E

"It's very much family [working at Headquarters in Virginia Beach]. Everybody looks out for each other. If you have problems you've been known to get money in the mail—inter-office. They do anything they can. It's like a big network system. Someone needs an apartment. It gets around. They find you one.

"I have a son who lost an arm at the age of seven. He went there [to A.R.E. camp] every year he could. He's been scholarshipped for a great part of it. And A.R.E. gives their staff a 50% discount. You know how mean kids are. They've teased him. When he goes to camp it's the only place he's an equal person with everyone else. Through the Cayce philosophy ... they all showed him that they loved you for the inside of you instead of how you look. So he learned a lot. That'd do him for a year.

The only way he could put himself back on track . . . is to go back again." G: 30's/GW: 4-1/E

"It answers so many questions—to everything." G: 30's/GW: 4-1/E

"The validity of the information by analysis and testing of it; to be able to have the understanding of reincarnation and some other psychic phenomena in a body of information that's been tested and validated; to go to a source that's done extensive research on it." G: 50's/GW: 4-1/W

"Reincarnation. Getting a real handle on reincarnation. To me it gives the answer to some very basic questions, i.e., who am I? Where did I come from and where am I going? What is the meaning and purpose to this life? Why is there pain and suffering?" G: 60's/GW: 4-2/W

"I think it's great to have such a big organization to turn to; it gives credibility to the whole study [of psychic phenomena] . . . so that people don't have to go to a booth [at a psychic fair]. Here is a foundation based on the study of psychic readings." G: 20's/GW: 4-2/W

"I'm excited about the resource of the library. I love to buy books but you can only put so many of them in your home. And most places, anyway, don't have such a vast resource of information. I'm just really appreciative that this exists. 'Cause it's just like a treasure. I haven't really been involved in anything else that's going on here. My parents read a lot of Cayce's books before I was born. The books were around and I remember seeing them around. And my father was a doctor. It was funny because I didn't know this—My mother told me when I moved here—that he used some of the Edgar Cayce remedies. I was never aware of it, really. I guess I just accepted it as an everyday thing." G: 20's/GW: 5/E

"His life. How he was ostracized by his peers, (if he had any) how he channeled basic tips for the human race, spiritually, physically, etc. [That] when he was asleep he ignored his own mortality—if that makes any sense. Well I mean, that's evidenced by his readings on tobacco and such vices as he had himself, from what I gather." G: Teens/GW: 5/W

**Question Two:
What has challenged you or been difficult in regard
to knowing Edgar Cayce and the Work?**

"Well I don't think he [Edgar Cayce] was too practical with money. I think he thought if he always spent what he had, that some more would come.
[Also he was not too practical in regard to] "talking on the porch, or living room too long without saying 'Good Night' to the people, and looking at her [Gertrude Cayce] and seeing how tired she was and what a

long, busy day they had had. But he had to be considerate to them, too. They had come a long way and were here for a short time. I suppose he just tried to be as reasonable about his family and the visitors as he could be.

"There was always as many as nine people and sometimes one or two more. So she [Mrs. Gertrude Cayce] was keeping house, buying groceries and cooking, taking readings two or three times a day. To me that was remarkable . . . to get up and serve nine people and then go to the grocery store and buy all the groceries, come home and do a reading, then give a lunch.

"Not only that, her attitude was so important as she sat down by him, with two or three people watching him give a reading. You see, if you had to clean a room, and there wasn't anybody here but you, it wouldn't be so hard. It was so hard for her to let people sit there and watch her and him when he gave a reading.

"I don't know, I never did see her lose her temper or complain. Maybe she just went off by herself in the corner of the bedroom or something. I never did see her show any temper. Now I didn't live down there, but I would go there.

"Yes, [during World War II] she wanted to help the people. It was a time of war; a time of sadness, fear and frightfulness, and she was hoping that the readings would help the people. She wanted to help Edgar, and her family, and friends who came. She just wanted to help the people."
G: Deceased/GW: 1-1/E

[Regarding challenges presented through the growth of the A.R.E.], "Well, like you coming from California to Atlantic University and coming here to talk with me—that's a warm and friendly thing to do . . . It has to be done just by two and two, and one and one. But you can't approach and touch 100,000 people. Well . . . how could you be warm and friendly with 100,000 people around the world? It's not quite as spiritual."
G: 80's/GW: 1-2/E

"Well, I'd say no." [There was nothing challenging or difficult.]
G: Centenarian/GW: 1-2/E

"What was difficult for me was going through my teen life and trying to find my own identity [and deciding whether there was] . . . any merit at that time to knowing what your past lives had been. The reason for that was that both my mother and my grandfather had been people you might call 'famous' [in past lives given through the Edgar Cayce readings] and I was confused as to what it was to be famous and what was expected of one. Was this the goal—to become famous in the earthly world? So, as a result, I rejected the whole need to know past lives until I could see them from an adult point of view." G: 60's/GW: 1-2/W

"By 1958, she [Jessica Madigan] was one of the most popular A.R.E. speakers on the west coast. After [years] of dedicated work, a key official [perhaps] out of jealousy, forced her to resign. [It was a] devastating mental and emotional ordeal ... Undaunted, she determined to continue lecturing on the spirit, meaning, and scope of the readings dealing with the 'why' of karma and suffering—the meaning and purpose of man in the earth." G: Deceased/GW: 2-1/W

"Jessica [Madigan's] story itself is heartbreaking, and probably told me more about the A.R.E. itself than anything else. Perhaps she seemed too eccentric for staid and solid and firm (unbudging) foundations—but she came from the heart. A 13th century mystic, Meister Eckhart, says, 'Where do we begin? We begin with the heart.' Rather than ostracizing those that appear to be in disagreement with you, it is always wise to listen to what this seeming shadow has to say. As dreams prove—it is Shadow that holds your gift." G: Deceased/GW: 2-1/W

"She [Jessica Madigan] was exiled because she believed in the ability to utilize the potential that was there." G: Deceased/GW: 2-1/W

"I feel I've been treated very fairly as a woman. What's been hard is knowing that I'm responsible for trying to live the principles that I believe." G: 80's/GW: 2-2/E

[After 46 years of marriage, when this individual's mate chose to end their union, the (Cayce-related) clinic they'd co-founded seemed, for her, 'empty' of its initial idealism and ethics. Rather than stay as a figurehead, this physician chose to strike out in vital new directions.] "It's a very painful, yet transformational time ... like going through a long labor ... I was ... thinking ... 'You know, God, what are you doing? Here I am almost seventy, and I am out here trying to do something' ... and I opened the Bible and I started reading about Moses. I thought, it's all right. There's a method to this madness, I'll go for it.

"I've been [her husband's] wife. He'd be out there doing these things—and that's fine—and I've let it go at that; but it has not been the A.R.E stopping me. They've invited me to do lectures right on a par with [her husband]. They've invited me to write things, so I haven't felt that from the A.R.E. [Now I realize that] I don't need to be the one in the background all the time." G: 70's/GW: 2-2/W

"The most challenging part of the Work has been to overcome my own weaknesses through attempting to apply the principles in the Readings in order to serve as an example for this Work. I am most disturbed at the idea that others may judge the Work based on their responses to me.

"It has also been a challenge not to get discouraged when others do not respond with enthusiasm to the Work, and are not ready to make a commitment to it ... over, and over, and over again." G: 60's/GW: 2-2/W

Appendix E

[This next individual felt that she was a part of the Work, though not always of the A.R.E.] "We (the younger women) weren't encouraged. I mean, I was not encouraged by Hugh Lynn. I was leading project groups; I was one of the best there through the 70's. Of course, he had a love/hate relationship with my dad all through the years.

[Also] "I think there's a real fear of being threatened by powerful women. It's very sad and I hope it changes. I'm not sure when and if I'll join the battle in terms of the A.R.E., but I know that I've tried to answer my calling, which means becoming a female minister and being able to bring the best that I can from the readings.

"I think Dad and Cayce both had this public image that there was no shadow side. And yet, I knew the private side of my dad, and there was definitely a shadow side and shortcomings. And I think that more and more as my dad was able to face his shadow-side he was able to face Cayce's shadow- side, which he had already experienced some as a young man when he worked with him.

"When he wrote his first biography of Cayce—which I read years before it got published—I just cried because I realized that Cayce was a man that I could relate to because he was human—not a God—he had problems, he had the same challenges I do and hard things to work through, and it just made him much more meaningful than this semi-god that I had grown up with.

"So I was real excited because then I could really relate to him and his journey. I think my dad, as much as anyone else alive or dead loved Mr. Cayce—still loves him—and was a son in one life—or believes he was; Cayce said he was. And I think that the best love can handle the darkness because the love is so strong. So my dad didn't get any pleasure out of that, but he feels that that is just a more real love; love that can face the darkness and walk with it and stand up to it.

"So I think my dad loves Cayce just as much as anybody and has the courage to not sell Cayce out or to sell God out by taking easy ways out or easy answers. What I want to do in my life is to try and have that courage—to see my own shadow and the shadow of any organization that I am a part of, and that includes the Church that I am a part of, as well as the A.R.E. I try to keep focused on the ideals." G: 40's/GW: 3-1/E

"It is my opinion that (a man in leadership) prefers men to women in the work situation. Obstacles or problems, for me, would have been personality problems that are actually—or part of them are—of my own doing. I could have done certain things that would have changed the course of what went on.

"I never understood why [a man in leadership] doesn't utilize the talent at hand. People have come to him—not to him, that's incorrect. The people have come to the organization that are so qualified it's ridiculous—that have tried to show them how to do certain things. [A woman], who used to be the editor of a couple of well known magazines, was down there trying to help, and finally she came to me and said, 'I'm going to have to go back to New York; my doctor said I'm going to have a heart attack if I stay any longer.'" G: 40's/GW: 3-1/E

" . . . And that's what I think is true of Cayce. That there are times when he gave incredible truths that are true for all time and times when I feel he was not able to transcend the limits of the culture and the sexism." G: 40's/GW: 3-1/E

"The challenge of the Edgar Cayce work that was the deepest for me was the revelation that I could no longer just accept what I was taught about life, religion, or man, but that I would have to question, probe, research, and challenge life to reveal itself to me—beginning a long quest.

"Again—his life. These experiences reveal possibilities far beyond the confines of the A.R.E. They open to mankind a revelation for deeper questing and questioning, a beginning of a desire to look within and see what might be written there, rather than to shove it away for common acceptance or taught behaviors—or past acceptables. The challenge to stay open in the face of closedness, to allow to be different rather than the acceptance of being the same. Exciting and scary." G: 40's/GW: 3-2/W

[This individual's extensive (sometimes paraphrased) remarks regarding challenges seemed to constellate around several core issues. She began saying she believed she is part of the Work, though not always part of the A.R.E.] "This is really hard for me to formulate because it's been so emotional for me."

1) First, related to the life of Edgar Cayce, the women were extolled for their self-sacrifice but there was a double standard. For example, Edgar Cayce was able to have adventures (at the oil wells) while his family went hungry. "I want to say that that is wrong." As a result, there are a lot of handmaidens at the A.R.E., but there is no matriarch. Where is the feminine wisdom?

   I'm looking at women traditionally being the handmaidens, being willing to work for nothing. Men who work for nothing are not respected. Men who are not in a high position are not respected. They have constantly tried to put women in key positions. But they keep choosing women who are . . . the father's daughter."

   [In regard to this, this individual felt that the young men of her generation had been especially fostered and encouraged as "Hugh Lynn's boys" whereas that was not so much the case for the young women of similar talent and ability.] "A lot of these men are puer eternas. That was a big consciousness for that [now 40's] age group. Women were coming into their own. You know . . . what do you mean, I can't do this?"

Appendix E

2) [Because of the early circumstances of Cayce's gift before metaphysics was accepted], "They (A.R.E.) want to be accepted. Why deny the wound of feeling like a stepchild... nobody wants to be a weirdo. As metaphysics is more accepted in the world, there could be less of this "credibility, Christianity and chastity' over-emphasis." Going back to one's church to "change what has been so rigidly patriarchal could be good, but it [A.R.E.] has often become a religious organization. I really haven't dared to say it that way."

3) Thus, there is an overall tendency to denial. "And that's the other thing about the A.R.E . . . It's as if you could only show one face. I think there is some splitting. You pray about it. You can't get angry. Rise above. Turn the other cheek. A lot of the Christian doctrine. Which is really very male. And here is an organization that is mostly women. You're seeing ... not a feminine viewpoint in an organization that is mostly feminine.

"For example, when I get metaphysical, A.R.E. types in therapy ... terrible pain, [saying] 'All I have to do is pray and meditate every day and it will all go away.' I know jerks who meditate every day. People need to face what's happening emotionally. The inner child has no voice, no abstract thought. Somebody comes in. They're denying, feeling guilty that they shouldn't feel 'bad things'. It becomes so compulsive and incredibly obsessive and neurotic. After you get through those feelings, then you have choice. People also remove themselves by using the metaphysical language, "So and so had such and such done to them but that's their karma."

4) Moreover, there seems to be a tendency to project the shadow, or unacceptable feelings or aspects of self, onto others. [Jeremy Taylor (1980) has a good explanation of this. He says the shadow is easily visible in the shape of those whom we most dislike and fear. We have to admit that we are as evil as we are good. Fears are projected outward onto the people who represent our own unintegrated element—in a patriarchal, white, technological culture, it is the non-male, the feminine, the non-white, the feeling, spontaneous, related-to-nature element. This justifies oppression and exploitation. Yet anything suppressed is going to rear up in its shadow.] Here for example, we have the splitting of the whole feminine force ... like an earthquake—they don't realize. Aphrodite versus Logos. Forget it. It's too powerful for the boundary of will.

5) This denial and outward projection of the shadow results in rigidity caused through the fear of change. As Taylor says, when acting out

of fear of change, or death, "the personality and its culture are held in some rigid, unchanging, image." (Taylor, 1980, p. 17) "That damn be careful, its dangerous stuff. Be only the way I want you to be.' That used to get to me. It used to be much worse than now. What I see happens is that new life comes in, gets used up, and leaves. The metaphor of sacrifices could be used."

In summary, this individual's identified areas of challenge included:
1) Areas of double standard regarding gender;
2) A group need for acceptance causes over-emphasis on conformity to conservative standards of credibility and religiosity;
3) Denial of the shadow, or unacceptable aspects of self;
4) Tendency to project the shadow onto others—particularly the feminine element; and
5) Some rigidity and fears that lead to difficulty integrating and fully utilizing the creative energies of new people as a result.

In conclusion, this individual reiterated her fundamental bond and commitment to the Work stating that "Its hard to criticize something that you care about. I'm going to be somewhat passionate about something or why get involved? Why should I criticize anything unless I care about it?" G: 40's/GW: 3-2/E

"The twin soul concept. I'm not real familiar with the readings on twin souls per se, but assuming that Jessica Madigan was a student of his [Work] and portrayed the same philosophy, I was in disagreement in part. [I believe] that the twin soul-in-the-earth relationship could pose as the most difficult relationship on earth. It was not at all times harmonious and forever appealing. The ultimate in the twin soul concept on earth is to let go totally and completely of that soul mate in order to pursue life—earth—goals." G: 30's/GW: 3-2/W

"The difficult part is the conservative approach to Spirit and the masculine language connoting that God is a 'he'. There's a strong current of fundamentalism in the people who've explored this Work perhaps more than in the readings themselves. The language of the readings has also bothered me. It continues to be a problem, and I think the wisdom of the readings has to be understood as having filtered through the mind-set of the belief system of the man, Edgar Cayce." G: 40's/GW: 3-3/E

"What has been difficult for me is the vision of regionalization versus the vision of centralization. It seems to me and many others that organizations will no longer work or be effective if all or most of the influence comes from a central location. I believe that for organizations to be healthy and vigorous, they need to see the organization as a living organism with the energy being shared. I felt by this time that A.R.E. would have begun to have centers in other locations than Virginia Beach.

This hasn't happened for many reasons. So this challenges me to broaden my view of the Work, which I know is a major source of Light in the Earth. Edgar Cayce and our soul group are not limited to a particular organization." G: 50's/GW: 3-3/W

"I feel that the A.R.E. would do well to pay the women who are out there in the field or find a way for them to get reimbursed more for all the work that they do for the organization, the same way that the churches today are finding the need to pay the women that are working in the churches. In the past it may have been appropriate for it to have been all volunteer work, but that is no longer the case today. The women are needing those incomes, and for their own self esteem also. Why shouldn't they be recognized monetarily also? Mainly, the men are in power positions and have been getting paid. The women who have been doing all the filing work and all the catechism classes and all the outreach haven't been getting paid." G: 30's/GW: 4-1/E

"It's terrible." [The salary at A.R.E.] G: 30's/GW: 4-2/E

"The reason that I haven't pursued it [the Cayce work] more. Part is that I haven't made the time commitment necessary. Part is that they would have you access the information through their own system and I would prefer to access it through my own understanding. It's only a piece of the puzzle for me, not the game." G: 50's/GW: 4-1/W

"Taking the principles beyond a beautiful esoteric theory and putting them into practice in daily life. Reconciling the suffering of innocent animals, particularly where man is not involved (i.e., fires, storms, food chain) into the reincarnational theme." G: 60's/GW: 4-2/W

"I think it [the Cayce material] needs to be more accessible to the everyday person—the kind of person who might say about someone who is psychic—Hey, look at that wacko,' that kind of thing. If they were made aware of the A.R.E., then that stereotype wouldn't present itself."
G: 20's/GW: 4-2/W

"It seems like there's so much more to take advantage of than I have [accessed]. I'm wary of getting involved with groups. It has to be an individual journey, really. One of the things that bothers me about any organization . . . it's always going to have human failings. I think one that comes up most frequently is just the commercialization and people frequently losing sight of the first reason that they wanted to have the organization and getting caught up in . . . And, this place to me, opposed to other places that I've been has more of that feeling about it. It's more of a business. It's a well-run business, and I don't find it to be a terrible business by any sense. But I was disappointed when I came here because I've been other places that I felt . . . people were more there for personal reasons.

"Because part of the reason I think someone goes somewhere is for the pilgrimage . . . sometimes you make a connection with another person that helps you along in your journey, and them also. By virtue of them being able to help you, I think it does something for them, and ah, it's a nice experience. I don't guess you can call up on demand; it's probably unrealistic to think you can go somewhere expecting that." G: 20's/GW: 5/E

"The attitudes of the people at A.R.E. itself—like he's some sort of deity. If you haven't noticed this, go to any A.R.E. lecture and listen to the context in which his name is mentioned. If he's not a god he must be a guru. (Yes, it's larger than him.)

"Everything I've learned has been second-hand. And I mean, things are a lot easier to accept when you're experiencing them in the flesh. It takes a certain amount of faith, just like religion does; to believe in and support the Edgar Cayce works.

"It parallels modern day religion. The question tends to arise: Is Cayce divine or simply an inspired mortal? And you know he intensely studied the Bible . . . and some of the devout Cayce followers (not that he should be followed) merely studied—and some of the intellectuals interested in Cayce. Are there different levels? Is it to be interpreted—his work—or is it to be taken literally?

"Or I think personally it would be interesting to see how he interpreted the Bible and saw—like—how much of it seeped into his subconscious—therefore, came out in the readings in different ways—so perhaps he's continued the Christ work. He studied the Bible all of his life. That made him that much closer to Christ's way of thinking and therefore to God—if there is a God—which enabled him to do things like God. If you're close to God, your perceptions are higher.

"He was able to help his fellow man in an unparallel manner. When he was meditating, it wasn't him; it was only a fraction of his mind. He had studied this work [the Bible] so much that he became unconsciously indoctrinated. It crept into his subconscious—not just his subconscious, his spiritual mind, or meditative states." G: Teens/GW: 5/W

Question Three:
How do you feel you've been able
to contribute to the Work?

"This Work would not have happened without women like Gertrude Cayce or Gladys Davis." G: Deceased/GW: 1-1/E and G: Deceased/GW: 1-2/E

"Gertrude Cayce's contributions to the Work of Edgar Cayce is discussed: "He would have given it up. A young couple with two little boys. He had to make a living, and if she had insisted that he give it up to make money and buy a home, he wouldn't have carried on his psychic

work. She had enough love and interest in him to talk to him, and I suppose, for them to decide, too, that he had a very unusual talent and that he should use it... that this should be his life's work."
G: Deceased/GW: 1-1/E

"She [his mother, Gertrude Cayce] held the family together. She never complained of what she was doing and she was satisfied and that was her part in keeping the household together. She didn't try to give readings and Dad didn't try to clean house. I think they had a very good balance. I think she was like a balance wheel that kept him from going off the end—like being too extravagant or trying to give too many readings.

"She purposely kept in the background. I think she realized that Dad was doing the work, and the people were interested in him and she wasn't trying to take the credit or anything, or take any of the glory, but I think she did an awful lot in the background, behind the scenes, so to speak. She participated in everything the family did. Organizing the Association, she would give Dad advice on how you could do this or that. I don't mean she was running everything behind the scenes, but she was a partner—she participated in everything that happened in the family.

"I think Mother was kind of on the forefront of the partnership. I mean in doing the things she did, like in driving, smoking, participating in organizing the Study Groups and taking part in it. Talking to Dad and keeping the family going, in the household, the budget—I think she was a strong person." G: Deceased/GW: 1-1/E

"I don't think the A.R.E. would be here at all if it wasn't for Gertrude. I don't think Hugh Lynn would have worked with the wealthy men who started the A.R.E. if it hadn't been for her. Well, I imagine they [Gertrude and Hugh Lynn] just talked, like we are talking and she would say this is a good way to increase the number of people. It was a hospital they started, and then it developed into the A.R.E. And you know, for a while, they had to close it. David Kahn, that's who it was."
G: Deceased/GW: 1-1/E

"They [Gertrude Cayce and Gladys Davis Turner] were always thinking of Mr. Cayce's welfare. It was a very delicate thing [the readings]. He could have not come back." G: Deceased/GW: 1-1/E and Deceased/GW: 1-2/E

"When I met Mrs. Sally Cayce it was the human being... I learned from being in her presence a whole bunch of things about her, about Gertrude Cayce, what a wonderful people they must have been, how really dedicated and aware whatever the constraints of the roles of the time. And I learned that by being with her, in her presence, seeing her kindliness, I could feel that there was a Cayce work of yesterday. It was much more sweet and spiritual and warm and gentle." G: Deceased/80's/GW: 1-2/E

"According to a family member, Hugh Lynn and Sally Cayce talked over their relationship many hours, making clear agreements. They would do it territorially ... separate turfs ... real partnership. This was a process passed down from one family (Gertrude and Edgar Cayce) to the another." G: 80's/GW: 1-1

"There were many people in the New York territory where we lived. We lived eighteen miles outside of Bronxville, New York. Everybody commuted by train. One year we opened our house for three weeks, and he [Edgar Cayce] came with his wife, his wonderful secretary, (Gladys Davis) and Hugh Lynn Cayce, and they lived in our home. People in the area would come out for a reading every morning and afternoon; these people could not afford time and money to go down to Virginia Beach, but they could afford to come out to be in a place in the vicinity of New York City." Age: Centenarian/GW: 1- 2/E

"I've been able to contribute in my own life by validating that life is a process and that the Work that Cayce began was opening consciousness into may realms. If he was the Father, he began a new paradigm. So if that's what he did, what I contributed was unconsciously being on the ground floor [as a child associated with him] and accepting this as a natural process so that I would operate in my own life's process from a more in-depth point of view." G: 60's/GW: 1-2/W

"In 1983 I had a serious illness. Two small children to raise and I didn't seem to be getting better after many months. I called my friend Jessica and told her that I couldn't find the herbs and remedies the Cayce readings had recommended for this condition—anywhere. Jessica suggested I contact 'the Saint of Virginia Beach.' She and Gladys Davis Turner had been friends, and if anyone would reach out to help a person in need, it would be Gladys Davis Turner, she believed.

"I called Gladys Davis Turner who kindly got everything that was needed from an old pharmacy in Virginia Beach and then sent it to me. When I got better and called Gladys Davis Tuner back to thank her, we talked briefly about Jessica. 'Once,' Ms. Turner stated, 'Hugh Lynn told me that, outside of his father, Jessica was the most psychic individual he had ever met.' Thus both Jessica Madigan and Gladys Davis Turner were very kind to me and helped me greatly that year to get well." G: Deceased/GW: 1-2/E, G: Deceased/GW: 2-1/W

"My experiences with Jessica (Madigan) were that she brought a heart energy to metaphysical information. And that operating from the heart energy is what's traditionally been viewed as a woman's strength. So she was able to convert some of the perhaps drier information into a way people could connect in their own heart level which led them to search the information for themselves." G: Deceased/GW: 2-1/W

Appendix E

```
                      To
               Gladys Davis Turner

    Who, more  than  any  other  individual,
    Has  given  years  of  dedicated
    And  devoted  service  to
            The  work  of
        E D G A R      C A Y C E
    America's    beloved    clairvoyant
           and    prophet    of
               our    time.
```

Madigan credits Gladys Davis Turner

"I loved her story of Twin Souls. I loved those lessons that I learned about Edgar Cayce from Jessica, and I'm sure that our souls—our life—continues to improve by knowing her." G: Deceased/GW: 2-1/W

"Jessica was not very practical, but she was very, very dear to me. A very advanced soul—and heart. Bless her! She would go anywhere, just about, to talk about Cayce and his readings. It was her work, too, just as much. And she was a very good reader herself. She's happy now on the Other Side of Life." G: Deceased/GW: 2-1/W

"One source that did spark a connection to me was the writings of Jessica Madigan. Being on a very parallel path to her heart's way was one reason. Her writings on Twin Souls . . . and her information on Dreams were very useful and meaningful to me. She is a very heart-based interpreter of Edgar Cayce's readings." G: Deceased/GW: 2-1/W

**Lynn Rogers' Mentor Jessica Madigan 1911-1986
(Photo Courtesy of Jery Stier)**

"She was the 'Grand Mother' of a new generation of students. Jessica was responsible for enlightening many women to the Cayce studies. Most definitely went on to elaborate Cayce's work in a way that anyone—particularly women—could relate to. I've always seen her as the Grand Mother who elaborated his work

"What we've attained as women will help balance the next generation. My sons certainly have been influenced. They've been given a different perspective than a patriarchal [one]. Cayce was more patriarchal Christian (from his generational roots). Jessica gave the women's perspective to this generation. We were able to take the both and give it to our children. So the new generation will have a real balance of these philosophies." G: Deceased/GW: 2-1/W

"What I liked mostly about Jessica was that she was open-ended . . . to any group that came to Asilomar. She did not shut out anyone. She was not orthodox in any way. And we had all kinds of groups. Although she was grounded in Edgar Cayce, she did what she could, but was not restrictive. I liked the open-ended forum. It was true—people could congregate there at every chance and have their say."
G: Deceased/GW: 2-2/W

"She's (Jessica Madigan) been a great source of inspiration and help—giving me a philosophy of life, besides reincarnation and life after death, Atlantis and all that sort of thing. It's been a great comfort, knowing her and I think she'll come to me in dreams, and personally, and so on." G: Deceased/GW: 2-1/W

"For years, my job was to travel—over 100,000 miles—to encourage people to set up Study Groups. I gave pep talks wherever they had a little group. My chief job was to visit the small towns that couldn't afford to pay to have somebody come. I'd plan a trip—write to them that I could give a little talk. Almost invariably, I'd have an enthusiastic response. I remember one—'It's beyond our wildest dreams that anyone from The Beach would visit York, Pennsylvania.'" G: 80's/GW: 2-1/E

"I think that's one of the most wonderful things Cayce readings share is the ideal, the importance of that, and community. And I do want to say this, that one of my heartbreaks has been that the A.R.E. has not been into service since I was a teenager (when I had so much feeling for the underdog) and felt in the readings that there was so much caring for the whole world and people and children.

"And then I felt that the A.R.E. as an organization, a community, had nothing in place to try to help those less fortunate—that we were all white middle-class. And that got me angry enough to leave it for a while and just feel that they were missing a big part of the readings. The readings have it there—to [be of] service.

"I used to remember the ideal was to grow up and perfect myself. I would work so hard; I would get my ideals. Work so hard on all the disciplines—perfect myself. And then I lost sight of how to also do service and that that will help perfect me. Salvation isn't just a personal 'me' thing.

"I think the A.R.E. has lost sight of that to a great degree. And that is one reason why we started our Church so that we could (do service). We didn't find the community that we longed for—and part of that element was service together—and so that's one reason we started the Church.

"I don't know how we can do it through the A.R.E. right now, but we have started our Church as an alternative and we really want to be open to networking with other churches like yours and we want to let you know that anyone who is working at the A.R.E. is certainly welcome at our Church. We try to announce those and keep some kind of flow there—some kind of dialogue—but it just does seem very limited in possibilities right now. They won't even put on their handout sheet of Churches that ours is a very Cayce-related church. I mean I'm [her father's (who was close to Edgar Cayce)] daughter! I mean it's really sad.

"So, they're either trying so hard to not be partial that they're totally missing an opportunity where we really want to help serve and minister to those people . . . or they're threatened, too. Some of the people (I won't name names) are threatened by me and by what we're doing.

"And that [sense of being a Prophetess in exile] is really sad. I wish everybody well, and I really do. I'm praying for the A.R.E., for all the leaders; but I also really feel that (given my ideals and insights and understandings) I have to put my life—my finite energy that I was telling you about—my time and money and everything into the Church and [help] in other kinds of ways. And in that way I feel like I've come home.

"I mean the larger Church community is the one that the Cayce work is supporting. It is not that God . . . I mean Cayce is not Christ . . . I mean he's Cayce Christ or Edgar Christ, but he's not The One we should be serving. So in a way, then, it's really good to be in exile because it's really not exile, it's really coming home." G: 40's/GW: 3-1/E

"Edgar Cayce would want us to continue to pursue, question, challenge, seek. In this way I feel I have helped the Work. Our need is to not settle or decide that all is set—or revealed, or experienced—but rather to encourage growth, revelation and experimentation. In this, my own life is an enhancement to the Work. What I discover is [that] I am willing to share. What I have experienced is available as research. Who I am is a reflection of a quest." G: 40's/GW: 3-2/W

"By continuing the growth of this work, by sharing it and giving it to my children, not only to my physical children, but to the children of the earth. By sharing as I go through everyday life. For example, at work there's always a little piece to give out." G: 30's/GW: 3-2/W

"I've held many volunteer positions and am now Regional Coordinator for Northern California. My work, as I see it, is to be a catalyst. I love to be part of a philosophy that empowers people to know themselves and remember they are co-creators with the Creative Forces." G: 50's/GW: 3-3/W

"The only way I feel I've contributed to the Work at all is to be able to incorporate pieces of it in my own personal growth. Then I offer my understanding of the whole picture to whoever comes to me for information.

So I'm not a traditional worker in their sense. And I don't offer the work exclusively, it's just part of a bigger package." G: 50's/GW: 4-1/W

"By living the principles; being an example wherever I can. We never know how or when a small thing we say or do touches another . . . for good or ill. By being willing and able to discuss my belief system (when appropriate) and how it enhances my life." G: 60's/GW: 4-2/W

"Even though I'm new to the Edgar Cayce philosophy, I've chosen to help my teacher put together work on women's spirituality and the Edgar Cayce material. I just feel this needs to be done." G: 20's/GW: 4-2W

"How can you contribute to a Work that was complete until it was interpreted by others? I can only hope to get (direct) knowledge from him because, even if we could communicate, as of yet I have no way to check and see if what I have said is understood." G: Teens/GW: 5/W

Question Four:
How do you see the woman of tomorrow contributing to the Edgar Cayce Work?

"We all have psychic abilities. And I was somewhere and this young teenage girl came up to me and said, 'You know, I enjoy reading and talking about the ARE. I think it makes living so much more practical.' You ought to put that down somewhere. It was a beautiful thing to say about the ARE . . .

"You want me to imagine a future life. Work with people, and maybe teach school. I used to teach school, and I really enjoyed it—and of course, work in Sunday School. I have to say, work with the children. Not too young, children, but maybe between ten and fourteen—that age when children are beginning to think, and beginning to make decisions . . . to work with children teaching." G: 80's/GW: 1-1/E

"I think Cayce is one of dozens of movements that women are interested that lean toward the goal of helping to educate the present peoples of the earth planet to get a new focus, a new perspective on what life is all about." G: Centenarian/GW: 1-2/E

"It is by getting in touch with their own power and acknowledging it and acting on it (that women of tomorrow can best contribute). I work with a group, 'Women's Issues', in Walnut Creek and my message to them is, 'claim your power'." G: 60's/GW: 1-2/W

"Well I'd like to see women take an equal part and have equal recognition, which I think is pretty much the case now. I think women are equal to men. We've all had the experience of being the other sex. So I don't think that gender is important. That's been my feeling. And I've had nothing but good treatment from everyone—Hugh Lynn and now C.T.—has treated me very fairly." G: 80's/GW: 2-1/E

"As for the contribution of women to the Work tomorrow, I think tomorrow is going to be vastly different than today and we will all be called upon to be our best selves as never before, living peace and unconditional love. If we and our organization can role-model that, by responding to the Spirit within constantly, we will indeed be leaders in the Golden Age." G: 60'/GW: 2-2/W

"This is where again I see the women's role. A mother does not neglect a child that is sick. So I see medicine moving into this role of nurturing, not curing. We try to cure illnesses, that's a masculine approach. Healing is something completely different. Healing has to do with accepting what's happening in a particular person's situation and working with it. It doesn't always mean curing the illness. A healing can come through death. A healing can come about through integrating with the whole life process. . . .

"There's a painting, which a friend of mine is giving me for our office, and it's magnificent. It shows Jesus and his female counterpart nose-to-nose, face-to-face, and you can tell by looking which is the female and which is the male, but they're exactly the same. They're on a balance nose-to-nose, face-to-face. To me, that's the most exciting picture because it doesn't say one is greater than the other—we're co-creators. It's essential in the 90's and to get into the next century. I think the 90's is when this is going to happen." G: 70's/GW: 2-1/W

"And that's what I think is true of Cayce. That there are times when he gave incredible truths that are true for all time and times when I feel he was not able to transcend the limits of the culture and the sexism.

[But "I wouldn't burn the bridge to the Cayce material, etc.], "oh, no, no, no. There's too much of value there. It's formed my whole life, in terms of the readings, and also, I must say, that when I was doing this research on the readings for my dad's book a year ago, that I found [Edgar] Cayce's letters so much more compassionate than his readings.

"If you get a chance to look at them . . . they're so humble. They're right there with the readings . . . all the correspondence Gladys put in right with the readings. Oh yeah! Gosh, sometimes I'd be weeping reading his responses to this person who'd be suffering, and saying, 'Oh, I wish I could be of more help; these are just my poor readings.' And it's such a spirit that they have lost there, but that I found in him just touched me so much that I loved him . . . I started to love him, you know, not just the things-the work, the readings were great—but the man . . .

"And I want to say about that comment [made by authoritative source in the Library] . . . that the person doesn't matter, that that's B.S. Because you know what he had in his study was photographs of everybody's face that he could get and Dad said that those were his icons . . . that's what gave him the purpose.

Appendix E

"Dad went in with my grandmother and said, [when Cayce was in trance] 'Let's give readings on the whole generic of diseases: epilepsy, cancer and everything. Let's not do it person by person, let's do the whole thing. We'll get more people healed.' And the response came back, 'How did Jesus take them? One by one as they came. Pretty good pattern to follow, huh?'

[Further, regarding women in the future:] "Leslie Cayce is a real neat woman and very strong and very gifted. There could be a pattern of co-partnership there in very exciting ways for women." G: 40's/GW: 3-1/E

"Women of tomorrow as women of today will always have a strong and vital role in 'the work of spiritual enlightenment'. They are the Mothers. Nurturing (a great act of Love) brings powerful revelations. The woman of tomorrow will be freer to reveal these to each other and men than those that have gone before, to cut the ground. Christianity, per se, has not been kind or accepting to equality of vision and awareness for both men and women. But through the Edgar Cayce work—a gentle gift to woman-the freedom to accept their own inner knowing, their dreams, their revelations, until the bonds of restrictions are broken and she can take her wisdom's flight, release her plight and know her co-heritage with the divine principles of being." G: 40's/GW: 3-2/W

"Relationships to me are it. That's what we're here for. To learn how to be with each other. Hugh Lynn's dream was to have a holistic clinic and I was always intrigued by that . . . but I'm scared of the way they'd do it. As long as it wasn't hierarchical. I like community. I like co-partnerships. I like individual responsibility. [With women's spirituality] you'd have a way of catalyzing, a congealing . . .
[Interviewer said, 'You're a holistic physician.']" I really like that."
G: 40's/GW: 3-2/E.

"To the Edgar Cayce work or to the Universe? I think that women will come to know their own strengths, their own totality, which will be in harmony with Cayce's philosophies. And there will be no differences between sexes in the work; in the Universe [in that] it will be total, complete. Souls as One. Period. No sexuality involved."
G: 30's/GW: 3-2/W

"We, each of us—men and women—must take what is helpful and hopeful to manifest it in our personal lives and reach out to our communities. I feel one of the most important works we can do is build community in small groups-retreats, community action; provide an environment where like-minded and 'hearted' souls can support each other and reach out to our human family with love and vision and hope."
G: 50's/GW: 3-3/W

"In terms of being in [A.R.E.] management, a woman like me just showing up and sticking it out and sticking through, going through management and not quitting, holding ground, I think has helped—I'm not sure ... it's been a tight. I'm not a traditional woman in any sense. So perhaps it has benefited to have someone like me fight about those issues-- the fundamentalist attitude, the patriarchal attitude." G: 40's/GW: 3-3/E

"Better pay scale." G: 30's/GW: 4-1/E

"I think the woman of tomorrow will contribute to the Edgar Cayce work as she contributes to every other work. And that is that the woman of tomorrow will have greater creativity and solutions to bring to all problems." G: 50's/GW: 4-1/W

"The A.R.E. has always seen women as equal partners in the work and life in general (reincarnation concept). Women have researched the work and written significant books. Women are officers and leaders in all levels of A.R.E. But even those who are not visible are very important. We are all points of light. Women are usually the inculcators of values and belief systems to the children. What a marvelous opportunity to help a soul remember who they are." G: 60's/GW: 4-2/W

"Today it seems to me that the world is going backwards as far as women's issues [are concerned]. Edgar Cayce had a lot of information about male/female energies, twin souls. Has A.R.E. had a lot of workshops on this? I think they should. Finally, I would like to see women in top, co-leadership roles in the future A.R.E., as in the world." G: 20's/GW: 4-2/W

"What I'd like to see is the feminine expression fully represented—equally represented in every sense of the word. As part of the Divine, as part of the Co-Creation, as part of every activity that we have here—the feminine fully expressed. And that would mean looking at the readings for the wisdom that's contained there, but interpreting it through our current experiences and understandings and not seeing the readings as dogma—as some do. If we don't move from an attitude of seeing the readings as dogma, the readings will die. The readings remain valid today only through what we bring to them from our experiences. And that would mean [also] that women would play a major role in every sense—creativity, leadership, work—in regard to the Cayce work and spirituality as a whole. (This would] keep the readings valid and continually helpful."
G: 40's/GW: 4-1/E

"I think there's a lot more concentration on women being able to be spiritual leaders, and the value of women's relationships to each other being important. I'm real pleased about that. As far as the integration of how we're supposed to fit together into a unified whole ... I think it's real important that women assume a more equal role. I think that anytime women are excluded from positions of power of this kind, of their rights, that men suffer as much people talk about women's intuition-I think women's intuition probably develops because of years of repression . . . if you weren't in positions of power you needed something else, another strength, and I think . . . that's why we have that strength more then men—they didn't need it. I don't think it's a quality that would be found in women more than men; it's a need that developed. [In the future] think that a woman could bring anything that a man could—in leadership, spiritual [areas], and I think that's happening more now." G: 20's/GW: 5/E

"I think it would be very helpful if everyone had access to it. Perhaps going back to Question Two—you know how I like to end on a positive note—how Edgar Cayce studied Christ. If one was to study his readings again and again perhaps that would seep into their consciousness and the work could be explained, or at least viewed in a different light. Their third eyes shall open." G: Teen/GW: 5/W

"There's still a few unsaid things for women, but I think that everyday it will get better. You know like, my daughters will have things that I didn't have, and it will be just totally different than today. I think it's a very good time to be a woman." G: Teen/GW: 5/E

Daughter of the Aquarian Age of Mary

APPENDIX F

AKASHIC RECORD READING BY JESSICA MADIGAN

Akashic Record Reading for Nancy Witt
by Jessica Madigan December 2, 1979

Through Maria Teresa, the Nun:

She is showing your aura. There is green of intellect and then there is the green of healing. There is a peripheral aura of silver, which means, at least to me, if she's letting me translate it, that you have many out-of-the-body experiences that would ordinarily be called a dream. A symbolic dream you may remember. I don't think you remember the others so well, but this is coming very close to your head, so I think you will remember out-of-the-body experiences. You have a deep layer of rose, a layer of gold, and what I call a Royal Blue, which means true blue, according to Edgar Cayce. She is showing a blending of blue/green which is intuition and memory, like a soul memory of a past life, and she's now beginning to write, and I will read and I make no translations, no observations.

This one, please repeat again, full name and birth date. Nancy responds: "My name is Nancy Jean Witt. I was born April 17, 1935, at 4:30 a.m. in Detroit, Michigan."

This one is a very old soul in the sense of having been many times in the earth. She has approximately 300 lifetimes in the earth and she, if she so chooses, at the end of this incarnation or the following incarnation, which will be one of great happiness and fulfillment, leave the body and go on to Arcturus and live in that realm, or she may choose to return to earth to do a service for mankind. We will give the highlights of her lives. This one was primarily an Atlantean coming in the first age of Atlantis—not in Lemuria—at the time that the celestial hosts were beginning to propagate the earth. She is one who came in with the one called Amilius. She is one who was creative to the extreme and one of those who actually, however difficult it would seem in the present, was of that celestial company who created planets, solar systems, stars, throughout the ages. In a sense this was almost negative, for in the very beginning there was Nirvana, as called by the Hindus, and then there was the birth of the elder brother who became the Christ, who is the Christ of all creations, and finally there was the creativity until, unfortunately, they came into what became the earth plane, the prison house of the universe. For only here, on this planet, is there physical flesh and blood life. It will not be found, as she well knows from her Atlantean lifetime when she (or he) was what would be termed an astronaut. It will not be found in outer space; however every portion of space is inhabited by spiritual beings.

We would go into this first coming in into Atlantis, with the other portion of her being, the twin soul. When there was separation and one chose the masculine polarity, the other the feminine polarity, but much more often than average these two have changed roles. They have been in a high place much more often than average and she (Maria Teresa) is going through this book of Atlantis very quickly. She's writing: This entity was in every age, favored of her father as an Atlantean high princess/priestess. The one who was with her father who was then her twin soul, coming again in the body when she needed to explore space, which was an ideal at that time. She chose the masculine vehicle and actually lost her life in exploration—quickly, suddenly, and throughout the ages she was one who did finally, in feminine form, go into the Yucatan area, along—as with several others—with Quetzalcoatl, a former incarnation of Jesus, to bury the records in that place, where one day, in this century, they can be found.

The entity knows of the truth of Atlantis. She will be able, if she wishes, to write of those things. In working with others, they too will remember Atlantis. There are basics which should be studied as almost a textbook, for they will bring to mind those truths that actually existed, and it will be easier for her to open up the vaults of her memory. The entity, for instance, is one who came in the beginning and came through error with the host which was led by the one who became Christ and after the entrapment in matter this entity chose, as with many of those who came with her, that until such time as there could be the return to the house of the Father, that she would come into the earth again and again and again to bring the truth.

High points of this one's life, and there are many, but those that relate to the present: She was in India, or what became India; she was one who traveled on a shoe ship, a large ship, and later a (small) shoe ship with the one who was called Ra, and in entering in India, she was chosen to bring forth the truth of Atlantis, for India was called the country of the long memory. Returning not in female form, but with seven others who were actually feminine souls, she chose to come into the masculine vehicle so

Appendix F

that centuries later she might work upon the Vedas. At times she should read these because they will stimulate the memory of those lifetimes.

Returning in feminine form, she came into the Temple Beautiful in Egypt, and here she was with one who had been her father in Atlantis—Ra Ta, called Ra, in the book of the Dead. She was one of his chosen daughters, one who came in late life, and one who was chosen to interpret his teachings. And this can be a portion of her work in the present, for that one was known as Ra Ta. Known by the name Iao, she worked with the little Isis in the Temple of Isis, after the death of Ra, and she often turned to Hermes, the black teacher who became Jesus, and listened to his teachings throughout her long life of 124 years. After the crucifixion upside down in the great pyramid, by his enemies [and those] of Hermes, this one, knowing that Isis too would be killed, went and taught in all of Egypt from place to place, of the mysteries of life in the earth. The entity has come forward into this life and those talents, and those abilities, and those memories, are uppermost.

For a time she lived in another life with Ra. She was a companion of the one called Nefertiti, when Aye was the father of Akhnaton and Nefertiti. And here from Aye, once again another time a high priest of the Law of One, she learned of the mysteries. And speaking of her, he told her that she had been in the Temple of History/in the Temple of Shadow Memory in Atlantis. For all things would come to those who meditated, to know the secrets of the past, and that one day, in another time and in another place, she could give forth these truths.

We go now, although there is so much to give her, into the land of Palestine. This entity was in that land more than once. She was a sister, one of eight sisters, of Solomon, and she had wisdom of the heart as well as wisdom of the mind—Solomon had wisdom of the mind and a tremendous masculine ego; however, he favored this sister and allowed her to be beside him in his consultations. And, as with one other, when she offered suggestions, he would say, "Sister, remember you are but a woman," and that would end the suggestions.

And this one, as with another sister, determined to return in the body and that of a man, and that she would use the wisdom that she had. But coming back, both sisters returned as brothers into a Roman family and both became what would be called Admirals (one in charge) on a ship, and both made errors, because in returning there was the over-emphasis on the masculine to outdo everyone else. Nevertheless, at the end of this entity's life, the entity had insight into the why of experiences, that is, into the Karmic patterns that had been created. She did not make the mistake of her (his) brother. The brother took women into white slavery, from Ireland,

and this was because he wished to prove his masculinity and in the following life met it, when he himself (she herself) was taken into slavery. This one, instead, met a philosopher who was then known as Phaeon and in conversation, listened and realized that the role should be reversed and came again in the body of a woman, this time to Palestine, and from childhood awaited the birth of the Christ. She was one who saw the star of Bethlehem on that night. She was one whose mother/father had each been in the Essenean Temple and had known, or knew, the birth date of the birth of the Christ. She stood by the window of the humble home all night long, listening not only with the physical ears, but with spiritual ears, to the hallelujahs of the angels. This was an actual event, not a legendary event, and she determined that she could be with him somehow, in some way. When she was 17, he was 12, and she learned from the house of Martha and Mary of Bethany, that he was going away—that he would go into India, into Persia, and into Egypt, there to take initiations and then he would return home.

And she waited, refusing matrimony twice for him to come back. And when he returned she was with a friend at the household of Mary and Martha where he gave the first talk and she heard that first sermon that was given on the mountain near that place. The entity was especially chosen and especially blessed. She married in the second year of his ministry, but the young husband died within a three-year period. And when the disciples and the apostles, so called, began their journeys into other places, this one went with them gladly, happily even, toward Rome. And it was in Rome, after eight years, again with a companion, that she lost her life. There is a subconscious fear of violence, of being set upon, of being caught in a moment, for the death came weeks before it should have occurred, but in those scenes, they were actually creatures of the wild. The entity had such a feeling, even for a wild animal, that when she was attacked, it was over in one instant. Again, she was above her body.

The entity has once had a life as a Guru in the India land and one who could control animals, and at the time of Zend and Zoroaster, in the Persian land. All of this has meaning, but the primary meaning of her life in the earth is, that in this time and in this place she came in for a purpose.

It is now the time that the public must learn of those people in even many churches and organizations however orthodox, must learn that there is a truth, that we can live again and again until we come to the place of love where we can leave this particular planet. Also, that there is no injustice in the earth.

She is not alone, she has had seven lives as, but she will not choose to have in the church—six times as a woman, once as a man, often turning to the intellectual type of writing. She was one close to Thomas Aquinas and one who suggested that he continue on with his work of writing, as she (he) was his scribe. But Thomas had had a vision. The vision was of the afterlife—suddenly, in a moment at the altar, a vision of another world, another time and place, where there were not the orthodox laws that were then in the church. This one, in dying, remembered that Thomas refused to write, or finish, the book that he had begun. He refused to dictate so that he (she) could not write the words, and in one moment, in contemplating this, the heavens opened, it seemed, and he was aware of the eternal quality of life—that there is no death and there is no birth—that birth is a moment of sorrow, that death is a moment of joy, and that life goes on, forever.

This entity again is at, if she so chooses, the high point, at the closing point of a long cycle of lives in the earth—as we have given, approximately 300, but there is yet a price to pay, for this one does have within her hands the possibility of bringing enlightenment on these truths to many. There will be, at times, rejections, or she will sense rejections, by those who have been more of her, more on the mental level (and she, Maria Teresa, is showing green). This one is called upon to use both sides of the nature, that which is the mental and that which is the intuitive and to use her talent, which is a great one, going back even into the Atlantean ages, of helping others to remember the past. Before her death, it will be virtually established, even in scientific fields, that it is a possibility and life after death, and death itself will not be feared. Again, she is one of those who failed in the beginning, in the sense of coming into the earth.

She is one of those who again, and again, and again, entered the earth for purposes of creation, creating even in the earth, and who was with Amilius, who became the Christ, on the day that the host could not return to him in the celestial spheres. She is one who heard his cry, "My God, my God, why did we forsake Thee?" And she is one who chose from that moment to become a teacher, to become a savior. She is also one who listened when Jesus told the story of the prodigal son, and knew that he did not speak of actual people, but that he spoke of lost mankind and of their finding their way back to the Father. This one has within herself the wisdom of the ages. She is one who knew him and has even been a sister in the time of Asaph, the leader of the choir—he who became called the teacher of righteousness. Asaph was Jesus. In that choir, in singing, they sang the creation, and of all the things of the spirit, and centuries later, in the Whitby Monastery, with two friends whom she knows now, once again she knew Cadmon, a stable man, who on Christmas Eve had the vision of the story of creation—that life is eternal is a part of her awareness forever, and this she can do, and, in His Name—we are finished.

The late Jessica Madigan in Los Angeles

Jessica Madigan and Jery Stier

Appendix F

In the course of Goddess studies I'd heard that our foreparents were land based and how they used feminine ritual to grow crops and heal. Coming from the Daughters of the American Revolution on my father's side, I doubted this applied to me.

But when my mother passed a couple of years ago, among the mementos she left was a haunting image of an ancestor I never knew. My Bohemian great uncle and aunt on the eve of their wedding. The background of the picture taken so long ago was the full moon. From her hair threaded garlands of herbs and flowers. Confirmation—this wasn't just in past lives but in our genes, my quest for the Divine Feminine had come full circle.

Coming Full Circle

REFERENCES

Amritanandamayi, Mata. (1998). *Awakened Children, Volume IV.* Mata Amritanandamayi Center, San Ramon, California.

Andrews, Lynn V. (1981). *Medicine Woman.* San Francisco: Harper and Row.

Ashton, Joan. (1989). *Mother of All Nations.* San Francisco: Harper and Row.

Assagioli, Roberto. (1965). *Psychosynthesis. A Manual of Principles and Techniques.* New York: Viking Press.

Assagioli, R., and Servan-Schreiver, C. (1974). A Higher View of the Man Woman Problem. *Synthesis, 1.*

Bach, Richard. (1984). *The Bridge Across Forever.* New York: William Morrow and Company, Inc.

Barnstone, Willis. (1984). *The Other Bible.* San Francisco: Harper and Row.

Birnbaum, Lucia C. (2002) *The Dark Mother, African Origins and Godmothers.* iUniverse.com Author's Choice Press

Blair, Nancy. (2002). *The Book of Godesses.* London: Vega.

Bodo, Murray. (1979). *Clare, A Light In The Garden.* Cincinnati: St. Anthony Messinger Press.

Bolen, Jean Shinoda, M.D. (1984). *Goddesses In Every Woman.* New York: Harper and Row.

Bolen, Jean Shinoda, M.D. (1989). *Gods in Everyman: A New Psychology of Men's Lives and Loves.* San Francisco: Harper and Row.

Bradshaw, John. (1991). "On the Family." KQED television series broadcast in San Franicisco.

Bro, Harmon Hartzell, Ph.D. (1989). *A Seer Out Of Season, The Life Of Edgar Cayce*. New York: New American Library.

Bro, Marguerite Harmon. (1943)."Miracle Man of Virginia Beach". *Coronet Magazine*.

Brondwin, C.C. (2002). *Clan of the Goddess: Celtic Wisdom and Ritual for Women*. Franklin Lakes, New Jersey: New Page Book.

Brown, Dan. (2003). *The Da Vinci Code*. New York: Doubleday.

Budapest, Z. (1980). *The Holy Book of Women's Mysteries Part I & II*. Los Angeles: Susan B. Anthony Press.

Budapest, Zsuzsanna E. (1989). *The Grandmother of Time*. San Francisco: Harper and Row.

Butler, M. A. and Goldstein, L. (1990). "Re-Membering the Goddess Within." Experiential workshop conducted in Virginia Beach.

Campbell, J. (1972). *Myths to Live By*. New York: Viking Press.

Campbell, J (1968). *The Hero With a Thousand Faces*. Princeton, NJ: Princeton University Press.

Campbell, Joseph. (1959). *The Masks of God: Primitive Mythology*. New York: Viking Press.

Cayce, Edgar. (1945). *Auras, An Essay on the Meaning of Colors*. Virginia Beach: A.R.E. Press.

Cayce, Edgar. (l946). *What I Believe*. Virginia Beach: Association For Research and Enlightenment, Incorporated.

Cayce, Edgar Evans; Cayce-Schwartzer, Gail; and Richards, Douglas. (1988). *Mysteries of Atlantis Revisited*. San Francisco: Harper and Row.

Cayce, Hugh Lynn. (1971) *Edgar Cayce's Story of Karma*. New York: Berkley Medallion Books.

Chernin, Kim. (1987). *Reinventing Eve*. New York: Harper and Row.

Chesler, Phyllis. (1972). *Women and Madness*. New York: Doubleday and Company, Inc.

Chew, Willa C. (1977). *The Goddess Faith: A Religion of the Mind*. New York: Exposition Press.

Christ, Carol P.; and Plaskow, Judith. (1979). *Womanspirit Rising*. New York: Harper and Row.

Church, W. H. (1989). *Many Happy Returns: The Lives of Edgar Cayce*. San Francisco: Harper & Row.

Daly, Mary. (1984). *Gyn/Ecology*. Boston: Beacon Press.

Daly, Mary. (1975). "The Qualitative Leap Beyond Patriarchal Religion." *Quest, 1*, (4).

Downing, Christine. (1987). *The Goddess: Mythological Images of the Feminine*. New York: Crossroads.

Doyle, Brendan. (1983). *Meditations With Julian of Norwich*. Santa Fe: Bear and Company.

Eichenbach, Louise and Orbach, Susie. (1983). *Understanding Women: A Feminine Psychoanalytic Approach*. New York: Basic Books.

Eisler, Riane. (1987). *The Chalice and the Blade*. San Francisco: Harper and Row.

Essene, Virginia. (1986). *New Teaching For An Awakening Humanity*. Santa Clara, California: S.E.E. Publishing Company.

Feinstein, David and Krippner, Stanley. (1988). "Bringing a Mythology Perspective to Social Change." *ReVision, 1*, (11).

Feng, Gia F. and English, Jane (Translators) with Jacob Needleman. (1989). *The Tao*. New York: Vintage Books.

Flexner, Eleanor. *Mary Wollstonecraft*. (1972). New York: Coward, McCann and Geoghegan, Inc.

Follis, Anne Bowne. (1981). "The Mother Love of God/I'm not a Woman's Libber, But . . ." *Catholic Digest*.

Fox, Matthew. (1983). *Original Blessing*. New Mexico: Bear and Company.

Fox, Matthew. (1990). "Towards a New Spirituality of the 90's." Lecture conducted at Holy Names College in Oakland, California.

Freedom,. Sonshine. (2004). *The Mystical Life*. First Books.com.

Gadon, Elinor W. (1989). *The Once and Future Goddess: A Symbol For Our Time*. San Francisco: Harper & Row.

Gilligan, Carol. (1982). *In A Different Voice*. Cambridge, Massachusetts, and London, England: Harvard University Press.

Goodman, Linda. (1978). *Love Signs*. New York: Fawcett Columbine.

Graves, Robert (Translator). (1951). *The Golden Ass by Apuleius*. New York: Pocket Books.

Graves, Robert. (1948). *The White Goddess*. New York: A. A. Knopf.

Grof, S. (1985). *Beyond the Brain: Birth, Death and Transcendence in Psychotherapy*. Albany, New York: State University of New York Press.

Gutpa, Bina. (1987). *Sexual Archetypes, East and West*. New York: Paragon House.

Hancock, Ann Marie. (1988). *Be A Light: Miracles at Medjugorje*. Virginia Beach: The Donning Company.

Herkless, D.D. (1901). *Francis and Dominic and the Mendicant Orders*. New York: Charles Scribner's Sons.

Houston, J. (1982). "The Psycho-Historical Recovery of the Self." *Association for Humanistic Psychology Newsletter, Special Issue*, 8–10.

James, E. O. (1935). *The Old Testament in Light of Anthropology*. London: Macmillan.

Johari, Harish. (1987). *Chakras*. Vermont: Destiny Books.

Jones, Gladys. (1979). *Mortal and Immortal Love*. Los Angeles: New Age Press.

Jones, Gladys. (1975). *The Greek Love Mysteries*. Los Angeles: New Age Press.

Jung, C. G. (1963). *Mysterium Coniuctiois*. Translated by R.F.C. Hull. New York: Pantheon Books Inc.

Jung, C. G. (1959). *The Archetypes and the Collective Unconscious*. Translated By R.F.C. Hull. New York: Pantheon Books Inc.

Kash, Sara. (1983). "Waitresses Fight Age Discrimination." *Ms.*, XI, (11)

King, Karen K. (2003). *The Gospel of Mary Magdalene: Jesus and the First Woman Apolstle*. Polebridge Press.

Leek, Sybil. (1971). *The Complete Art of Witchcraft; Penetrating the Mystery Behind Magic Powers*. New York: Harper and Row.

Lerner, Mark. (1974). *The Egyptian Heritage*. Virginia Beach: A.R.E. Press.

Lewin, Miriam. (1984). *The Shadow of the Past: Psychology Portrays the Sexes*. New York: Columbia Press.

MacKinnon, M.H. Alexi and Rogers, Rev. L. (1987). "Re-Search Series: Atlantis." Experiential workshop conducted at the Creative Resource Center in Campbell, California.

Madigan, Jessica. (In Press). *Edgar Cayce: New Psychic Revelations*. Los Angeles: Mei Ling Publications.

Madigan, Jessica. (1970-1972). *The Past Lives of Jesus and Mary (vols. 1 & 2)*. Los Angeles: Mei Ling Publications.

Madigan, Jessica. (1965). *Twin Souls, The Eternal Love*. Los Angeles: Mei Ling Publications.

Madigan, Jessica (1965) *World Prophesy (vol. 3)*. Los Angeles: Mei Ling Publications.

Mansbridge, J.J. (1980). *Beyond Adversary Democracy*. New York: Basic Books.

Maslow, Abraham. (1971). *The Farther Reaches of Human Nature*. New York & London: Penguin Group: An Esalen Book.

May, R. (In Press). *The Cry For Myth*. New York: W. W. Norton.

Meador, Betty De Shong (2001) *Inanna, Lady of Largest Heart, Poems of a Sumerian High Priestess* University of Texas Press

Muten, Burleigh, editor. (1994). *Return of the Great Goddess*. New York Random House.

Nelson, Kirk. (1986). *The Second Coming*. Virginia Beach: Wright Publishing.

Olson, Carl. (1987). *The Book of the Goddess. Past and Present*. New York: Crossroad.

Pagels, Elaine. (1979). *The Gnostic Gospels*. New York: Random House.

Pogrebin, L. C. (1983). *Family Politics: Love and Power on an Intimate Frontier*. New York: McGraw Hill.

Pursel, Jach. (1988). *Lazaris Interviews Book 1*. Beverly Hills: Concept Synergy Publishers.

Read, Donna (Director). (1990). "Goddess Remembered." Canada: Studio D, National Film Board of Canada.

Reif, Jennifer. (2001). *Morgan Le Fay's Book of Spells and Wiccan Rites*. Citadel Press, Kensington Publishing Company

Richards, Douglas G. (1990). "The Bimini Discoveries." Interview: Douglas G. Richards. *Venture Inward*, 6, (6), pp.

Roni, Jay. (2000). *The Book of the Goddess*. London: Quarto.

Rosser, Phyllis. (1983). "The Beauty of Health: Brain." *Ms.*, p. 76.

Rouse, Lawrence David. (1985). *Validation of a Clinician-Client Typology Model*. Doctoral Dissertation, Pacific Graduate School of Psychology.

RSCJ: (1988). *A Journal of Reflection*. 9, (1).

References

Rubik, Beverly. (1990). "Science: A Feminine Perspective." *Creation, 6,* (6), pp. 6–7.

Ruether, Rosemary Radford. (1990). "Creation Spirituality: The Message and the Movement." *Creation, 6,* (6), pp. 20–37.

Ruether, Rosemary Radford. (1983). *Sexism and God-Talk.* Boston: Beacon Press.

Sanderfur, Glenn. (1971). *Lives of the Master.* Virginia Beach: A.R.E. Press.

Schiffman, Muriel. (1967). *Self Therapy.* Berkeley, California: Wingbow Press.

Shelley, Violet. (1965, 1976). *Symbols and the Self.* Edgar Cayce Foundation: Virginia Beach.

Sjoo, Monica, and Mor, Barbara. (1987). *The Great Cosmic Mother.* New York: Harper and Row.

Smith, Houston. (1958). *The Religions of Man.* New York: Harper and Row.

Sparrow, Lynn. (1988). *Reincarnation: Claiming Your Past, Creating Your Future.* San Francisco: Harper and Row.

Starhawk. (1987). *Truth Or Dare.* San Francisco: Harper and Row.

Starhawk. (1979). *The Spiral Dance.* New York: Harper and Row.

Stassinopoulos, Agapi (1999). *Conversations with the Goddesses.* New York: Stewart Tabori and Chang.

Stern, Jess. (1967). *The Sleeping Prophet.* New York: Bantam Books.

Stier, J. and Rogers, Rev. L. (1988). "Edgar Cayce's Atlantis." Interactive workshop conducted in Campbell, California.

Stier, Jery. (1985). "67th Philosophical Roundtable." Conference conducted in Santa Maria, California.

Stone, Merlin. (1984). *Ancient Mirrors of Womanhood.* Massachusetts: Beacon Press Books.

Stone, Merlin. (1978). *When God was a Woman.* New York: Harcourt Brace Jovanovich.

Taylor, Jeremy. (1980). *Basic Hints for Dreamwork.* San Rafael, CA: Dream Trees Press.

Taylor, Jeremy. (1990). "Sexism Hurts Men, Too!" *Creation,* 6, (6), p. 31.

Teish, Luisah. (1990). "Wisdom of Native Sprituality." Seminar at Holy Names College, Oakland, California.

Telesco, Patricia. (1998). *365 Goddess.* San Francisco: Harper.

"The Edgar Cayce Readings." (1971). Virginia Beach: The Edgar Cayce Foundation.

Thurston, Mark, PhD. (1984). *Discovering Your Soul's Purpose.* Virginia: A.R.E. Press.

Thurston, Mark, PhD. (1991, May/June). "The Great Readings/The Story of Atlantis: An Interpretation by Mark Thurston." *Venture Inward,* 7, (3), pp. 32–34.

Tyson, Michael E. (1990, October/November). "The New Hero's Journey: Men and the Men's Movement." *The Well Being Journal.*

Van Hoose, Larry. (2004). *The Voice: How The Bible Reveals Reincarnation.* Palm Desert, Ca: We Publish Books.

Waldherr, Kris. (1997). *The Book of Goddesses.* Oregon: Beyond Words

Walker, Barbara G. (1983). *The Woman's Encyclopedia of Myths and Secrets.* San Francisco: Harper and Row.

Whitmont, Edward C., M.D. (1980, Fall). "Reassessing Femininity and Masculinity: A Critique of Some Traditional Assumptions." *Quadrant.* pp. 109–122.

Wilber, K. (1981). *Up From Eden: A Transpersonal View of Human Evolution.* Garden City, NJ: Anchor, Doubleday.

Wilner, E. (1975). *Gathering the Winds: Visionary Imagination and Radical Transformation of Self and Society.* Baltimore, NY: John Hopkins.

Zimmer, Heinrich. (1946). *Myths and Symbols in Indian Art and Civilization*. Princeton, N.J.: Princeton University Press.

Harmon Hartzell Bro, Ph.D. and Edgar Cayce

About the Author

Lynn Rogers was born in Berkeley, California where she became active in the peace and civil rights movements as a teenager. She received her bachelor's degree in transpersonal psychology at Antioch University in San Francisco and her masters in transpersonal studies at Atlantic University in Virginia Beach, Virginia. She took additional graduate studies with theologian Matthew Fox at The Institute for Culture and Creation Spirituality in Oakland California.

Based in San Jose, California, Lynn is a lecturer, teacher and counselor for diverse groups, including philosophical foundations, colleges, churches and media, integrating the Edgar Cayce and other traditions with that of the reemerging Divine Feminine.

Previous publication includes:

Articles such as "Vanessa, Sojourn With An Autistic Child" for Venture Inward Magazine.

Short stories such as "A Woman On The Side" for True Love Magazine.

Books: *Born In Berkeley* (inklingpress.com), which gives voice to a young girl's coming of age at a pivotal time.
Valley of Heart's Delight/Chapbook, an anthology made with her diverse creative writing students.

Many of her efforts are on behalf of what Fox called "the anawim" or voiceless ones of our society, starting with blacks in the sixties. To that end she served as a spokesperson for autistic youth in the eighties helping establish group homes in the community for autistic young people who would have otherwise languished in state hospitals. She now enjoys encouraging America's least understood resource, its older adult population, to capture its memories and consciousness through creative writing. Her ongoing Wise Women's circle classes empower women.

She looks forward to the completion of her most recent work *Valley of Ashes*. After the dot com crash and terrorist paranoia, Silicon Valley outcasts search for a safe place which may only be found in each others hearts.

Further titles may include:

The Rainbow's Daughter. In which nineteen year old Page is pulled into a seventies occult group led by a charismatic priestess.

Where The Flowers Have Gone. Set in the San Francisco Bay Area between the eighties and the sixties.

In the contemporary *Soul Mate Quartet.* Lara and Swan meet at the millennium when soul mates must reach for each other in order to bring the light.

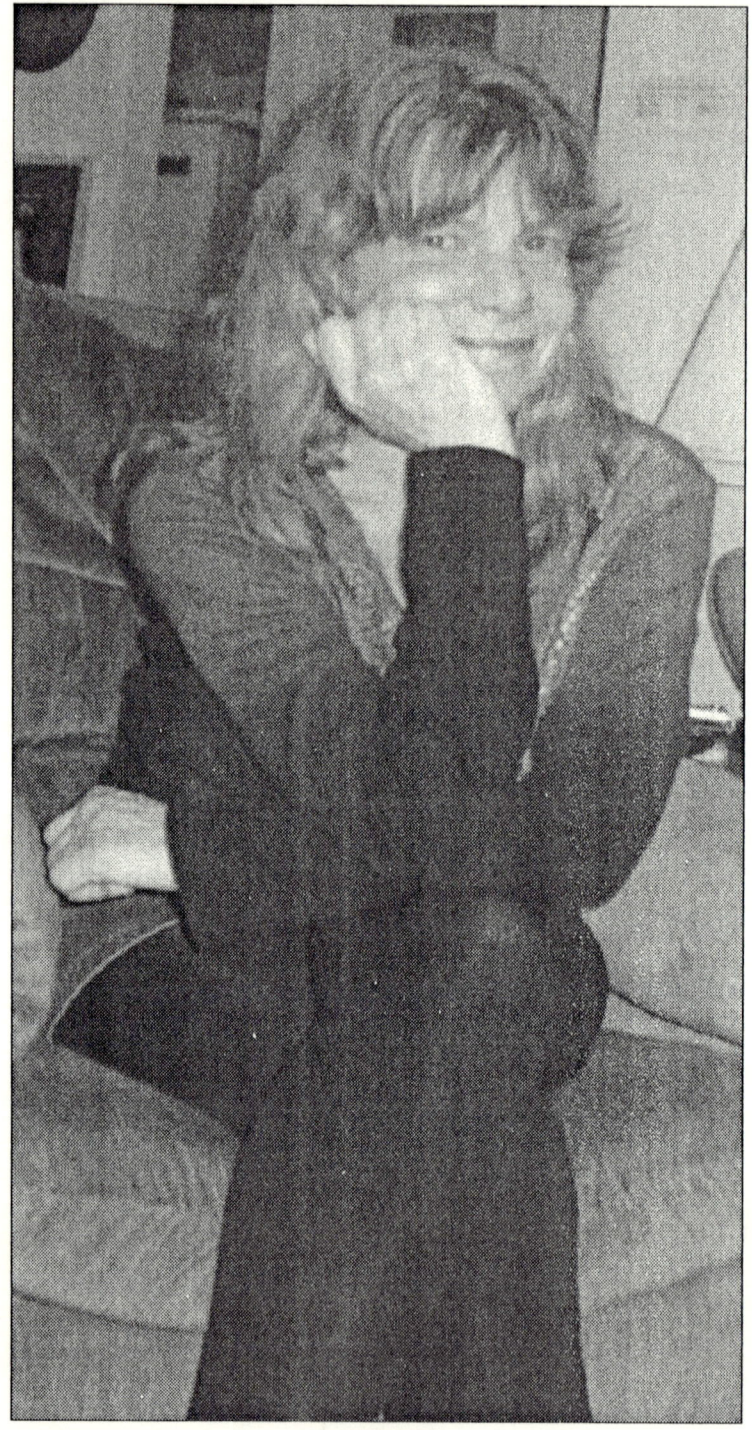

Lynn Rogers

Printed in the United States
18363LVS00003B/58-510